A Closer Look at the Evidence

" . . . be ready always to give an answer
to every man that asketh you
a reason of the hope that is in you,
with meekness and fear . . . "

1 Peter 3:15 KJV

Richard L. & *Christina E. Kleiss*

Search for the Truth
Publications
3275 Monroe Road
Midland, MI 48642
SearchfortheTruth.net

A CLOSER LOOK AT THE EVIDENCE

First printing - June 2003
Second revised printing - March 2004
Third revised printing - January 2006
Fourth printing - December 2008
Fifth printing - May 2011
Sixth printing - February 2015

ISBN: 0-9715911-1-0
Library of Congress Catalog Card Number: 2002094427
Copyright 2003 by Richard L. & Christina (Tina) E. Kleiss
Poetry by Christina Kleiss
Background Photographs by Bruce Malone
Cover and Graphic Design by Janell Robertson
Subject Illustrations by Joel Seibel
Edited by Bruce Malone

Unless otherwise indicated, all Scripture quotations are taken from the Holy Bible, New International Version. Copyright 1973, 1978, 1984 - International Bible Society.

Reproduction Rights

Dedication

We dedicate this book to those students who truly desire to know *why* the belief in a Creator, Lord, and Savior is *so credible*. May you be encouraged in your faith by these evidences and develop a real passion to study further and live for Christ.

I PETER 3:15

Acknowledgments

We extend our deepest appreciation and gratitude to those who helped make this book possible. We can truly see how God used the talents of the many friends who helped us with the typing, proofreading, praying, setup, artwork, design, and timely words of encouragement. We also thank God for bringing us together with Bruce Malone, who shared our vision for this book. May God bless each of you for your selfless service, and may He truly be honored through this book!

RICH AND TINA KLEISS

About this Book

The primary purpose of this book is to help people understand what makes Christianity so trustworthy. Many books are available on the scientific evidence for creation, but most are difficult to share due to the technical nature of the subject matter. This book is written to be enjoyed as a daily devotional, but can also serve as an easy-to-read resource on the physical evidence that our Creator exists.

God's desire is that the knowledge of what He has done through both the cross and creation is for everyone. We must not keep this knowledge to ourselves. The evidence that He is our Creator is so overwhelming and encouraging that it desperately needs to be shared in the world today. *A Closer Look at the Evidence* **is designed to be an affordable resource to both reinforce our individual faith and facilitate sharing the reasons for this faith.** Consider praying about how God could use you to utilize the truths found within these pages.

Each page summarizes interesting facts about God and/or creation. The reader is encouraged to find more extensive and detailed information through the sources listed at the bottom of each page. Occasionally the source is quoted directly, but more often the material is summarized.

Because this book contains much **scientific evidence** supporting the reality of creation, it is possible that some of the more speculative conclusions could change over time. It is not the intent of the authors or publisher to distort or mislead in any way. Therefore, we will correct any confirmed technical errors in subsequent printings. If you find any technical errors, please contact the publisher at **SearchfortheTruth.net**.

About the Authors

The book's authors, Richard and Tina Kleiss, have been public school science teachers for many years. Richard holds a B.S. degree in Mechanical Engineering and worked as an engineer for 13 years before returning to school to earn a teaching degree in chemistry, physics, and mathematics. He taught both junior and senior high school science and math courses for 15 years. Tina has a B.S. and M.A. degree in education. She has taught elementary and junior high science for over 32 years.

As science teachers, the Kleisses had a particular interest in the question of origins. Their research led them to the discovery that the scientific evidence overwhelmingly supports creation. After witnessing evolution being presented as a fact in the media and textbooks while the evidence for creation was being systematically excluded, the authors decided to continue their study, compile their findings, and write *A Closer Look at the Evidence* as a resource for others. For over a decade the Kleisses have taught classes and given seminars on creation/evolution to audiences ranging from kindergarten to adult. The authors have currently retired from public education in order to devote full time to bringing seminars on the evidence for creation to both students and adults.

The authors' desire is not that this book be used for the purpose of ridiculing the beliefs of evolutionists, but that it would strengthen our faith in the Word of God. Their hope is that this book would be a useful tool for *parents* who need to find answers to their children's questions, *students* who want to investigate the credibility of Christianity, and *teachers* who want to study the problems with evolution. Rich and Tina reside in Gladwin, Michigan.

About the Editor/Publisher

Bruce Malone worked as a Research Leader for the Dow Chemical Co. for 27 years specializing in new product developments. Mr. Malone has a B.S. in Chemical Engineering and holds 18 patents on various aspects of foam extrusion and polymer technology. However, his passion is writing and teaching about the evidence for creation. Bruce is interested in every aspect of science and has been studying, lecturing, and writing on the harmony of the evidence for creation with science for almost 20 years. Bruce lives in Midland, Michigan with his wife Robin.

In 2008 Bruce took early retirement from Dow Chemical in order to serve as full time executive director of Search for the Truth Ministries. Search for the Truth is a non-profit 501(c)(3) organization started to distribute interesting and technically accurate books on creation to students, teachers, prisoners, pastors, and missionaries. Naturalistic evolutionary presuppositions have a lock upon our education system, museum system, and media but the courts have yet to prevent the free distribution of technically accurate and fascinating books on the evidence for creation. Our goal is to circumvent the censorship which is happening within our schools by distributing over a million books on the evidence for creation over the next ten years. *A Closer Look at the Evidence* is one of these books.

Foreword

It is critically important that each of us is able to **explain why we believe** that Jesus Christ is our Creator and Savior. Merely saying that we believe is not an adequate answer in today's world of sophisticated technology and skepticism.

Since Darwin published *On the Origin of the Species* in 1859, evolutionists have spent millions of hours researching reasons to reject God as Creator. Over the same period, many Christians have rested on "blind faith." This trend is changing, thanks to the work of organizations such as the Institute for Creation Research, Answers in Genesis, Creation Moments, the Center for Scientific Creation, the Creation Research Society, and many others. These organizations are headed by men and women committed to helping Christians obey God's command in 1 Peter 3:15, " ...*be ready always to give an answer to every man that asketh you a reason of the hope that is in you with meekness and fear...*" KJV The dedication and diligence of these Christians to further scientific research and education is tremendous. They merit our prayers, encouragement, and financial support.

This book barely scratches the surface of the evidence which reveals the truth and authority of the Bible. It is built upon the work of others and will hopefully serve as a vehicle for whetting your appetite as **you prepare** to give a **ready answer** for why you believe in the Creator. As you familiarize yourself with the evidence in this book, we encourage you to study and further research these evidences on your own. God challenges us to examine and discern the Scriptures (Acts 17:11, 1 Thessalonians 5:21), and we will find that they are true. We believe you will find that the evidence supports a clear and straightforward understanding of God's Word. Taking time to study this evidence will bless you and will greatly encourage your faith that the Lord God is real and exactly who He says He is in the Bible. We have been working on this project of love for many years, and it has **truly changed our lives**. Our discoveries have given us a passion to serve God and commit ourselves to the obedience of His Word! We hope our efforts will be a blessing to you.

In Christian love,
Rich and Tina Kleiss

Introduction

There is a cultural war raging in Western Civilization and the outcome of this war is far from certain. There are many hotly contested battlefronts, but at the root of each battle is man's desire to replace God with himself. Self-centeredness and mankind's desire to escape accountability to the Creator is apparent everywhere. Whenever clear biblical teaching on the evidence for creation is presented, it is opposed with passion. The intensity of the opposition to the biblical viewpoint is an indication of mankind's lack of humility and hatred for moral accountability. It is also an indication of the importance of this issue.

Evolution lays the groundwork for rejecting any absolute standard of behavior, because it undermines the Bible as a source of authority. The Bible makes it quite clear that God created everything, life only reproduces after its own kind, and that He sent a global flood as judgment for man's sin and rebellion. If these facts are denied, then people will draw the wrong conclusions about their origin. Why, then, should they trust anything else the Bible has to say?

There are many wonderful, well-documented, and highly technical books on the scientific evidence supporting biblical creation. However, the battle will not be won in academic towers but in our homes, schools, and neighborhood living rooms. This compilation of evidence for the truth of the Bible can have a tremendous impact. Why? Because this book shares "the rest of the story" and exposes the fallacy behind many of the ideas and beliefs we have been taught to blindly accept. This volume is filled with awe-inspiring examples of God's handiwork, making it almost impossible to resist turning the page to find out what comes next.

There are **only** two possible alternatives for the origin of mankind–creation or evolution. Many people like to believe that God used evolution to "create" us. However, this just sidesteps the real issue by assuming that evolution has happened. Such a false compromise leads people away from, not toward, the personal God described in the Bible. To understand whether the scientific evidence from the observation of the world around us fits best into the evolution or creation model for our origin, the reader must understand the very different (and mutually exclusive) models for our origin. Evolution masquerades as science by using scientific terminology and teaching that small observable changes in organisms prove that one type of creature has turned into a completely different type. In reality, evolution is based on a religious concept which has been summarized as follows by Philip Johnson in his book *The Right Questions*:

> "In the beginning was no intelligence or purpose; there were only particles and impersonal laws of physics. These two things plus chance did all the creating. Without them nothing was made that has been made. The particles combined to become complex living stuff through a process called evolution. Primitive humans, not having science to tell them what had happened, dreamed up a creator they called God."

This religious belief is taught as a fact within public school textbooks throughout the world. We need to prepare our children if they are going to resist the one-sided indoctrination which they are receiving in schools, museums, movies, and science programs. The biblical explanation for life is radically different:

> In the beginning was God. God created all space, matter, and time in a brief creation period not so long ago. He created distinctly different kinds of creatures to reproduce after their own kind and placed mankind on a planet designed for him. The entire universe was created for man's pleasure in order to reveal God's glory, majesty, and character.

> Yet mankind rebelled and rejected God. In response God did not destroy man, but all of creation started a downward spiral of disorder and death (referred to as "*the Fall*"). Later, in response to the almost total depravity of mankind, a worldwide flood was sent to wipe out virtually all life on the planet. The effects of this judgment provide undeniable evidence of the hatred a holy God has toward sin and rebellion. This flood is what created the worldwide fossil record.

> In an incredible display of mercy, God forewarned the entire world as to what was coming. Yet only one family believed God and was saved on a giant

floating vessel. A few generations after the flood ended, mankind was dispersed around the world as evidenced by the explosive growth of highly advanced civilizations approximately 5,000 years ago. God did not leave mankind without hope for reconciliation with Himself. He inspired the Bible as an authoritative record of both physical and spiritual reality. The Creator God became man and took upon Himself the penalty which we deserve for our rebellion. He did this so that we may be reconciled with Him.

From the first rebellion of mankind in the Garden of Eden (when man tried to cover his sin with a fig leaf) to the crucifixion of Jesus on the cross (when mankind tried to wash his hands of the responsibility for his actions), God has been reaching out to mankind. It is only by placing our faith in what Jesus has already done that we may return to fellowship with the Creator of the universe. We can never be "good" enough to earn our way to heaven.

These are the two competing viewpoints for understanding our universe. Scientific exploration should not start by eliminating consideration of the biblical model. There are innumerable scientific observations which agree perfectly with a straightforward understanding of the Bible's model. Science should consider *all of the data* to determine which model is best supported by the evidence. Was there a worldwide flood or not? Do random changes add useful information to an organism? Can chemicals come alive? Does the fossil record show the transformation from one form of life into another? Do the majority of dating methods reveal a young or an old earth? The answers to these questions are found through scientific investigation, not religious discussion.

This book is about the evidence. Each reader must determine for him/herself which concept of our origin is best supported by the evidence. **Share this book with every person you know, especially young people.** Many of them are looking for meaning and purpose in life. The evidence presented here, tied to God's Word, will be *"a lamp unto their feet and a light unto their path"* through this spiritually dark and confusing world.

> To Jesus be the glory,
> Bruce Malone, Editor and Publisher

Which Came First, the Chicken or the Egg?

Which came first, the chicken or the egg?
  This question we must pose.
The answer rests upon God's Word
  And what the evidence shows.

Evolution says it was the egg;
  Pure chance brought us the bird.
The Bible says God made the bird
  In Genesis One of His Word.

These views we know can't both be true,
  No matter what men say.
So we must lay out all the facts,
  And let them point the way.

If we look closely at what's found
  In fossils, stars, and cells,
They point out there's a Master Mind;
  And He designed them well.

Of course, mankind just laughs at this.
  They won't admit it's true.
They know that if there is a God,
  Accounts to Him are due.

As Christians, here's where we can't fail
  To know God's world and Word.
Our reasons for belief in Him
  By no means are absurd.

The Bible says to seek out truth;
  Foundations must be strong.
So when men say they have the facts,
  We'll know what's right from wrong.

Let's read God's Word, apply our minds,
  And seek Him with all our heart.
God said He'd teach us wondrous things
  And truth to us impart.

So when we're asked to clarify
  That eggs weren't first and why,
We'll know God's Script, point to the facts,
  And have a sound reply.

If we can spur man to rethink
  His views on evolution,
Perhaps He'll see the facts show *God*
  As the correct solution.

Evidence From CREATION FOUNDATION

True Christianity, as set forth in the Bible, is **a credible faith and not one based on emotions, superstitions, or groundless belief.** Christianity is founded on truth that can be tested and is for the thinking person. God does not ask us to check our brains at the church door. Followers of other religions can quote their texts and give glowing testimonies of how their religions make them feel, but their beliefs are based on feelings, rather than historical facts. It is quite possible to be devoted and sincere about a religious belief, while wholeheartedly believing a lie. How can a person know that what they believe is actually true? Although some beliefs can bring comfort, will they ultimately help or harm us if they are false?

Christianity alone is based on verifiable historical truth. The Bible states in Romans 1:20 that no one has any excuse for disbelief in the one true God, because God clearly makes Himself known to everyone through what He has made (His creation). This can be verified through the study of creation using the tool of science.

God also makes Himself known through His Word, the Bible. He challenges us to examine and test it. Each person is responsible to investigate the Bible's claims of authenticity. Our eternal destiny depends upon it.

MANY INFALLIBLE PROOFS, P.7

...Always be prepared to give an answer to everyone who asks you to give the reason for the hope that you have. But do this with gentleness and respect.

1 PETER 3:15

Evidence From
BIOLOGY

Although the original world was created perfect and without death, our fallen world requires creatures to adapt to difficult situations in order to survive. Even in the current world full of death and competition, the smallest of creatures exhibit amazing capabilities for survival in harsh environments. The female snowshoe rabbit is one such creature.

During extreme drought or harsh winters, the stress of finding food triggers a chemical process in the pregnant female that stops an embryo's growth. Her body then responds to this condition of physical weakness with a process called resorption. In this process, **the mother completely reabsorbs the growing embryo.** This mechanism allows the rabbit to survive by replenishing her own strength. She can later become pregnant during more favorable conditions.

The number of chemical and physical changes required for a rabbit to **reverse a pregnancy** is mind-boggling. There is no scientific evidence which explains how this remarkable resorption process could have evolved. The creativity of God to have provided for the common rabbit in this way is truly amazing!

Character Sketches, Vol. II, p.66

The LORD is gracious and righteous; our God is full of compassion.

Psalm 116:5

Evidence From
PROPHECY

The prophet Ezekiel prophesied that the city of Sidon, twenty miles north of Tyre, would have a miserable and bloody future due to its horrible sinfulness. A study of history shows that this prophecy (precise future events foreseen and predicted) came true exactly as predicted.

Throughout the centuries, Sidon has indeed been one of the bloodiest locations in history. Soon after the prophecy was given, the city was captured by the Babylonians. Later, over 40,000 died in a rebellion against the Persians. The Greeks then captured it under Alexander the Great in 330 B.C. It continued to be the scene of many fierce battles during the Crusades and various Turkish wars. Today, this city is part of Lebanon, only twenty miles south of Beruit. **This area seems destined to continue its unhappy history (indefinitely), just as the Bible predicted over 2,000 years ago.**

As much as one-fourth of the Bible consists of prophetic statements. **Every single prediction has come or is in the process of coming true–with 100% accuracy.** This is true because the Bible is inspired by the Holy Spirit (who is God). Only God is outside of time and capable of seeing all of time, from the moment of creation until He wraps up history, in advance. This is possible as time is part of the physical universe and God (who created the entire universe) is outside of time. Only the Bible validates itself by predicting the specific future events in advance!

SCIENCE AND THE BIBLE, P.118-119

"...I am against you, O Sidon...I will send a plague upon her and make blood flow in her streets. The slain will fall within her, with the sword against her on every side...."

EZEKIEL 28:22,23

Evidence From BOTANY

On a hot summer day, one large tree can pump over a thousand gallons–that's four tons–of water from the ground to its leaves. The water is collected from the soil through the roots. But the real work of pumping four tons of water, often 100 feet into the air, occurs at the top of the tree. The water is suctioned toward the treetop by three remarkably efficient mechanisms–capillary flow, osmosis, and vacuum pressure. Osmosis and capillary action act in concert to move the water partway to the top of the tree, but the real driving force is a pressure differential created by the leaves within the vessels of the tree. This pressure differential is a result of water evaporating from the leaves of the tree, creating a suction throughout the vessels. This suction (measured as low as 1/20 of atmospheric pressure) helps to draw water from the roots all the way to the top of the tree. If you were to cut one of these vessels, you could actually hear (using extremely sensitive equipment) a hissing sound as air rushed back into these vessels.

The **engineering excellence** of this silent pumping system, which efficiently delivers moisture to the very top of trees, is a not-so-silent witness against the idea that chance evolutionary processes (such as mutations) could have developed it.

LETTING GOD CREATE YOUR DAY,
VOL. 4, P.79

Do you not know? Have you not heard? The LORD is the everlasting God, the Creator of the ends of the earth. He will not grow tired or weary, and His understanding no one can fathom.

ISAIAH 40:28

Evidence From
CHEMISTRY

The existence of life depends upon a substance which chemists call the universal solvent. This magnificent molecule, with its many unique properties, is ordinary water. Unlike almost all other liquids which contract upon changing from liquid to solid, water stops contracting and starts expanding at 4°C. This results in solid water (ice) being less dense (lighter) than liquid water. Thus lakes and rivers freeze from the top down instead of from the bottom up. **If lakes froze from the bottom up, life within every lake in a freezing climate would be destroyed.**

Water also has a unique ability to conduct electricity at just the right resistance to make the processes of life possible within cells. In addition, its unique surface tension insulates some animals, while its inability to mix with body oils insulates other animals by keeping them dry. Water is only one of the special substances that God created to enhance and enable life.

From the properties of the smallest molecule to the complex interrelated systems of life, the entire universe has every appearance of being designed to work together in **perfect harmony**. This is one of many ways in which creation provides a vivid testimony to our Creator's attention to the details of life.

LETTING GOD CREATE YOUR DAY, VOL. 4, P.49

Come and see what God has done, how awesome his works in man's behalf!

PSALM 66:5

Evidence From
BIOLOGY

The Couch's spadefoot toad of the Sonoran Desert is an example of how God takes care of creatures under extreme conditions. **This toad lies dormant in the hot desert eleven out of twelve months each year.** It has built-in sensors that tell it when a violent desert rainstorm occurs. The toad can detect vibrations of pounding rain miles away. It somehow knows to emerge from the sand when it rains so that the male toads can call for females as soon as pools of water form. Shortly afterwards the egg-laying is completed and the toads return to the sand, safe from the heat of the burning daytime sun. Most of the time the desert pools rapidly dry up, killing the eggs. Only under ideal conditions will some of the eggs hatch–nine days later. The young toads have at most a few weeks to eat enough food to survive before burying themselves in the sand for the next eleven months while awaiting another rainstorm.

Such survival instincts and mechanisms were probably not required before the Fall, when the world was designed as a paradise. In the current world, with its severe climates, such instincts and abilities seem to have been specifically designed for animals such as the spadefoot toad. How could this ability to adjust to such harsh weather conditions have evolved? **Unless all of the abilities, instincts, and timing of the toads' reproductive cycle were in place, the toads could never have survived** the first severe season.

LETTING GOD CREATE YOUR DAY,
VOL. 4, P.48

The wild animals honor me...because I provide water in the desert and streams in the wasteland...

ISAIAH 43:20

Evidence From
ANATOMY

Human hair is actually a complex functioning feature, not just a simple cosmetic addition to our bodies. Not only does hair provide warmth and enhanced appearance, but it has multiple design functions to enhance life. For instance, **hair is an integral part of the body's protection system.** Eyelashes protect our eyes by triggering them to almost instantly and involuntarily close when dust strikes the lashes. Body hair serves as tiny levers. Each hair is connected to a muscle which squeezes oil from adjacent glands that keep our skin from drying out. Hair even acts as a filter for particulates caught in the nose and ears.

Hair is also "programmed" to grow to specific lengths and thicknesses in various places on the body. Eyelashes, for example, do not grow as long or thick as scalp hair. They grow to a certain length, fall out, and are replaced by new hair. Who planned it this way? Clearly, one can see evidence of design in both the function and placement of even the simple hairs on our bodies.

Evolution does not explain where the complex programming to create even a single hair came from. Human hair is not a leftover skin covering from our "ape ancestry."

The Human Body: Accident or Design?, p.17

Are not two sparrows sold for a penny? Yet not one of them will fall to the ground apart from the will of your Father. And even the very hairs of your head are numbered. So don't be afraid; you are worth more than many sparrows.

Matthew 10:29-31

Evidence From THE FOSSIL RECORD

We are repeatedly told that dinosaurs died out around 60 million years ago. **Yet there have been many reports of dinosaur bones which have been dated quite young.** Carbon-14 (^{14}C) analysis of dinosaur bones reveals that they can contain measurable amounts of ^{14}C. This is impossible if the bones are over 60 million years old but makes perfect sense from a biblical perspective. The ^{14}C concentration for organisms alive before Noah's Flood would have been greatly reduced compared to modern levels, but ^{14}C should still be present in small amounts. This is exactly what we find and does not indicate a great age but a recent burial by a worldwide flood.

According to the March 1992 ABR Newsletter, Hugh Miller of Columbus, Ohio had four dinosaur bone samples carbon dated at a university laboratory. Each of the bones were "dated" at an age of under 20,000 years. These bones were not identified as dinosaur bones because the labs would not agree to test bones which their evolutionary presumptions tell them could not contain any ^{14}C. Yet the same level of ^{14}C found in the bones of a more "recent" creature would be assumed to be correct.

In an even more amazing discovery, both DNA fragments and unfossilized red blood cells have been found within dinosaur bones. Neither of these fragile organic molecules could exist after millions of years. Yet it is quite reasonable to expect to find such fragments to remain if they were buried during Noah's Flood–less than 5,000 years ago.

NOAH TO ABRAHAM: THE TURBULENT YEARS,
P. 36

Recent dates on dinosaur bones should be no surprise to Christians. In Genesis 1:21 God says he created "great whales" (KJV). Elsewhere this Hebrew word, tannin, is translated "dragon." Job chapters 40 and 41 describe powerful creatures which could only be dinosaurs.

Evidence From PROPHECY

There are over 300 distinct prophecies in the Old Testament that were literally fulfilled by Jesus Christ. These prophecies, given hundreds of years before Christ was born, were very specific and could not be fulfilled by any other man in history. The prophecies include the time, place, and manner of Christ's birth, including specifics about His ministry and genealogy. Also predicted were details about His miracles, His trial, His death, His resurrection, and the events after His resurrection. **The probability of all of these prophecies being fulfilled by any other person is an absolute impossibility.**

These predictions concerning the life of Jesus Christ were recorded in the sacred books of the Jewish people–now commonly known as the "Old Testament." Copies of these ancient documents, identical to the modern texts, were buried hundreds of years before the birth of Christ. They were found sealed in clay jars near the Dead Sea in Israel. These "Dead Sea Scrolls" and other manuscripts recorded specific details about Jesus long before they actually occurred. Only a Creator God who is outside of time could have inspired these hundreds of specific details to be written down prior to their fulfillment.

THIS INFORMATION IS CONDENSED FROM
EVIDENCE THAT DEMANDS A VERDICT, P.141-176.
THIS BOOK IS AN EXCELLENT RESOURCE ON BIBLICAL ACCURACY.

"...Surely, just as I have intended so it has happened, and just as I have planned so it will stand."

ISAIAH 14:24 NAS

Evidence From
BIOLOGY

Human engineers did not design the first cooling system. Every living warm-blooded creature has mechanisms for controlling its body temperature. **The design of the gazelle's cooling system is among the most ingenious in nature.** The gazelle must run at high speed in order to escape predators. This exertion of energy raises the gazelle's body temperature to such an extent that for the gazelle to survive, its brain must be cooled. The solution to this problem is a special cooling system built right into the gazelle's head. Gazelles and similar animals have hundreds of small arteries that pass through a large pool of blood in the nasal passage. Inhaled air cools this nasal blood pool, which in turn cools the blood in the tiny arteries passing through the pool. [In industry, these specifically designed pieces of equipment are called heat exchangers.] After the blood has been cooled, it recombines in a larger blood vessel and circulates into the brain. Without this system for cooling the brain, the gazelle simply could not survive in the current fallen world which requires the gazelle to escape from predatory animals.

It takes a team of engineers using sophisticated calculations to design heat exchangers for use in industrial processes. Since it had to work perfectly from the outset, creation is the only logical explanation for the design and function of the gazelle's far more intricate heat exchange system.

It Couldn't Just Happen, p.108-109

"...Who is like you–majestic in holiness, awesome in glory, working wonders?"

Exodus 15:11

Evidence From ASTRONOMY

In the writings of virtually all civilized nations going back to Rome, Greece, Egypt, Persia, Assyria, and Babylonia, there exists a description of the major star systems. Mankind has called these 12 star systems the "Constellations of the Zodiac" and has attached mystical meanings and powers to them. It is intriguing that nearly all nations had the *same 12 signs*, placed in the *same order*, all representing the *same things*. Secular archeologists, who deny the dispersion of man from a single source (the tower of Babel), cannot explain how so many nations have the same signs for the constellations which bear no resemblance to the pictures they supposedly represent.

The Bible sheds light on this mystery in several places:
1. In Genesis 1:14-16 God is in the midst of creating the heavens when he says He made the sun, moon, and stars for the purpose of *"Signs,* and for seasons, and for days, and years."
2. In Job 38:31-32 God asks Job if he could bring forth the "Mazzaroth" in his season. Mazzaroth is Hebrew for the constellations of the Zodiac. Pleiades, Orion, and Arcturus are specifically listed.
3. In Psalm 147:4 God tells us He not only *created* the stars, but He *numbered* the stars and calls them by their *names*.

Some believe a study of the constellations reveals the gospel through the heavens. Each constellation, from Virgo (meaning "virgin") to Leo (meaning "he that tears apart"), unfolds the story of Christ. Christ was the God-man who came to die in payment for man's sins, redeem those who make Him Lord of their lives, and conquer the serpent, Satan.

THE REAL MEANING OF THE ZODIAC

And God said, Let there be lights in the firmament of the heaven to divide the day from the night; and let them be for signs, and for seasons, and for days, and years...

GENESIS 1:14 KJV

Evidence From BIBLICAL ACCURACY

The belief in **uniformitarianism** (that the past history of our planet can be explained by slow processes over long periods of time) is not a new scientific revelation. Belief in evolution is built upon this foundation of uniformitarianism by denying that there have been major interventions by God in the past. **God knew and forewarned mankind of this errant viewpoint thousands of years ago in 2 Peter 3:3.**

1. **Evolution denies** the instantaneous creation of very different forms of life.
2. **Evolution ignores** that there was ever a curse on man and nature as a result of mankind's rebellion.
3. **Evolution suppresses** the evidence for the worldwide Flood in spite of enormous geological support testifying to the reality of this event. This global Flood explains the fossil record without the need for evolutionary concepts or time scales and must be denied in order to accept evolution.
4. **Evolution undermines** Christianity by assuming that death has always been around and is the natural order of things. If this is true, then Christ did not die as a final payment for Adam's (and our) sin because death is normal and not a specific penalty for our rebellion. Adam and Eve simply becomes a fanciful, imaginary story.

Once evolution is accepted as a fact, is it any surprise that Christianity rapidly becomes irrelevant? Is it any surprise that Europe became almost devoid of true Chrisitian faith in the same time frame in which it totally embraced evolutionary theory as fact?

BRUCE MALONE

First of all, you must understand that in the last days scoffers will come, scoffing and following their own evil desires. They will say, "Where is this 'coming' he promised? Ever since our fathers died, everything goes on as it has since the beginning of creation."

2 PETER 3:3-4

Evidence From COMMON SENSE

Life shows every possible characteristic of design by an intelligent designer. If you ask any person to define what characteristics would indicate that an object has been made by an intelligent designer (such as form, complexity, independence of parts, integrated components, etc.) life exhibits these same characteristics. In addition to this, all basic types of animal life appear completely developed, not partially developed. There are no examples of half-developed feathers, eyes, skin, arteries, veins, intestines, or any other vital organ.

Actually, **if a reptile leg were to evolve into the wing of a bird, it would become a bad leg long before it could become a good wing.** How could such a reptile survive an attack from a predator or catch prey while its legs were in the process of evolving? Before it turned into something else, the animal would become extinct. Adherence to the teachings of evolution, masquerading as science, has blinded even highly intelligent people to the truth. The Bible says it best–claiming to be wise, mankind has become foolish.

IN THE BEGINNING, 7TH ED., P.7

REASON EMOTION

For since the creation of the world God's invisible qualities–His eternal power and divine nature–have been clearly seen, being understood from what has been made...but their thinking became futile and their foolish hearts were darkened. Although they claimed to be wise, they became fools....

ROMANS 1:20,21,22

Evidence From HISTORY

Jesus Christ is *not* a *mythological character.* **Evidence of His existence can be verified by many sources.**

First, there is the testimony of the <u>New Testament documents</u>. All 27 New Testament books were completed within 60 years of Christ's resurrection. Ten of these books were written by Christ's personal friends. At least thirteen were written by Paul, an eyewitness of Christ's life.

Second, <u>the Jewish Babylonian Talmud</u> and the <u>writings of the famous Jewish historian Josephus</u> bear witness to the historical presence of Christ. Their testimony to Christ's existence is all the more valuable, because the Jews not only rejected Christ, but were extremely hostile toward Him. Many of these writings contain lies and distortions, but the very fact He merits attention supports His historical existence.

Third, <u>ancient nonreligious historical writings</u> also bear record of Christ. For example, Pliny, the governor of Bithynia (around 112 A.D.); the Roman historian Tacitus (115 A.D.); and the popular Roman writer Seutonius (about 120 A.D.) all acknowledged the existence of Christ.

A Study Course In Christian Evidences, p.140-141

After Jesus was born in Bethlehem in Judea, during the time of King Herod, Magi from the east came to Jerusalem...

Matthew 2:1

THE WORLDWIDE FLOOD

Evidence From

How could the Ark have survived a year-long water catastrophe without sinking? The study of hydrodynamics (the branch of physics having to do with the motion and action of water) has demonstrated that a giant boxlike vessel the size and shape described in the Bible would be almost unsinkable. **Even in a sea of gigantic waves, the Ark could be tilted to almost a 90° angle and would always tend to right itself again.** A vessel of this shape also aligns itself with the waves so that it experiences the least amount of pitching. Recent studies indicate the large fins on the front and back of many ancient vessels functioned to keep these vessels pointed into large waves during windy, stormy seas. This design may have started with the original design of Noah's ark, made necessary during the massive storm which it experianced.

In 1604, a Dutchman named Peter Jansz, built two smaller ships with the same proportions as the Ark. These small "arks" could carry one-third more cargo than regular ships without requiring any additional crew and quickly became a popular cargo carrier.

The perfect engineering of the Ark, with the exact characteristics necessary to survive the Flood, points to God as the ultimate Designer. **Every detail of the Bible** *confirms* **its accuracy and supernatural origin.**

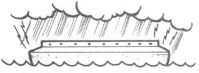

THE CREATION, P.150-151
THE GENESIS RECORD, P.181

"This is how you are to build it: The ark is to be 450 feet long, 75 feet wide and 45 feet high."

GENESIS 6:15

Evidence From BIOLOGY

The ironic life cycle of a toad-eating horsefly was first documented in the Arizona desert by Dr. Thomas Eisner of Cornell University. Eisner noticed this unusual drama at a muddy desert pond that had a large population of spadefoot toads. Upon close inspection of the pond, he noticed that some of the **toads were being pulled down into the mud as they hopped across the surface.** A little digging revealed that the predator was the horsefly larva. The larva burrows into the soft mud until its head barely sticks out. When an unsuspecting toad wanders by, the larva grabs him with its powerful jaws and pulls him into the mud. The larva injects the toad with poison and drinks the toad's body fluids. Eventually the larva grows into an adult horsefly, but now it must avoid becoming a meal for the toads that have survived the larva attack.

Even in the desert where food is scarce, God has designed an incredible circular food chain that works in perfect balance. Although mutually beneficial relationships such as this may not have been required before mankind rebelled, God has provided mechanisms to insure the survival of animals within His creation.

LETTING GOD CREATE YOUR DAY, VOL. 3, P.127

These all look to you to give them their food at the proper time.

PSALM 104:27

Evidence From
GEOLOGY

Buried in an eroded hillside at Yellowstone National Park are petrified tree trunks protruding through multiple layers of earth. For many years a geological marker at this site (Specimen Ridge) stated that the trees were buried and petrified in place. The parallel layers were interpreted as successive forests buried by volcanic activity. It was claimed that after each volcanic eruption, the volcanic-ash layer slowly weathered into suitable topsoil and hundreds of years passed as subsequent forests grew to maturity. This pattern supposedly happened 27 times spanning at least 30,000 years. This interpretation seemed to present a problem to biblical accuracy, which indicates there has been less than 10,000 years of Earth history.

However, this interpretation ignores several important observations. The roots of the tree stumps are broken off with only the root balls left. **The stump size, tree ring pattern, and number of tree rings throughout all 27 layers are remarkably similar.** What the evidence really supports is the rapid burial of a single massive forest by a flood of worldwide proportions. Trees are buried at different levels because they sank into the sediment at different times. Apparently the majority opinion has moved toward this better interpretation because the "multiple-forest" interpretive sign has been removed. Unfortunately, the reality of a worldwide Flood is still not mentioned. It is because the Bible can be trusted when it speaks on physical matters (such as the reality of a worldwide Flood) that we can trust what the Bible has to say about spiritual matters (morality and salvation).

THE YOUNG EARTH, P.113-115

It is the glory of God to conceal a matter; to search out a matter is the glory of kings.

PROVERBS 25:2

Evidence From GENETICS

The belief that mutations could slowly change one type of animal into a completely different type of animal is analogous to believing that you could change a black-and-white television into a color television by randomly changing parts. The random addition of parts will definitely produce *change;* but they will never produce an improved television, a color television, or a television that is slowly being transformed into some other useful device. Even if the correct color television parts were randomly placed into the television, the complexity required to change the television into some other useful device would not allow it to happen. It would become a nonfunctioning piece of junk long before it could have evolved into a more complex piece of machinery. Mutations cause a loss of information and do not explain where the information present within every living organism originated. This is a fact of science, regardless of how many parts are added without an overall plan.

Evolution relies on billions of years to explain the transformation of life. But even if zillions of parts are randomly added to trillions of televisions for billions of years, not a single improved television will result. In the same way, **mutations will produce changes, but they will never enable one type of creature to turn into a completely different type.** For that to happen, useful information would have to be added to the DNA of the creature. This simply does not happen as a result of random mutations.

SEARCH FOR THE TRUTH, P.23

And God made the beast of the earth after his kind, and cattle after their kind, and every thing that creepeth upon the earth after his kind: and God saw that it was good.

GENESIS 1:25 KJV

Evidence From GENETICS

One of the most common questions asked of biologists is the origin of races. This question produces confusion concerning the origin of mankind. If humans evolved from apes, should not some humans be closer to their apelike ancestors than others? If so, why not consider them "less human"? This logical conclusion of evolutionary thinking led directly to historical atrocities such as Hitler's elimination of the Jews and the genocide of Australian aborigines. Historical statements such as the following 2/24/1924 *New York Tribune* description of aborigines reveal the evolutionary-driven prejudice of the day:

> *"They appear to be a race totally incapable of civilization...these people are from a lower order of the human race."*

In contrast, the Bible states that all people have equal dignity, because all mankind descended from a single pair of humans. **Gregor Mendel, a Christian monk and the father of modern genetics, proved that the genetic variability of different characteristics (such as skin color and body shape) was present in the very first human created.** Skin color, eye color, etc., are not indications of our evolutionary past but are inherited characteristics from our parents. The only reason "white" people have "white" babies is that generations of light-skinned people married each other and the genes producing more melanin (dark skin pigments) became recessive or lost. The Bible stated that **ALL people are of one blood** long before science proved it.

ONE BLOOD: THE BIBLICAL ANSWER TO RACISM, P.7-88
THE REVISED ANSWER BOOK, P.219-236

And He has made from one blood every nation of men to dwell on all the face of the earth, and has determined their preappointed times and the boundaries of their dwellings...

ACTS 17:26 NKJV

Evidence From
THE FOSSIL RECORD

For over 200 years paleontologists and geologists have been digging in the hills, valleys, and plains of the earth. **During this time, they have uncovered and cataloged over a billion fossils.** Thousands of fascinating plant and animal fossils from extinct organisms have been found. Fossils, like living organisms, are found fully formed and distinctly different in structure. Evolutionists claim to have found animal bones having features intermediate between similar creatures, proving that evolution has occurred (e.g., small horses to big horses). Yet there are no examples in the fossil record of one animal slowly changing into a different kind of animal. Diagrams have been made which show variations within the same type of animal in an effort to organize them into a supposed evolutionary order. Textbooks promote this type of evidence because no transitional evidence showing one animal slowly changing into another has been found.

It is astounding that over a billion fossils have been found, yet there is no undisputed transitional form between very different types of animals or even animal features (such as a reptile's scale turning into a bird's feather). How can we say that evolution–the idea that man is the result of slow changes over time from earlier creatures–is a reasonable theory in light of this lack of evidence?

LETTING GOD CREATE YOUR DAY, VOL. 3, P.213

All flesh is not the same flesh: but there is one kind of flesh of men, another flesh of beasts, another of fishes, and another of birds.

1 CORINTHIANS 15:39 KJV

Evidence From GREAT SCIENTISTS

It is false to say that you cannot be a true scientist if you believe in creation. **The very founders of the scientific method and the scientists who developed some of the most important foundational principles of modern science were primarily creationists.** Creationists find themselves in the company of great men of science such as Robert Boyle, George Washington Carver, Michael Faraday, John Ambrose Fleming, James Joule, Lord Kelvin, Carolus Linneaus, Matthew Maury, Joseph Clerk Maxwell, Gregor Mendel, Samuel F.B. Morse, Isaac Newton, Louis Pasteur, William Ramsay, and Leonardo da Vinci. Many scientists (such as Carolus Linnaeus, George Washington Carver, and Matthew Maury) claim to have received their inspirational ideas directly from the Bible. There are also many creation scientists today who are top in their fields. Their belief in creation and a young earth has not proven to be a hindrance, but actually an asset to their scientific endeavors.

The discoveries of these great men of science are a testament to their belief in the Creator of a designed universe. Their confidence to pursue scientific discoveries was and continues to be a natural outcome of their belief that discovering how the world works is possible because the universe is the product of an intelligent and all-powerful Designer of order.

MEN OF SCIENCE, MEN OF GOD, P.1-3

The unfolding of your words gives light; it gives understanding to the simple.

PSALM 119:130

Evidence From
COMPARING RELIGIONS

Christianity is unique over all other religions because it is based on historical *facts*. Other religions are primarily centered on the ethical and religious *opinions* of their founders. Christianity is based on the character of Jesus Christ and what He said and did. Jesus repeatedly claimed to be the Creator God and acknowledged the accuracy of every part of Old Testament Scripture. Christianity's truth and validity rely on real events of the past such as: the Fall as a real event which explains why we need a savior and are incapable of saving ourselves; Noah's Flood as the best explanation the geology of the world around us; the specific predictions of future events, before they happened, such as the birth and crucifixion of Christ. The historical truth of these events can be objectively investigated from not only one source, but from multiple sources across time.

Christianity is the only religion which offers the possibility of physically investigating its factual nature, because it makes specific claims about the world around us. It also addresses where we came from. If one of these claims is false, then other biblical claims are also suspect. But if these claims are scientifically valid, there is every reason to believe all of the Bible's claims (such as what happens after death or what God requires of us in order to spend eternity in His presence).

Many Infallible Proofs, p.10

All your words are true; all your righteous laws are eternal.

Psalms 119:160

JANUARY 23

Evidence From
BOTANY

The Venus fly trap is a wonder of God's engineering. It has an ingenious method, quite different from other plants, for getting food. This **meat-eating plant** usually lives in mineral-poor soils. Therefore, it catches its food in order to provide the needed nutrients for survival. When an insect touches the tiny trigger hairs inside the trap, an electric signal is sent to cells on the outside of the trap. This impulse almost instantly causes the outer cells to secrete an acid which breaks down the cell wall. This, in turn, causes cells to expand, closing the trap at high speed. The more the insect fights, the more tightly the trap closes. Six to twelve days later, after the insect is digested, the plant receives a chemical signal and the trap opens to await its next meal.

Why do animals, and even plants, have to fight each other for their very survival? Is this really the creation that God described as "very good"? Actually, it is not. All of creation exhibits a fallen, aggressive nature due to the actions of Adam and Eve in the original garden paradise. It is unknown whether the complex mechanisms of survival demonstrated by the Venus fly trap were present but dormant before the Fall, or were designed within the plant for survival after the Fall. Either way, **the Venus fly trap is a marvel of purposeful design** which gives testimony to the genius behind its creation.

LETTING GOD CREATE YOUR DAY,
VOL. 4, P.46

Many, O LORD my God, are the wonders you have done. The things you planned for us no one can recount to you; were I to speak of them, they would be too many to declare.

PSALM 40:5

Evidence From ANATOMY

Our blood vessels are an incredible pipeline system which networks our entire body. These vessels come in three basic types: arteries, veins, and capillaries. Capillaries are microscopic vessels that link the smallest arteries to the veins. They are the most abundant type of blood vessels. About 40 capillaries laid end to end measure only one inch. Yet they are so numerous that if **all of the capillaries in our body were laid end to end they would stretch around the equator two times!**

Blood is pumped into the capillaries with enough force to drive the plasma through the porous walls of these tiny vessels, thus nourishing surrounding cells. However, the pressure is not so great that the red and white blood cells are lost or the capillaries burst. **There must be an absolutely perfect balance** of pressure between the blood flowing within the vessel, the blood being forced through the vessel walls, and the blood in and around the body's cells. Without question, the design of our blood vessels and the perfect balance of pressure required to maintain life is testimony to our Designer.

THE HUMAN BODY: ACCIDENT OR DESIGN?, P.42-44

To Him who alone does great wonders, For His lovingkindness is everlasting...

PSALM 136:4 NASV

Evidence From GEOLOGY

The evolutionary model assumes that coal formed gradually over long time periods from decaying plants. Coal deposits are believed to be the compacted accumulation of generations of swamp plants which were covered by other sediments over millions of years. **In reality, the nature of coal deposits contradict this slow and gradual model.** For example:

1. Well-preserved remains of leaves and insects are frequently found in coal. This requires that the vegetation was buried very quickly (such as would have happened during a massive flood) in order to have prevented the remains from rotting.
2. Coal deposits covering thousands of square miles are found hundreds of feet thick. This testifies to a flood of worldwide extent. The "swamp model" of coal formation does not explain the massive extent of coal reserves.
3. Coal seams are found in repeated overlying layers, often separated by sterile rock types with no sign of soil. This indicates burial under water (with sediment washing in between layers), not slow accumulation from swamps.

Coal is **a buried testimony** to both the **Worldwide Flood** and the incredible hatred God has of sin.

UNLOCKING THE MYSTERIES OF CREATION, 1ˢᵀ ED., P.131

"...I will send rain on the earth for forty days and forty nights, and I will wipe from the face of the earth every living creature I have made."

GENESIS 7:4

Evidence From
THE FOSSIL RECORD

What does the fossil record show concerning the appearance of all basic animal body types? The following quotes are representative of what has been found after extensive searching by an army of evolutionary paleontologists over the last 150 years. These statements by evolutionary scientists are both contextual and relevant to what the fossil record actually reveals:

" *All paleontologists know that the fossil record contains precious little in the way of intermediate forms; transitions between major groups are characteristically abrupt.*"

" *Despite the bright promise that paleontology provides of 'seeing' evolution, it has presented some nasty difficulties for evolutionists, the most notorious of which is the presence of 'gaps' in the fossil record.*"

" *No real evolutionist, whether gradualist or punctuationist, uses the fossil record as evidence in favor of the theory of evolution as opposed to special creation....*"

" *The known fossil record fails to document a single example of phyletic evolution accomplishing a major morphologic transition.*"

Evolutionists have lined up some fossils which seem to fill small gaps between closely related creatures. However, accepting small transitions as evidence in support of the grand evolution scenario is like believing a single stepping stone proves that a bridge once spanned the Mississippi River in the same location.

Evolution requires transitional forms between the most basic animal groups–yet none exist. Creation asserts that there never were transitions between basic kinds of life. This is exactly what the fossil record shows. What better evidence for creation could there be?

Search for the Truth, p. 43

For the foolishness of God is wiser than man's wisdom....

1 Corinthians 1:25

JANUARY 27

Evidence From
CREATION FOUNDATION

What kind of God would make creatures whose only function seems to be devouring and feeding upon other creatures? Sir Dave Attenborough, who has produced the acclaimed *Life on Earth* and *Living Planet* series for BBC, states it this way:

"When creationists talk about God creating every [type of animal] in a separate act, they always instance hummingbirds... and beautiful things. But I tend to think instead of a parasitic worm that is boring through the eye of a boy sitting on the bank of a river in West Africa, and [I ask them], 'Are you telling me that the God you believe in, who you also say is an all-merciful God, who cares for each one of us individually–are you saying that God created this worm that can live in no other way than in an innocent child's eyeball? Because that doesn't seem to me to coincide with a God who's full of mercy.'"

Evolutionists do not believe that all of creation has developed a fallen nature. Creatures originally created to live in harmony have become deadly competitors. Mankind chose to reject God and died spiritually. It is only by being "born again" that this spiritual union with God can be restored. God cursed creation as an act of mercy. It would have been intolerable for fallen mankind to exist in the midst of perfection. Furthermore, God has given us the ability to prevent and cure many diseases (when we choose to spend our time and resources to do so). At times He even provides supernatural healing. Most importantly, God has provided a pathway to spend eternity in paradise after our short time here on Earth. God became a human in order to take the penalty which we deserve. **What more could He have done?**

THE REVISED ANSWERS BOOK, p.103 -113

"For my thoughts are not your thoughts, neither are your ways my ways," saith the LORD.

ISAIAH 55:8 KJV

Evidence From
BIOLOGY

The eagle's diving speed can exceed 100 miles per hour. At this speed, the eagle's eyesight must be perfect in order to know exactly when to pull out of a dive. **Its eyes are designed to spot a rabbit or fish up to one mile away.** The eagle also has remarkably designed wings, each covered by over 12,000 feathers. Aircraft designers are still trying to copy this engineering marvel.

Besides the ability to climb to 10,000 feet within minutes, the parent eagle also assists its young in flight. **As it flies alongside the eaglet, whirlpools of air formed by its primary feathers provide the eaglet with additional lift.**

In speaking of His protective care over the nation of Israel, God states, "...I bare you on eagles' wings...." (Exodus 19:4 KJV). The Hebrew word for "bare" is *nacah,* and its primary root means "to lift." This is exactly what the parent eagle does to help its young in flight.

The precise selection and meaning of words used in the Bible is a testimony to both the **accuracy and precision** of this remarkable book.

Character Sketches, Vol. III, p171-174

You yourselves have seen what I did to Egypt, and how I carried you on eagles' wings and brought you to myself.

Exodus 19:4

Evidence From BIBLICAL UNIQUENESS

Any study of man's history will prove that the Bible had (and still has) a unique and profound influence. The Bible gives us a proper perspective on all vital human issues, including marriage, raising children, finances, government, the judicial system, equal rights, aging, poverty, health, work, ecology, education, entertainment, etc. **The basis for the world's laws and ethics all originate in God's Word.** Even the seven-day week, which was given at creation, has become the worldwide standard pattern. No other source for this cycle has ever been offered.

The Bible tells us that God is good and there is absolutely no darkness in Him (Mark 10:18, 1 John 1:5). **Throughout history whenever Christianity has been blamed for atrocities, one always finds major deviations from God's Word.** Conversely, wherever the Bible is *believed* and *followed,* people live in harmony. Even a skeptic has to stand in awe of the Bible's unique influence and profound insight.

RICH AND TINA KLEISS

All Scripture is God-breathed and is useful for teaching, rebuking, correcting and training in righteousness, so that the man of God may be thoroughly equipped for every good work.

2 TIMOTHY 3:16-17

Evidence From GEOLOGY

If, as evolutionists say, the earth formed as a hot molten mass, it should have cooled to its present temperature in far less than 4.5 billion years. Evolutionists believe that radioactive decay accounts for the still-elevated temperature of the earth's core. Yet estimates of the amount of heat created by radioactive decay cannot account for the heat present in the earth's core–unless the earth is much younger than assumed. The high temperature at the core of the earth testifies to a young earth. Lord Kelvin used this argument to show that evolutionary geologists of his day were wrong about the age of the earth and his conclusions are still accurate today. In spite of this type of evidence, evolutionists continue to claim that the earth is about 4.5 billion years old.

The vast majority of scientific dating methods indicate that the earth is quite young. Since the earth was created as a fully formed and functional planet, its core temperature would have been very high–similar to today–from the very beginning. The fact that the core of the earth is still quite hot confirms what Christians who take the Word of God seriously have believed all along–both the earth and the entire universe were formed quite recently.

In the Beginning, 7ᵀᴴ Ed., p.33

...speak to the earth, and it will teach you....

Job 12:8

Evidence From
BIOLOGY

One type of female angler fish grows to approximately three and one half feet, and its mouth takes up much of its size. Just above its top lip the angler fish has been designed with a six-inch-long fishing pole. This pole has a little orange light on the end of it. The angler fish lives a mile beneath the ocean where it is dark. It attracts other fish with its light. When creatures move in to strike at the light, the angler fish grabs them with its long, sharp teeth. When not in use, its fishing rod fits into a groove on the top of the angler fish's head.

Yet the strangest part of the angler fish's life is its mating practices. While the female is over three feet long, the male angler fish is only one-half an inch long. He has no fishing pole or light. Mating starts when the tiny male swims up to the female and sinks his teeth into her side. He never lets go the rest of his life. In fact, soon his skin and circulatory system actually join the female's. All that is left of the male is a small pouch on the female's side containing the male's reproductive organs, which continue to fertilize the female's eggs.

Apparently, these strange reproductive and predatory habits were given to the angler fish after the Fall. What is the mathematical probability that any of these unique characteristics could have developed by random step-by-step changes? How wonderful is God's creativity!

LETTING GOD CREATE YOUR DAY,
Vol. 4, p.195
ANGLER FISH (CREATURES THAT GLOW) P. 8-9

How great are your works, O LORD, how profound your thoughts!

PSALM 92:5

Before I Find a Boy I Love

Oh Lord, I have a *big* request
　Which I must ask You now.
Before I find a boy I love,
　I *pray* You show me how.

I know Your Word is very clear
　On what a boy should be.
Don't let my feelings mix me up,
　But give me *eyes* to see.

Keep me from boys who turn my heart
　From You with looks or charm.
Protect me from temptations and
　Those things which bring me harm.

Help me discern all those sweet words
　And actions which are fake.
Guide me to see what's right,
　What's wrong;
　My *love* for *You* is at stake.

Help me consider only boys,
　With lives that would please You,
Whose focus is to serve You well
　And do what *You* would do.

Lord, help me find a boy that's wise,
　That seeks and does what's right;
So if I choose to follow him,
　We'll *both* walk in Your light.

Show me a boy that knows You well,
　That spends much time with You;
So he can *know* and *do* Your will
　And *love* just like *You* do.

I know that if I follow You
　And put *You first* in all,
The boy I find will be *Your* choice;
　Our *purity* won't fall.

Prepare *me*, Lord, to be a girl
　That such a boy will choose;
To grow with him, close to Your heart—
　With You, we cannot lose!

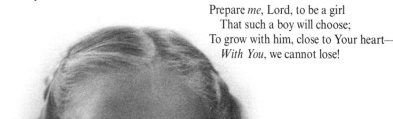

Evidence From
GREAT SCIENTISTS

If the evidence for creation is so strong, why don't more scientists accept this evidence and reject evolution? The primary reason is that **science has been defined to eliminate the consideration of God's interaction in creation**. Richard Dickerson, a prominent biochemist and member of the elite National Academy of Science, states it this way:

"Science, fundamentally, is a game. It is a game with one overriding and defining rule: **Let us see how far and to what extent we can explain the behavior of the physical and material universe in terms of purely physical and material causes, without invoking the supernatural.** Calling down special-purpose miracles as explanations constitutes a form of intellectual 'cheating.' A chess player is perfectly capable of moving his opponent's king physically from the board and smashing it in the midst of the tournament. But this would not make him a chess champion, because the rules have not been followed."

Evolution is not promoted because of the overwhelming evidence supporting this concept. Nor is creation rejected because it is a poor explanation for life's origin. Creation is simply ignored by most scientists because they have been trained to ignore this possibility. They would be **accused of "cheating"** if they did accept evidence for creation!

DARWIN'S BLACK BOX: THE BIOCHEMICAL CHALLENGE TO EVOLUTION, P.238 - 243

"If you abide in My word, you are My disciples indeed. And you shall know the truth, and the truth shall make you free."

JOHN 8:31-32 NKJV

Evidence From GENETICS

It is commonly assumed that the wide variety of life on Earth proves that evolution has taken place. Darwin proposed that small changes, similar to what is possible by selective breeding, can be extended to produce completely different kinds of creatures. Selective breeding, which has produced our many dog varieties, is quite common.

Within every type of living organism, wide variation is possible and many varieties may be developed. An example is the one million varieties of rice that have been developed. The information needed to create this wide variety of rice was already present on the rice DNA at the moment of creation. Selective breeding can definitely produce the wide variety and diversity we find in such plants as rice. **However, a limit is always reached**—rice stays rice and reptiles never turn into birds. This is true, regardless of how much time passes. **With time, creatures actually degenerate by birth defects rather than turning into new types of creatures.**

There is no observable scientific evidence to support the idea that evolution of completely different types of creatures can take place. The science of genetics wasn't formally introduced until the early 1900s. Since then intensive breeding experiments have failed to show how even one kind of animal could ever change into another kind of animal.

Many Infallible Proofs, p.251-255

And God said, "Let the land produce living creatures according to their kinds...."

Genesis 1:24

Evidence From
PHYSICS

If the sun were closer, **we would burn up**; if farther away, we would **freeze**. If our atmosphere was thinner, the meteors that now harmlessly burn up **would constantly bombard** us. If the moon was not precisely its current size and distance, the **ocean tides would flood** the land twice a day. If the continental shelf was smaller, the oceans would be deeper near shore. This would lower the **oxygen level in the atmosphere** making life much more difficult.

A study of the ecological processes in nature (water, oxygen balance, seasons, day/night cycles, etc.) **show that they must be maintained in delicate balance** or Earth would just be another lifeless planet. The forces, speeds, and distances that hold our planets within our solar system, galaxy, and universe are all in delicate balance. The mechanisms that cause our bodies to function and reproduce are all finely tuned. The very constants that hold atoms together and keep the universe from flying apart or imploding are all in perfect balance. These are just a few examples which point to God's perfect "maintenance plan." These and thousands of other variables seem to be held in precise balance to make both the earth and our universe a perfect habitat for human life. It is totally outside the realm of reason to assume that all of these perfectly balanced systems just happened by chance.

God: Coming Face to Face with His Majesty, P.78

If it were his intention and he withdrew his spirit and breath, all mankind would perish together and man would return to dust.

JOB 34:14-15

Evidence From
BIBLICAL ACCURACY

Prothrombin is a chemical in our body which is absolutely critical for blood clotting. Without it, we would bleed to death with even the smallest cut. Vitamin K is vital for the production of prothrombin by the liver. Therefore, both vitamin K and prothrombin are necessary for life. Newborn boys begin production of vitamin K on day five through day seven after birth. On the eighth day, a newborn male child reaches his lifetime maximum level of prothrombin. Therefore, **on the eighth day after birth, a male baby has the highest clotting rate** of any time in his life. If a male baby is going to be circumcised, the eighth day after birth would be the safest day for this to take place.

Isn't it interesting that **over 4,000 years ago God told Abraham to have newborn males circumcised on the eighth day!** Before God told Abraham to undergo this procedure, there was no trial-and-error testing to find the best day on which to circumcise a baby. Only our Creator could have known this biological fact and have made sure that it was included in the Bible.

A STUDY COURSE IN CHRISTIAN EVIDENCES, P.130
*REASON AND REVELATION,*13[7], JULY 1993, P.55
APOLOGETICSPRESS.ORG/FAQ/R&R9307B.HTM

"And every male among you who is eight days old shall be circumcised throughout your generations...."

GENESIS 17:12 NAS

Evidence From
PHYSICS

Most students assume that because a theory is taught in textbooks–especially theories as widely believed as quantum physics, special relativity, or the big bang–it must be true. Yet how many people understand how these concepts explain reality or the many unsolved problems with each theory? If we are perfectly honest with ourselves, **we really don't even understand what an atom is,** so how can we state that we know where, when, and how the atom was created?

A fascinating model of the atom has been developed by David Bergman which attempts to explain the observable properties of the electron, proton, and neutron based purely on Maxwell and Faraday's equations for moving charges. According to this Electric Theory of Mass (ETM), **all energy and matter can be explained in terms of circular rings of the moving positive and negative charges.** This theory claims to accurately model the dual particle/wave properties of electrons; the stability, spin, and mass of elements and subatomic components; and the mechanisms of covalent and ionic bonding.

The implications of this model are staggering. If it is correct, then everything physical is an electromagnetic field created by moving positive and negative charges. In essence, **physical reality may not be made out of tangible matter at all.** This presents several interesting questions–who created the moving charges, what is a "charge", and why are they in constant motion? Perhaps our physical world is really just an electromagnetic field simulating solid objects. But who is maintaining the simulation?

WWW.COMMONSENSESCIENCE.ORG

He is before all things, and by Him all things hold together.

COLOSSIANS 1:17 RSV

Evidence From ARCHAEOLOGY

For many years **biblical critics have doubted the existence of writing before the time of Moses.** This is one of the reasons given for not believing that Moses wrote the first few books of the Bible. These critics teach that the original books of the Bible were written much later and just attributed to Moses.

Archaeologists, however, have **unearthed an ancient library in the city of Ur.** This library contains thousands of stone "books." Ur of Chaldees was Abraham's home before he moved to Canaan, and some of these stone books were written even before Abraham's day. These books consist of both scholarly subjects and books that an ordinary tradesman would read. **This was at least 4,000 years ago and a full 1,000 years before Moses was born.**

If the common man on the street of 4,000 years ago could read and write, why should we doubt that a highly educated man like Moses could have compiled the accounts from Adam to Abraham into the first book of the Bible? Jesus Christ accepted and confirmed that Moses wrote the first books of the Bible. To believe otherwise is to doubt what we find in archaeology, the authority of the Bible, and Jesus Himself.

The Bible has the Answers, p.66

[Jesus said,] "If you believed Moses, you would believe me, for he wrote about me."

John 5:46

FEBRUARY 7

Evidence From ANATOMY

All efficient machines have control systems to regulate their operation. **The human body also has control systems.** For example, the endocrine system is one type of control center that uses chemical stimulation. It puts more than 100 different chemicals (called hormones) directly into the blood stream to trigger specific bodily activities. Humans could not survive without this system.

Even more complex is the fact that the endocrine system must coexist with the circulatory and nervous systems. **Each chemical hormone is so specialized that it transmits its message to only certain target cells** that have special receptors capable of recognizing the specific chemical. The hormone molecules have a specific shape that only allows them to attach to other molecules with a corresponding shape, much like a lock and a key. The hormones have no effect anywhere else in the body.

Hormones are basically coded messages sent out at the right time, to the right place, and in the right amounts to regulate the functions of our body. Common sense tells us that all messages require an intelligent originator. How does evolution explain the programmed messages used by our hormonal system?

THE HUMAN BODY: ACCIDENT OR DESIGN?,
P.72-73

"Your hands shaped me and made me."

JOB 10:8

Evidence From COMMON SENSE

If life is the result of random-chance processes, then so are our very thoughts. Therefore our thoughts–including what you are thinking right now–would merely be the consequence of a long series of accidents. In other words, **your thoughts would have no connection with reality**–including the thought that life is a result of chance natural processes–because they would be random occurrences resulting from random processes. In a very real sense, evolution undercuts the very basis for all human understanding, because it destroys the basis for believing that truth could exist.

The concept of evolution even undercuts the mechanisms proposed for evolution. It has been said that humans use only a small fraction of their mental abilities. If this is the case, how could our unused abilities have evolved in the first place? Certainly not by natural selection. Natural selection will only select an existing characteristic or ability which has some use. If unused mental ability is not used, it can never be selected for an advantage. Evolution teaches that any capabilities which are not used by a creature will waste away and become lost over time. The idea that natural selection is supposedly driving evolution upward is an illogical concept that contradicts the observation from the world around us.

In the Beginning, 7ᵀᴴ Ed., p.18

For the LORD gives wisdom, and from his mouth come knowledge and understanding.

Proverbs 2:6

THE FOSSIL RECORD
Evidence From

One of the premier fossil evidences for evolution found in every textbook on the subject is the fossil remains of a bird known as **Archaeopteryx** (meaning ancient wing). Creationists claim that gaps exist in the fossil record because all major animal groups were created as distinct kinds. Textbooks present Archaeopteryx as a prime example of a fossil that fills the gap between reptiles and birds. Yet a closer look at the evidence reveals that this icon of evolution does not fill the huge gap between birds or any other creature.

Almost all paleontologists now agree that Archaeopteryx could not be the link between birds and reptiles. It is acknowledged that this fossil was a creature with fully formed and functional feathers, wings similar to modern birds, and a wishbone needed for flight muscle attachment. In other words, **Archaeopteryx is simply an extinct species of bird.** The fact that the Archaeopteryx fossils have minor variations from modern birds–such as teeth and claws on the wings–is irrelevant because other modern birds (hoatzin, ostrich) have some of these same features.

So why is this bird fossil still presented in textbooks as evidence that reptiles have turned into birds? Could it be because intensive searching has turned up nothing better? After almost two centuries of scientific investigation, creation is still the best explanation for the widely diverse types of living and fossil animals found on the earth.

REFUTING EVOLUTION, P.57-59
ICONS OF EVOLUTION, P.111-136

A discerning man keeps wisdom in view, but a fool's eyes wander to the ends of the earth.

PROVERBS 17:24

MATHEMATICS

Evidence From

The present human population of the world supports the Genesis record. According to known historical records, the **world's population doubles approximately every 100 years.** This population doubling has happened even faster in the last few hundred years, taking place about every 60 years.

Starting with an original population of eight people from the Ark (Noah's family), one can easily calculate that the population would have to double itself a little over 30 times to produce the present world population of 7 billion. If the most straightforward understanding of the Bible is correct, Noah lived about 4,500 years ago. This gives an average doubling interval of almost 150 years, which is very conservative when compared to the observed doubling rate of approximately 100 years.

Now let's assume that evolution is correct and that some apelike creatures turned into people approximately 1,000,000 years ago. You can calculate how many people there should be on Earth based on the historical rate of a population doubling (once every 150 years), starting with two ape-people, and doubling their population every 150 years for 1,000,000 years (6,000 times). **The result is more people on the earth than there are atoms in the entire universe.** If people have been around for as long as evolutionists tell us, there should be more people and lots more bodies. The observable facts perfectly fit a biblical time frame.

SCIENCE AND THE BIBLE, P.86

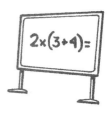

Thy word is true from the beginning: and every one of thy righteous judgments endureth forever.

PSALM 119:160 KJV

Evidence From
BIOLOGY

Painted turtles live farther north than any other North American turtle. The baby turtles hatch in the late summer but stay buried in the ground, safe from predators all winter. However, the turtle's nest is not deep enough to keep from freezing solid during frigid winter weather. So how do the turtles survive?

As the baby turtles freeze, their blood circulation concentrates on preserving the action of the heart and brain. Eventually even these freeze solid. There is no breathing and no heartbeat. **Only a tiny bit of electrical activity in the frozen brain reveals that life remains in the body.** Normally, when living cells freeze, long sharp ice crystals form, puncturing the cell membrane and killing the cells. This is one reason that cryogenically frozen people cannot be revived. The presence of a special *protein*, which is made by the painted turtle's liver and circulated to every cell in the turtle's body, prevents the ice crystals from becoming large enough to puncture delicate cell walls.

How could random processes have produced this protein? Either it was present the moment the turtle was created, or the turtle would have died during the first hard freeze. Only God could have invented such a unique method of protecting tiny painted turtles.

LETTING GOD CREATE YOUR DAY,
VOL. 3, P.47

...There is none like unto thee, O Lord; neither are there any works like unto thy works.

PSALM 86:8 KJV

Evidence From
CHEMISTRY

As we learn more about the chemistry of life, the similarity of living cells to complex machines is becoming increasingly obvious. **Even at the microscopic level, scientists have found that the intricate parts of each cell are fashioned like irreducibly complex machines.** Although these machines are made of proteins instead of metal, their complexity is proof that they could only have been produced by an intelligent designer. The simple *mousetrap* is an example of an irreducibly complex machine. This machine consists of a *platform, spring, hammer, catch, and hold-down latch-bar*. The absence of any one of these five components will turn this machine into a piece of useless junk. Thus, this functioning machine is "irreducibly complex." It is this interdependence of the individual parts which makes it obvious that the simple mousetrap has a designer.

Living things are made from far more sophisticated irreducibly complex parts. For instance, within certain single-celled organisms there are complex structures called cilia. These spinning fibers allow the organism to move about. Scientists have discovered that cilia have the same irreducibly complex interdependence of parts as an electric motor. The cilia spin within sealed shafts as charged particles are alternatively repelled and attracted in the same way the rotor and stator of an electric motor work. **If any part of the cilia are removed, they will cease to function.** Only the spiritually blind can deny God's handiwork as we discover tiny electric motors placed inside of microscopic organisms!

DARWIN'S BLACK BOX: THE BIOCHEMICAL CHALLENGE TO EVOLUTION, P.39-73

Know that the LORD is God. It is he who made us, and we are his...

PSALM 100:3

Evidence From THE FOSSIL RECORD

The very nature of the fossil record testifies to a worldwide water catastrophe in the past. In *Germany* there are lignite beds (a form of brown coal) which contain large numbers of fossil plants, animals, and insects from various regions and climates of the world. The detailed structures of these animals have been remarkably preserved and are striking proof of sudden burial. Huge diatomite deposits near *Lompoc, California,* contain millions of beautifully preserved fish, usually in positions indicating sudden death. Masses of fossilized fish have been found washed together and suddenly buried in *Scotland,* while 70 tons of dinosaur fossils were found at a 13,000 foot elevation in *China.* How did they get buried so high?

These evidences are exactly what one would expect to find after a worldwide flood like the one recorded in the Bible. They are not a result of natural death over millions of years. There is not a single example of a massive fossil graveyard with large varieties of animals currently forming anywhere in the world. The rapid burial of life by the worldwide Flood of the Bible is the best explanation for the geologic and fossil observations we see in the world around us.

THE CREATION, P.89

The waters rose and covered the mountains to a depth of more than twenty feet.... Everything on dry land that had the breath of life in its nostrils died.

GENESIS 7:20,22

Evidence From GEOLOGY

The fossilization of large organisms such as dinosaurs and whole trees presents a problem for the traditional evolutionary approach to fossilization. **Some of these fossils (called polystrata fossils) are found intact and poking through multiple rock layers.** Organisms of this size could never have been fossilized by a slow burial over time. Observation of the world around us shows that **organisms decay rather than fossilize.** Think how long it would take to bury a huge dinosaur body by slow sedimentation over large periods of time. The body would be long gone before it was ever buried. One must conclude that these types of fossils were rapidly buried under large amounts of sediment.

In Newcastle, England, a fossilized tree 59 feet long and almost six and a half feet in diameter was found buried at a 40° angle. **The tree goes through ten separate layers of coal.** This evidence fits the biblical flood model, but cannot possibly be explained by slow burial over millions of years. It is the extent, character, and number of these types of geological formations that testify to the worldwide Flood spoken of in the Bible.

THE CREATION, P.89-90

...the waters stood above the mountains. But at your rebuke the waters fled...they flowed over the mountains, they went down into the valleys, to the place you assigned for them.

PSALM 104:6-8

Evidence From
COMMON SENSE

There are hundreds of methods for dating the age of the earth. However, none can scientifically prove how long ago the earth formed. We can look at objects and determine their mass, color, composition and rate of change, but none of these things will determine the object's age. To determine a date, we must know how much of something was present at the beginning and how it has changed since formation. In other words, all dating methods depend on assumptions and any date we get depends upon the assumptions that are made. It is impossible to "scientifically" prove the age of an ancient object.

However, if unbiased observers make the same assumptions that evolutionists routinely make (extending present measured rates of change into the distant past), the vast majority of dating methods indicate that the earth and solar system were formed quite recently. For example, scientists have been able to calculate the rate at which certain elements (aluminum, antimony, calcium, chlorine, copper, cobalt, gold, iron, lead, mercury, nickel, silicon, silver, sodium, tin, zinc, etc.) flow into the ocean. **By dividing the amount of these elements in ocean water by the measured rate at which the same elements are flowing into the ocean, we can estimate an age for the ocean.** It turns out these methods date the oceans (and the earth) far too young for evolution to have happened.

In actuality, the most reliable method of determining the age of an object is to research written historical records concerning the object. This is exactly what we have in the Bible.

THE ILLUSTRATED ORIGINS ANSWERS BOOK, P.18-20

...He has also set eternity in the hearts of men; yet they cannot fathom what God has done from the beginning to end.

ECCLESIASTES 3:11

Evidence From
COMPARING RELIGIONS

The Bible is unique among all the religious writings of the ancient world in the following ways:

1. **It is the only book** that gives an account of the creation of all things from nothing.
2. **It is the only book of ancient history** that reveals a meaning and purpose behind events of the past.
3. **It is the only book** that gives a continuous historical record from the first man to the present era.
4. **It is the only religious book** which sets the moral standard required by man at an impossible level and explains why man, by his efforts, can never achieve this standard.
5. **It is the only book** containing detailed prophecies of future events that have come true with 100% accuracy.

The very words of the Bible are God-breathed. The Old Testament alone states approximately 2,600 times that it is God's Word. No other religious work claims this.

MANY INFALLIBLE PROOFS, P.156-157

Above all, you must understand that no prophecy of Scripture came about by the prophet's own interpretation. For prophecy never had its origin in the will of man, but men spoke from God as they were carried along by the Holy Spirit.

2 PETER 1:20,21

Evidence From BIOLOGY

One of nature's masters of disguise is the stick insect. Stick insects are leaf eaters designed to look like little twigs. One tropical stick insect is as thick as a finger and the same color as the bamboo on which it is found. It even has swollen ridges just like bamboo! Other types have leafy flaps that **match the leaves** of the plants which they like to eat. Some stick insects even lay eggs that **look exactly like the seeds** of the plant on which they feed. A stick insect that's found in New Mexico **glues its eggs to grass stems**. The position and shape of their pointed eggs exactly imitate the seeds of the grass!

Although stick insects don't fly, some of them have brightly colored wings that can fold very quickly to scare away nervous birds who want to investigate them for lunch. Some stick insects will often **sway with the breeze** to make their illusion even more effective. Others will sit motionless for hours as if they are just another **piece of dead wood**.

Stick insects are even geniuses at using their predator's weakness for their own protection. Birds understand this and will closely examine non-moving twigs in search of a meal. **Stick insects will not even move when being carried away by a bird,** thus fooling many birds into dropping them. Although these defense mechanisms were likely designed after the Fall, stick insects are clearly not the result of random mutations, but the intelligent design of a Creator.

LETTING GOD CREATE YOUR DAY,
VOL. 3, P.194

Ascribe to the LORD the glory due his name; worship the LORD in the splendor of his holiness.

PSALM 29:2

Evidence From ASTRONOMY

In 1979, the Voyager space probe filmed a volcano erupting on Io, one of Jupiter's inner moons. This discovery amazed the NASA scientists who believe in the evolutionary concept that the solar system is billions of years old. **Small bodies such as this moon should have cooled off long ago.** Io, however, was not found to be cold and dead, but was literally bubbling with volcanoes. The cameras on Voyager even recorded one volcanic eruption on the moon's rim that sent fire and brimstone more than 100 miles into space. Where did this interior heat come from? Before this observation, the earth was considered the only geologically active body in the solar system, but Io was found to be even more active.

The fact that Io still has volcanic activity when it is supposedly almost 5 billion years old has no adequate explanation. Scientists have scrambled to find explanations, attributing the heat to Jupiter's gravitational pull or to radioactive decay in Io's core, but neither explanation fits the observations. It is only the assumptions of evolution that blind researchers to the most obvious solution. Perhaps Io is still hot because it is simply not very old!

IT'S A YOUNG WORLD AFTER ALL, P.43-44

The heavens declare the glory of God; the skies proclaim the work of his hands. Day after day they pour forth speech; night after night they display knowledge.

PSALM 19:1-2

Evidence From
BIOLOGY

Extra nitrogen dissolves into the blood of divers who breathe compressed air while diving deep underwater. If the divers return to the surface too quickly, the dissolved nitrogen bubbles out of their blood. These bubbles block blood flow to muscles, organs, and the brain, often leading to death. For many years, scientists could not understand why other mammals such as seals **could make extended dives into deep water and not develop this condition called "the bends."**

They found the answer by using a backpack to monitor the seal's heart rate, sample its blood, and record its diving depth. True to the laws of physics, nitrogen accumulated in the seal's blood as it descended deep into the ocean. However, the nitrogen concentration leveled off in the seal's blood just before reaching a dangerous point. **Scientists discovered that the tiny sacks in the seal's lungs, which absorb air in order to pass oxygen into the blood stream, simply shut down once the nitrogen level in the blood gets too high.** At the same time, the seal's heart, liver, and blubber begin to absorb the nitrogen from the blood. As the seal ascends to the surface, the air exchange sacks in the lungs reactivate. A complex system like this could only be the result of design.

LETTING GOD CREATE YOUR DAY, VOL. 3, P.79

"Ah, Sovereign LORD, You have made the heavens and the earth by your great power and outstretched arm. Nothing is too hard for You."

JEREMIAH 32:17

Evidence From
PROPHECY

Even the most mundane parts of Scripture can have great significance. One example is the list of ancestors leading from Adam to Noah, which can be found in Genesis Chapter 5. Ancient names were not just randomly selected but chosen to convey a meaning. For instance, Adam means "man" and his son Seth means "appointed," because he was appointed to take the place of Abel. Looking at the entire list:

Adam means *"Man"*
Seth means *"Appointed"*
Enosh means *"Mortal"*
Kenan means *"Sorrow"*
Mahalalel means *"The blessed God"*
Jared means *"Shall come down"*
Enoch means *"Teaching"*
Methuselah means *"His death shall bring"*
Lamech means *"The despairing"*
Noah means *"Comfort (or rest)"*

Putting it all together, we find that the very names of the first 10 generations of mankind form the promise of our coming Savior. **"Man [is] appointed mortal sorrow; [but] the Blessed God shall come down, teaching [that] His death shall bring the despairing comfort (or rest)."**

Could this be a coincidence, or can we see that the Holy Spirit truly directed both history and the writing of every detail of Scripture?

HIDDEN TREASURES IN THE BIBLICAL TEXT,
P.11-18

...Who foretold this long ago, who declared it from the distant past? Was it not I, the LORD? And there is no God apart from me, a righteous God and Savior; there is none but me.

ISAIAH 45:21

Evidence From
PROPHECY

"The implication of the Gospel message within the very names of the first ten generations of mankind is staggering. It demonstrates that from the beginning of time God had already laid out his plan of redemption for the predicament of mankind. It is the beginning of a love story, ultimately written in blood on a cross."

"This simple list of names is one of many evidences that the Bible is...the product of supernatural engineering. This punctures the presumptions of most people who view the Bible as mere stories–as a record of an evolving cultural tradition. The Bible claims to be authored by the One who alone knows the end from the beginning. The One who is not just watching time pass by but instantaneously knows every detail of the past, the present, and the future...because **He is the Creator of time itself.**"

"It is astonishing to discover how many Bible controversies simply evaporate if one simply recognizes the unity and the integrity of these 66 books. **Every number, every place, every name, every detail—'every jot and tittle'** (the smallest space of the Hebrew language)—**is part of a tightly engineered design**, tailored for our learning, our discovery, and our amazement."

Hidden Treasures in the Biblical Text, p.17

...I say unto you, till heaven and earth pass, one jot or one tittle shall in no wise pass from the law, till all be fulfilled.

Matthew 5:18 KJV

Evidence From
BIOLOGY

Evolutionists teach that small changes (which are actually just genetic variations) over vast amounts of time can produce large genetic shifts, eventually producing completely new creatures. This belief ignores a major problem with evolution; **where does the *useful* information come from?** Failing to ask this question prevents students from questioning which direction mutational changes are driving an organism. This omission (not telling students **which way** mutational changes are heading) leads them to the wrong conclusion concerning what evolutionary change can or cannot accomplish.

It is conceivable that small changes could yield a new creature if these changes added useful information to the existing creature. Let's pretend evolutionary change is like a journey by train. The journey from Atlanta to Chicago would be like the upward advancement from a single-cell organism to a man while the journey in the opposite direction–from Atlanta to Miami–would be like multiple birth defects leading to the extinction of a species. Each foot along the journey is like a small mutation in a creature's transformation. You would only need to see the beginning of the trip to trust that the train *could* arrive a thousand miles away. However, if the train were actually heading south instead of north, you would have no reason to believe it would end up in Chicago (as a new type of creature). The same is true of mutational changes used to support evolutionary development. Information is *always* lost. For a protozoa to turn into a pony, enormous amounts of *useful* information would need to be added. All examples of evolution are in the wrong direction–yielding a loss of information.

Creation Magazine, *March 2002*,
p.16-19.

The first to present his case seems right, till another comes forward and questions him.

Proverbs 18:17

Evidence From BIOLOGY

Many high school biology textbooks still contain a section on *comparative embryology*. This is the idea that humans and animals have a common ancestor because their embryos have a similar physical appearance. In other words, as a human baby forms, it goes through a fish stage, amphibian stage, and finally becomes human at birth. This concept was popularized in 1866 by Ernst Haeckel as he traveled throughout Europe lecturing on the subject and showing drawings of how different animal embryos had similar appearances. **However, it was shown that he had used false drawings as early as 1874.** Although the specific drawings used by Haeckel have long since been discarded, **his teachings remain in textbooks to this day.**

Why is this poor science still found in textbooks? Could it still be there because it leaves the impression that developing babies are mere globs of matter? Over 50 years ago, Francis Crick won the Nobel Prize for the discovery of the structure of the DNA molecule. **This scientifically proved that a woman's fertilized egg is a complete human being with a full set of instructions.** Only time and nutrition are required for it to grow larger. From the moment of conception, a pregnant woman's body is home to a completely unique person. The Bible acknowledged this fact long before it was proven by modern science.

Search for the Truth, p. 26

...you knit me together in my mother's womb. I praise You, because I am fearfully and wonderfully (*this word in Hebrew can also mean differently or separately*) **made....**

Psalm 139:13-14

Evidence From HISTORY

Starting in the early 1800s, **geologists have chosen to interpret fossils and sediments based on a presupposition of slow accumulation,** or more recently, multiple local catastrophes over billions of years (uniformitarianism). Thousands of geologists have been indoctrinated in this belief and have spent the last 150 years fitting the evidence into this interpretation of Earth history. Yet there remain many facts unexplained by this interpretation of geology. Almost all of these mysteries disappear once the reality of a recent Worldwide Flood is acknowledged.

In addition to the Bible, which clearly presents the Worldwide Flood as a factual event in which eight humans were saved on a floating Ark, **every culture in the world has a flood story.** The very symbol in the ancient Chinese language for "*boat*" is a combination of the symbols for "*eight*," "*people*," and "*vessel*." Every culture from the Chinese to the Aztecs, Aborigines to the ancient Greeks, Eskimos to the Africans, have an ancient account of a universal Flood. Many of these stories include details of a righteous man being saved on a floating vessel and attribute the event to judgment from God. If this really happened, people would have spread across the globe after the catastrophe. **As centuries passed, the account of the Flood would have been distorted, but remembered.** This is *exactly* what we find. The Worldwide Flood is a fact of the past as revealed by archaeology, geology, and the Bible.

Search for the Truth, p. 65

And on that very day Noah and his sons, Shem, Ham, and Japheth, together with his wife and the wives of his three sons, entered the ark.

Genesis 7:13

Evidence From ANATOMY

The 206 bones in the human skeletal system are an engineering marvel. It is a *rigid support* for the body's organs and tissues and serves as protection for the brain, lungs, heart, and spinal chord. Bones also act as *levers,* enabling muscles to move the body. They provide a *reservoir of essential minerals.* Bones contain 99% of the calcium, 88% of the phosphorus, plus many other trace elements needed by the body. In addition to support and storage, bones act as *chemical factories* producing red blood cells, certain white blood cells, and platelets within their marrow.

Incredibly, when a bone is broken, it immediately starts to repair itself. Engineers are continually trying to develop strong, lightweight structural materials, **but have yet to devise a substance that grows continuously, lubricates itself, requires no shutdown time, and repairs itself when damaged.** Man's framework is the most suitable that could be devised in material, structure, and arrangement.

It would seem total foolishness to accept the teaching that our bones had no designer except mutations, natural selection, and time.

THE HUMAN BODY: ACCIDENT OR DESIGN?
P.19-21

Declare his glory among the nations, his marvelous deeds among all peoples.

1 CHRONICLES 16:24

Evidence From
BIBLICAL ACCURACY

Matthew Fontaine Maury (1806-1873) **dedicated his life to finding out if there really were "paths of the sea" as stated in Psalm 8:8.** During a long illness, Maury's son read the Bible to him and Maury was drawn to this verse. After recovering, he began to make the study of the oceans his life's passion.

Maury was the first to recognize that the seas contained circulating systems with interaction between wind and water. He spent decades collecting thousands of ships logs from captains and compiling their weather/travel information into a systematic understanding of the ocean's circulating patterns.

His book on physical oceanography is still considered the foundational textbook on this subject. In 1927, the United States Naval Institute issued a book by C.L. Lewis titled *Matthew Fontaine Maury: Pathfinder of the Seas*, which describes Maury's work and inspiration. Maury trusted God's Word and as a result, **developed the science of oceanography**.

A STUDY COURSE IN CHRISTIAN EVIDENCES, P.127-128

...**the birds of the air, and the fish of the sea, whatever passes along the paths of the sea.**

PSALM 8:8 RSV

Evidence From BIBLICAL UNIQUENESS

One profound evidence of the authenticity of biblical Christianity is its unique treatment of women. The Bible clearly states God created men and women with different functions, but as equals. This delegation of different roles is necessary so that harmony and order can be established.

Biblical Christianity *elevates* the woman, whether married, single, or widowed. It *recognizes her* moral and social influence, *encourages her* use of reason and intellect, *restores her* plundered rights, and *challenges her* to be a woman of grace, purity, self-control, humility, compassion, commitment, and love. **Christ's own treatment of women and the Bible's remarkable accounts of godly women attest to the dignity of the woman.** Biblical Christianity also changes the hearts of men and teaches men to treat women with the utmost love and respect–as Christ treats His church. In practice, other religions do not uphold women's dignity. Women are abused and exploited in almost every society which is not governed by Christian principles.

Scripture sets forth marriage between one man and one woman as a central foundation upon which society rests. When the institution of marriage fails, all of society begins a downward slide. The history of all past civilizations bear witness to this fact.

FEMALE PIETY: A YOUNG WOMAN'S FRIEND AND GUIDE, P.7-32

You are all sons of God through faith in Christ Jesus.... There is neither Jew nor Greek, slave nor free, male nor female, for you are all one in Christ Jesus.

GALATIANS 3:26,28

THE WORLDWIDE FLOOD
Evidence From

Many critics question the possibility of so many animals living in the confinement of the Ark for a year. In nature, however, God provided animals with the ability to hibernate *(to spend winter in a dormant or inactive state)* or estivate *(to spend summer in a dormant state)*. During periods of unsuitable temperature, many animals often live in very confined quarters with little to no food intake or bodily excretions. **It is logical to assume many of the animals behaved similarly during their stay on the Ark.**

Even if the animals on the Ark did not hibernate, it has been shown that **eight people could have adequately cared for all of the animals on the Ark using simple and ancient principles of animal husbandry** that have been practiced throughout the world for thousands of years. Over the years a variety of challenges have been raised in an effort to show that the account of Noah's Ark, which is recorded in Genesis, could not be factual. A thorough investigation shows that virtually every one of these objections has been fully and adequately explained by a combination of modern science, archaeological discoveries, and history.

THE GENESIS RECORD, P.186
NOAH'S ARK: A FEASIBILITY STUDY, P.45-127

...two of every sort shalt thou bring into the ark, to keep them alive with thee...

GENESIS 6:19 KJV

Evidence From BOTANY

Scientists have discovered that red algae plants grow almost 1,000 feet below the surface of the ocean, where it is pitch black. Scientists estimate that the light intensity at this depth is reduced by 99.95%. How can red algae, which requires light for photosynthesis to make food for survival, live at such depths?

The unique structure of these deep-water plants allow them to be 100 times more efficient at catching and using light than shallow-water plants. Plants, including most types of red algae, line their cell walls with calcium for structural strength. This prevents some light from getting into the cell. The red alga plant, however, only lines the vertical walls of its cells with calcium so that more light can enter. Because of this, the cells are much more transparent to available light. In addition to this marvelous engineering design, the red alga's cells are internally arranged in such a way that the light that does make it through the cell membrane can penetrate deep into cach cell.

Good engineering, not chance mistakes, created the red algae plants.

LETTING GOD CREATE YOUR DAY, VOL. 3, P.176

Nothing in all creation is hidden from God's sight.

HEBREWS 4:13

Remember the Rooster

The rooster is mentioned in God's Holy Book;
   He was given a special part.
The Lord used him to remind a man
   Of his terribly sinful heart.

Now Matthew, Mark, Luke, and John
   All wrote about this bird.
They said the rooster made his sound,
   And by Peter it was heard.

Poor Peter was clearly told that he,
   Like us, was prone to sin.
How often Christ said, "Without my help,
   A sinful person can't win."

With a heart full of pride, Peter replied,
   "Your side, I'll never leave."
Jesus then warned him to watch what he said,
   For his words would make him grieve.

Late that night, Peter got his chance
   To say, "Yes, Jesus I know."
But he failed three times and denied his Lord
   When the rooster began to crow.

Let the rooster be both to you and me,
   A warning to *run* from sin.
Let us seek the Lord's help and follow His Book,
   So the devil cannot win.

Evidence From
PSYCHOLOGY

Man was created with a conscience. No other living creature exhibits this built-in sense of right and wrong. **No beast feels guilt or sheds a tear as it wipes out weaker creatures.** No animal thinks about why things are or are not "fair." No other living organism values selfless sacrifice and condemns selfishness.

The Bible says God wrote the law on man's heart. In Romans 1:19-20, God says *He makes Himself evident to everyone so that no one can claim that He does not exist.* Our conscience is one of these undeniable evidences. The intricate design of nature is another. If evolution is true, there is no evidence for the existence of God from the observation of nature, because the origin of everything can be explained by natural laws of science. The real goal of evolution is removing any accountability to our Creator by denying the obvious evidence from creation that points to His existence. To this the Psalmist replies in Psalm 14:1, that the *fool* says in his heart, "There is no God." The biblical meaning of a fool in this passage is a person who goes about life acting as if God does not exist. This is as true of the scientific conclusions we reach as it is of our moral behavior.

RICH AND TINA KLEISS

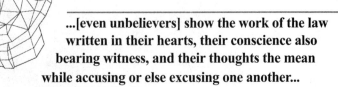

...[even unbelievers] show the work of the law written in their hearts, their conscience also bearing witness, and their thoughts the mean while accusing or else excusing one another...

ROMANS 2:15 KJV

Evidence From ANATOMY

Our **eye's lens** is truly a marvel of chemistry. It contains a very high concentration of protein molecules in a transparent water solution. This discovery amazed scientists, because protein molecules in water solutions are not transparent, but opaque. However, for the lens of the eye to work properly, it must be transparent. After much research, scientists discovered that the concentration of protein molecules in the lens of the eye is so high that they pack together like the molecules of window glass. **This results in the normally opaque protein solution becoming transparent.**

For how many years was an evolving creature forced to stumble around half-blind before random mutations happened upon the perfect protein, in the perfect concentration, to pack together in exactly the right way, to make his eye lens transparent? Why didn't natural selection drive the creature to extinction before the lens developed properly? Once again, creation makes sense, while evolution leaves us questioning the logic of its conclusions.

LETTING GOD CREATE YOUR DAY, Vol. 3, p.104

Understand, you senseless among the people; and you fools, when will you be wise? He who planted the ear, shall he not hear? He who formed the eye, shall He not see?

PSALM 94:8,9 NKJV

Evidence From PHYSICS

The second law of thermodynamics states that all things naturally move from a higher to a lower state of order. A law of science is only established when no exceptions are found after years of study. Albert Einstein called the second law of thermodynamics, "the premier law of science" upon which all other processes are based. Scientists are finding that the entire universe, including the sun and the stars, are subject to this law. All processes are slowly winding down.

Things can only move to a state of increased complexity with the *addition* of controlled energy and intelligent guidance, such as when a pile of bricks is turned into a building. Natural processes will do the opposite–tear buildings down, not build them up. The same is true with life. Mistakes and extinctions are happening all around us, whereas new life forms are not developing. Observations agree with the second law of thermodynamics–life is heading in the direction of increasing disorder. This means there must have been more order in the past. Where did this original state of extremely high order originate?

LETTING GOD CREATE YOUR DAY, VOL. 3, P.96
IN THE BEGINNING, 7TH ED., P.24-25

...for the creation was subjected to futility... We know that the whole creation has been groaning in travail...

ROMANS 8:20,22 RSV

Evidence From
EARTH'S ECOLOGY

When Adam and Eve sinned, biological life was changed causing weeds and thorns to appear on Earth for the first time. Both plant and animal life were changed with defensive and offensive survival mechanisms. For many years modern agriculture has relied on herbicides and insecticides to protect crops from pests. God's marvelous foresight included many natural ways of controlling pests, which modern science has only recently learned to copy. The spined soldier bug (also known as the **stink bug) is one of these natural pest control systems. It eats over a hundred different pests,** including commercially damaging insects such as the cotton bollworm and the gypsy moth. Researchers have found that spraying crops with a natural chemical made by the stink bug attracts stink bugs to the fields. The stink bugs then devour the harmful insects without harming the crops. The added bonus is a *natural solution* which doesn't harm the environment or other creatures.

God told Adam and Eve in the beginning that they were to have *dominion* over all creation. This word in Hebrew means "to understand, care for, and control." We have much to gain when we realize that all creation is a designed system from which we can learn.

*LETTING **GOD** CREATE **YOUR** DAY,*
VOL. 3, P.100

Oh, the depth of the riches of the wisdom and knowledge of God...

ROMANS 11:33

Evidence From GENETICS

It would take thousands of carefully directed changes to the genes of an eyeless creature for it to possess a crude light-sensitive patch or a compound eye. It would take countless more to turn a light-sensitive patch or compound eye into a fluid-filled eyeball. **Since an eye that is not fully developed does not provide sight, any mutation not providing some advantage would be useless.** These mutations would be eliminated by natural selection rather than developing in a step-by-step manner into the complex eye. So how did the eye develop?

Neither living nor fossil animals show any evidence for the gradual development of an eye. Every known creature either has a fully developed compound eye, a fluid-filled eyeball, or a light-gathering spot. No adequate mechanism has been proposed as to how any one of these types of eyes could have turned into another by random step-by-step mutational changes.

There are no adequate mechanisms explaining how an eyeball developed over time and no examples in the fossil record indicating that it has ever happened. The most reasonable scientific conclusion is that there is a Creator who designed and created each type of eye.

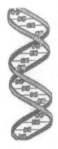

LETTING GOD CREATE YOUR DAY, VOL. 3, P.104

Let them give thanks to the LORD for his unfailing love and his wonderful deeds for men.

PSALM 107:8

Evidence From
BIOLOGY

Hot air can be cooled by the evaporation of moisture. **This principle is used by the desert pack rat to air-condition its underground nest.** Any source of water can be used, even water contained in freshly cut grass. The pack rat gathers and stores vegetation within the compartments of its nest. Tunnels connect these compartments to the rest of the nest and allow the moist air to circulate and cool the entire nest.

The pack rat's own body waste is even used as a source of moisture for cooling. The tunnel first passes though the pack rat's bathroom, and the body waste is not removed from the nest until all of the water has evaporated. During long hot spells, the pack rat even brings droppings of larger animals into its nest to provide additional water for its air conditioning system. One can't help but wonder how the little guy figured all this out. Maybe he had some help from his Creator!

Character Sketches, Vol. III, p.86

...O LORD, you preserve both man and beast. How priceless is your unfailing love!

Psalm 36:6-7

Evidence From
BIOLOGY

The rare Australian aquatic frog uses one of nature's most amazing methods of reproduction. If other creatures attempted this same method, it would be fatal to their young.

After the eggs of the Australian aquatic frog are laid and fertilized, the female swallows them. Sometimes she waits until they have started to develop, but once the young are in her stomach, the mother stops eating for the next eight weeks. After eight weeks, fully-developed little frogs come out of the mother's mouth!

What other creature can swallow its young, discontinue eating for eight weeks, and incubate its offspring within its stomach? The young Australian frogs can do this because they release fine threads of special chemicals which prevent the mother's stomach from making digestive acids. These tiny frogs actually change their mother's stomach from an organ of digestion into a comfortable, protective nursery. How did the first baby frogs which were swallowed learn to turn off their mother's digestive acids? How did they learn to pass this ability on to the next generation?

Our Creator loves to amaze us with His creativity!

Letting God Create Your Day,
Vol. 3, p.105

Sing to him, sing praise to him; tell of all his wonderful acts.

1 Chronicles 16:9

Evidence From ANATOMY

In order for our eyes to see, many chemical and electrical reactions must take place in the proper sequence. Even more importantly, these reactions must happen almost instantaneously for us to see what is happening, while it is still happening.

Researchers have recently discovered just how quickly light causes the first chemical change within our eye. In order for our brain to see an image, a chemical in our eye which is sensitive to light must respond as soon as a photon of light strikes it. This type of chemical change is called a photochemical reaction. Photochemical reactions are the basis of how photographic paper works, but the reactions that result in a printed picture are extremely slow compared to the photochemical reactions in our eye. The fastest photographic film requires the camera lens to remain open for about 1/10,000 of a second. Biologists have found that the eye's photo-chemistry is so fast that the first reaction in the sequence takes place in approximately 1/5,000,000,000 (one-five billionth) of a second. **This is 500,000 times faster than our best film capabilities.**

Our attempts to duplicate the processes in our eyes fall short of God's original design by such an extreme amount that Darwin himself admitted that the human eye seemed to defy his theory of evolution.

LETTING GOD CREATE YOUR DAY, VOL. 3, P.108

Oh that men would praise the LORD for his goodness, and for his wonderful works to the children of men!

PSALM 107:15 KJV

Evidence From
BIBLICAL ACCURACY

Genesis 3:15 tells us that a female, like the male, *also* has the "seed of life" or a necessary part in the making of a baby. **This wasn't believed in Moses' day when it was told to Moses by God.** Ancient writers believed only the male had the seed of life and that the female was just the incubator of the baby. One ancient Greek writer, Democritus, even suggested that male semen placed in warm mud would result in a human life in the same way sperm deposited within a female can result in a baby.

These writers were wrong, while Genesis proved to be correct. Today we know that it takes the 23 chromosomes found in the female egg (seed) plus the 23 chromosomes found in the male sperm (seed) to make a normal human. **How could Moses have known this without God's divine guidance?**

A STUDY COURSE IN CHRISTIAN EVIDENCES, P.130-131

And I will put enmity between thee and the woman, and between thy seed and her seed....

GENESIS 3:15 KJV

Evidence From
ANATOMY

One of the many incredible chemicals produced by our bodies is a complex sugar called hyaluronic acid. This sugar is an effective lubricant that is found in both people and animals. What makes this molecule so versatile is its elasticity, which allows it to absorb shock and return to its original shape. It is hyaluronic acid which lubricates our joints, makes our skin elastic, and protects delicate tissues within our eyes. Because of its many unique and desirable properties, hyaluronic acid is added to cosmetics, skin moisturizers, and shaving creams. In addition, it has been found useful in areas varying from the treatment of arthritis to eye surgery.

The primary problem with putting this marvelous chemical into even more widespread use is that it is tremendously expensive to obtain. Chemists are diligently trying to find less expensive methods for producing this complex natural lubricant, but have yet to succeed. **Does it make logical sense to believe that random-chance processes created chemicals that scientists must spend years of study and planning to duplicate?**

LETTING GOD CREATE YOUR DAY, VOL. 3, P.112

**For you make me glad by your deeds, O LORD;
I sing for joy at the works of your hands.**

PSALM 92:4

Evidence From GEOLOGY

Textbooks have taught for generations that the massive coal formations, which are found around the globe, have taken millions of years to form. Creation scientists have refuted this claim, citing multiple experimental evidences showing that coal can be produced in much less time under high pressure and temperature conditions. It has recently been shown that under certain conditions high pressure is not even necessary.

Scientists at the Argonne National Laboratory took ordinary wood fragments mixed with acid-activated clay and water, and heated it at 300 °F for 28 days in an air-free quartz tube. **They obtained a high grade of black coal, even without the addition of pressure. This proved millions of years are not necessary to explain the formation of coal.**

Sadly, the standard textbook model involving **millions of years and gradual formation of coal by peat swamps remains the only model presented to students**. One wonders why this is the only possibility presented. Why is the possibility of a worldwide flood and rapid formation ignored? Sound scientific practice requires the consideration of all theories of coal formation, rather than teaching a single possibility as if it were a fact.

LETTING GOD CREATE YOUR DAY,
VOL. 3, P.114

He made the earth by his power; he founded the world by his wisdom....

JEREMIAH 51:15

Evidence From LANGUAGE

According to evolution, the development of human language began when apelike creatures grunted and made simple noises at each other. Supposedly these ape-men agreed on meanings for these sounds, and language was born. **This view does not explain why ancient languages are more complex than modern languages.** Furthermore, for any apelike creature to develop complex language, not only would the structure of its throat need to change, but simultaneously its brain would have to develop the ability to convert abstract sounds into symbolic meaning.

Other than the assumption of evolution, there is no reason to believe ancient man was not completely capable of complex communication. **From the intricate artwork of cave -dwelling people to the massive engineering marvels of the earliest civilizations, it is quite apparent that ancient man was both intelligent and fully able to communicate.**

The Bible clearly states that humans were created with an inherent ability to use and understand complex language. God gave us language both as a method of fellowship and as proof that we have been made in the image of our Creator. From the earliest signs of human civilization, it is apparent that humans have always possessed complex linguistic abilities. When people draw conclusions based on data, rather than preconceived beliefs, one can see which model of origins is best supported by science.

LETTING GOD CREATE YOUR DAY,
VOL. 3, P.115
CREATION EX NIHILO MAGAZINE, VOL.23, NO.2,
MARCH-MAY 2001, P. 42-45

So the man gave names to all the livestock, the birds of the air, and all the beasts of the field.

GENESIS 2:20

Evidence From
BIOLOGY

Researchers are gaining insights into new drugs by observing animals. *Chimps in Tanzania* were seen swallowing the unchewed leaves of a tree they normally avoided. Intrigued by why the primates would eat these particular leaves without chewing them, biologists studied the chimp droppings and found that the leaves were not digested. **The chimp's digestive system simply removed chemicals from the surface of the leaves, and these substances killed parasites within the chimp's intestinal tract!**

Another insight learned from the interaction between animals and their diet was found in the habits of the *Brazilian woolly spider monkey.* The female monkey does not ovulate for about six months after she gives birth so that she has time to raise her baby before becoming pregnant again. After six months, however, the female will travel outside of her territory to gorge on the fruit from a specific tree. **Biologists found that this fruit is rich in the exact chemical the female needs to ovulate.**

God tells us in His Word that we should study the animals so that we can learn from them. How true His words have proven to be!

LETTING GOD CREATE YOUR DAY, VOL. 3, P.120

"But ask the animals, and they will teach you..."

JOB 12:7

Evidence From BOTANY

Mistletoe is a common plant parasite found in various places throughout the world. While it uses its green leaves to make its own food, it gets its water and minerals through roots attached to a host. Many species of the *Australian mistletoe* are unique in that they mimic the host on which they grow. The *drooping mistletoe* is so named because its leaves look like its host, the eucalyptus tree. The *box mistletoe* and the *pendulous mistletoe* both have hard, sickle-shaped leaves that look like the trees on which they grow. The *buloke mistletoe* has long, thin, grayish-green leaves that are similar to the pencil pine on which it grows. **How can we explain this mimicry?**

God states in His Word that He created everything and that He loves and cares for His creation. Mistletoe cannot see its host nor can it change form like an amoeba, yet it manages to survive by exactly duplicating another organism. The mistletoe was designed to adapt to the appearance of its host. **Only a creative and intelligent Designer could accomplish such a task.**

LETTING GOD CREATE YOUR DAY, VOL.3, P.121

For by him all things were created: things in heaven and on earth, visible and invisible....

COLOSSIANS 1:16

Evidence From PROPHECY

God left us with many evidences to show that His Word is true, but prophecy is one of the strongest. More than 25% of the Bible is prophecy. God set a stringent standard on prophecy: it must be *100% accurate,* or the prophecy is not of God. **This is a unique characteristic of the Bible, not found in the Veda (Hindu writings), the Koran (Islam's holy book), or any of the other writings of mankind.** The so-called prophecies of Nostradamus, Jeanne Dixon, and others are of a completely different class than the Bible. Not only are these prophecies vague (leaving possiblity of being interpreted to fit numerous events), but more often than not their predictions of the future prove to be wrong. Biblical prophecies, however, are both specific and accurate.

When we hold the Bible, we are holding a collection of 66 books written over a period of about 1,500 years by more than 40 authors. Yet this book reveals a single coordinated message. The Bible repeatedly authenticates its uniqueness by describing history in exact detail before it happens. How else could God authenticate his message and prove that He created everything and inspired the Bible? God is not subject to constraints of time any more than He is subject to constraints of mass, gravity, or acceleration. He knows all of history before it happens. **Prophecy is merely God's demonstration t h a t because He is the Creator, He is outside of time.** The prophecies of the Bible are proof of this fact.

MANY INFALLIBLE PROOFS, P.14-15
HIDDEN TREASURES IN BIBLICAL TEXT, P.17

You may say to yourselves, "How can we know when a message has not been spoken by the LORD?" If what a prophet proclaims in the name of the LORD does not take place or come true, that is a message the LORD has not spoken....

DEUTERONOMY 18:21-22

Evidence From
COMMON SENSE

Imagine that you are the child of the famous painter, Michelangelo. You grew up watching your father paint the ceiling of the Sistine Chapel. Each stroke of the brush revealed his love, creative genius, and masterful perfection.

Years later as you're walking beneath your father's great work, a guide enters leading a group of tourists. As they stand in awe under the grandeur of the artistic work, you hear the tour guide boldly state that the ceiling occurred by naturalistic processes over countless years as water leaked through the roof and stained the plaster. The people are told by their expert guide that what appears as an intentionally designed work of beauty is strictly a chance occurrence.

Would you not, as Michelangelo's child, rise up in righteous indignation at the telling of such a flagrant lie? If the guide said that your *father* had used the random procedure of dripping water through the plaster to create the masterpiece, would that lie have been any more palatable?

The modern "tour guides" of our world are **evolutionists** who would have us believe that all of the purpose, eloquent design, and astronomical complexity of life *just happened* as chance naturalistic processes (such as mutations) formed life over billions of years. **Liberal theologians** would have us believe that God used such a process to make things.

Should not Christians boldly proclaim the truth so that more people may come to know the true Master Artist and come to trust His written revelation to mankind (the Bible)?

BRYCE GAUDIAN,
THE GREAT WORKS CATALOG, P.22

By wisdom the LORD laid the earth's foundations, by understanding he set the heavens in place.

PROVERBS 3:19

Evidence From
MICROBIOLOGY

The bdella is an impressive microscopic chemist. During its short four-hour life span, it manages to survive in environments as diverse as fresh water, salt water, or raw sewage. In the first stage of its life cycle, it uses a flagellum (a long whiplike tail) to swim ten times faster than its favorite food, E. coli bacteria. When a bdella spots an E. coli, it rams the bacterium and uses at least six different enzymes to bore a hole through the outer membrane of the bacterium. The bdella then drops its flagellum, penetrates the bacterium, and starts the second stage of its life.

As soon as the bdella gets between the inner and outer membrane of the bacterium, it injects a chemical into the bacterium that kills it. In order to keep the dead bacterium for its own use, the resourceful parasite injects yet another chemical into the bacterium's cell membrane that causes the outer coat of its prey to harden so that no other bdella can enter the bacterium. Over the next two to three hours the bdella eats the bacterium and reproduces. The new bdellas break through the dead bacterium's hardened membrane to start the cycle all over again. Even in our fallen world the evidence for design is undeniable.

What enormous faith to believe all of this is a result of random mutations! No wonder Scripture says that only the foolish can deny that God exists.

LETTING GOD CREATE YOUR DAY, VOL.3, P.131

The fool says in his heart, "There is no God."

PSALM 14:1

Evidence From BIOLOGY

Common Puerto Rican forest frogs (called coqui) are very important to the tropical forest, because they are one of the forest's primary insect predators. This type of frog is active and hunts at night because it is extremely susceptible to dehydration during the day. The frog's eggs must also be kept from drying out. Researchers have found that the frog population is directly related to the number of sheltered spots available. The female coqui cannot protect her eggs after laying them, because **she has totally expended her available energy** and must leave to find insects to replenish herself. The eggs are laid on land and would die within hours without immediate attention. **The dedicated father immediately moves in to keep the eggs moist at all times and safe from predators.** To do this, the male coqui will sit on the eggs 23 hours a day for up to three weeks.

One has to wonder how this coordinated effort between the male and female frog could possibly have evolved. How would the male frog know to take on the sacrificial incubation process as soon as the female disappeared? What told the female to abandon its eggs as soon as they were laid? Instincts, even in our fallen world, *must* have been programmed by a Creator.

LETTING GOD CREATE YOUR DAY, VOL.3, P.132

Even the sparrow has found a home, and the swallow a nest for herself, where she may have her young....

PSALM 84:3

Evidence From ANATOMY

David L. Berliner, University of Utah anatomist, discovered the purpose of the vomeronasal organ—VNO for short. In animals the VNO detects odorless pheromones (chemicals used to communicate messages such as the readiness to mate). For many years evolutionists thought that the human VNO was a useless vestigial organ left over from our distant past. Berliner discovered that **the centimeter-long organ in our nose detects odorless human pheromones using a totally different detection system from our sense of smell.** This specifically designed organ sends its messages to the hypothalamus (which is responsible for our drives and emotions), while our noses are wired to other sections of the brain.

The discovery of the purpose of the VNO shows that there is still much to learn about our bodies. With continued research, scientists are learning that the organs they once thought to be useless are proving to have very important functions. This is no surprise to creation scientists, who understand that our Creator would not have made anything without a purpose.

LETTING GOD CREATE YOUR DAY, VOL.3, P.135

Can you fathom the mysteries of God? Can you probe the limits of the Almighty? They are higher than the heavens–what can you do? They are deeper than the depths of the grave–what can you know?

JOB 11:7,8

Evidence From
MICROBIOLOGY

The 1/50-inch-long iceplant scale is the scourge of a common landscaping plant. Since this creature is wingless, it was thought to spread from plant to plant by contact. This idea has turned out to be totally incorrect. Biologists have discovered that the iceplant scale sails the wind from plant to plant. **This insect not only has the ability to accurately sense wind velocity and direction, but can turn itself into a tiny bug-shaped parasail.**

Once the insect senses a wind velocity of 10 miles per hour, it determines the wind direction with its antennae. It then proceeds to turn its back to the breeze, rear up on its hind legs, and extend its antennae and legs. This doubles the iceplant scale's surface area and makes it possible for the insect to be lifted and carried by the wind. In essence, the scale makes a parasail out of its body. Scientists found that even one-day-old insects are knowledgeable about flight and ready to migrate. Both the intricate design and instincts within the smallest creatures testify to programming by their Creator.

LETTING GOD CREATE YOUR DAY, VOL. 3, P.140

Let them know that you, whose name is the LORD–that you alone are the Most High over all the earth.

PSALM 83:18

Evidence From
THE WORLDWIDE FLOOD

Sedimentary rock covers almost three-quarters of the earth's surface, including the tops of most mountains. Sedimentary rock forms as sediments (such as sand, silica, and other minerals) settle out of water to later solidify into rock layers. If this sedimentation happens rapidly, as occurs during a flood, organisms can become trapped and later fossilized in the rock layers. These sediments were eroded from previous locations, transported, and then deposited. If a worldwide flood has occurred on the earth, it is not at all surprising that geologists would find fossilized shells and sea creatures all over the earth, including at the tops of the highest mountains. Fossilized sea shells have indeed been found at the very top of Mt. Everest.

This evidence fits perfectly with the description of the worldwide Flood described in the Bible. Geology based on evolutionary assumptions is simply wrong as it makes illogical assumptions in order to account for the worldwide appearance and extent of these sedimentary rock layers without a worldwide Flood.

Bone of contention, Is Evolution True?, p.32
In the Beginning, 7ᵀᴴ Ed., p.37-41

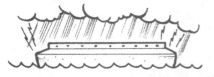

The waters rose and covered the mountains to a depth of more than twenty feet.

Genesis 7:20

Evidence From GEOLOGY

In public schools, children are usually given only one possible explanation for the geologic features of our planet. **Leaving out alternative evidence, their thoughts are guided toward only one conclusion.** A prime example is the earth science teaching on continental drift. Students are shown that there is a roughly matching fit between the North and South American continents with the African and European continents. They are then told that the rock layers at the edges of these continents match. Finally they are told that the continents are moving apart at approximately 3 cm per year. Under the "critical thinking" questions, students are told the continents are 3,000 miles apart and asked to calculate the time required for them to have reached their present positions.

The problem with this type of teaching is that it sounds logical and scholarly, but fails to give students *all* the information they need to draw the correct conclusion. **Left out is the evidence that mechanisms have been identified showing how the continents could have moved apart rapidly in the past.** No mention is made of the evidence showing that the Mid-Atlantic Ridge reveals enormous and rapid geologic activity. Withheld is the evidence indicating rapid formation of mountain ranges. Nor are students exposed to the evidence that current erosion rates show that the continents could not possibly be millions of years old. If students were given all of this additional information, would they still arrive at the conclusion that the earth formed billions of years ago?

BRUCE MALONE

To Eber were born two sons: the name of one was Peleg, for in his days the earth was divided....

GENESIS 10:25 NKJV

Evidence From
MICROBIOLOGY

Even the "lowest" forms of life, such as bacteria, have built-in abilities and intelligence. Some bacteria can move toward the food they like and away from enviroments which are harmful to them. The E. coli bacterium is so tiny that it has difficulty moving through water in the same way a human would have trouble swimming through molasses. Therefore, E. coli was designed with whiplike hairs called flagella which allow it to move.

E. coli can only move when its flagella are rotating. When rotated counterclockwise, its six to eight flagella wind together, forming a propeller that rotates at a fantastic 18,000 revolutions per minute. This allows the bacterium to move in a straight line. Sometimes the E.coli reverses its propeller, causing the whiplike hairs to unwrap and spin the bacterium into a tumble.

Microbiologists have yet to figure out how a bacterium knows where it wants to go in order to find food. The bacterium must have both sensors and a memory in order to know whether or not the location it is traveling to is better than where it came from. These remarkable abilities of even a tiny bacterium should cause anyone to question how it could possibly have evolved by random-chance mutations.

DARWIN'S BLACK BOX, P.51-73

Let them know that it is your hand, that you, O LORD, have done it.

PSALM 109:27

Evidence From
BIOLOGY

The spider and its silk are exquisitely designed engineering marvels. The spider has the ability to produce a variety of different kinds of silk strands for its web. **These different kinds of silk, woven into the spider's web, serve remarkably different functions.** Some lines are sticky to catch prey, while other strands are non-sticky so that the spider can approach its prey without becoming stuck to its own web. The drag line is a third kind of silk that the spider uses to lower itself from its web to the ground.

Scientists report that spider silk is made from a combination of crystalline and amorphous (randomly arranged) materials which combine the best characteristics of wire and rubber. Usually when you make something stronger, it becomes more brittle and resistant to being elongated. Yet spider silk is just the opposite–as the threads become stronger, they also become more elastic.

The complexity of the spider and its ability to produce marvelously designed webs could not have happened by random-chance; they point to their Designer.

LETTING GOD CREATE YOUR DAY,
VOL. 3, P.146

He performs wonders that cannot be fathomed, miracles that cannot be counted.

JOB 5:9

Evidence From
ARCHAEOLOGY

Archaeological discoveries show that ancient man was both highly intelligent and skilled. In France fifty years ago, the Lascaux Cave paintings that are thousands of years old were discovered. Researchers have found *scaffolding* and *stone lamps* used to light the work area. They have also discovered the original *palettes* used by the artists with *dried paint* intact. This has allowed researchers to study the pigments used by the ancient artists. Using scanning electron microscopes and other high-tech equipment, researchers learned that the artists collected local minerals to make their paints. Within 15 kilometers from the cave, mineral deposits were found which were able to provide the full range of colors.

These **ancient artists had the technology** necessary for *obtaining* the minerals, *grinding* them into fine powders, and *mixing* them to create pigments that hold their color and beauty to this day. Evolutionary thinking has led many to assume that just because man lived in caves, he was primitive. The actual evidence indicates otherwise.

LETTING GOD CREATE YOUR DAY, VOL. 3, P.147

"...and every skilled person to whom the LORD has given skill and ability to know how to carry out all the work...."

EXODUS 36:1

Evidence From
BIOLOGY

Scientists have known for a long time that moths communicate with each other using hormones called pheromones. A female moth who is ready to mate releases a scent (pheromone) into the air which is picked up by the male. It has been discovered that the pheromone is not released randomly, but in a series of pulses at a frequency of at least one pulse per second. The pheromone can be propelled for up to a meter from the female moth. This is like a human blowing out a candle from 60 feet away. **Researchers have also discovered that the male is not only drawn to the female by the scent of the pheromone, but also by the pattern in which the chemical is sent.** The male's antennae receive and then send the signal to its brain with the same frequency as the female's pulses. The scent itself acts as a carrier for a Morse Code-like message!

The more we study creation, the more we find that even the smallest details of creation reveal amazing complexities which point to a Master Designer.

LETTING GOD CREATE YOUR DAY, VOL. 3, P.148

...In putting everything under him [Jesus Christ], God left nothing that is not subject to him....

HEBREWS 2:8

Evidence From
MICROBIOLOGY

Sulfate-reducing bacteria love metal. Using complex chemistry, they are capable of dissolving objects made of metal. **These bacteria can make a sixteenth-of-an-inch hole in an inch-thick pipe within six months.** Even stainless steel and titanium can't stand up to them. The sulfate-reducing bacteria often attach themselves to the inside of a pipe or tank and seal off their colony from the liquid inside. Once sealed off, the bacteria start to form hydrogen gas. Sealed under a miniature biosphere, the hydrogen accumulates and is absorbed by the metal. The absorbed hydrogen begins to corrode the metal, making it brittle.

Isn't it interesting that this so-called simple organism can produce complex chemical reactions that can eat away man's strongest metal alloys? **Simple organisms are anything but simple!**

LETTING GOD CREATE YOUR DAY, VOL. 3, P.217

"Do not store up for yourselves treasures on earth, where moth and rust destroy, and where thieves break in and steal."

MATTHEW 6:19

Evidence From
ASTRONOMY

The *big bang* theory assumes that the universe is infinite in extent and that the earth is randomly located in space. In other words, there is nothing special about the earth or its location. In contrast to this philosophical viewpoint, **the *Bible* clearly states that the universe was created to show God's glory and character to mankind and that mankind is the focus of God's attention.** Thus, placing the earth near the center of the universe would seem quite logical.

Evidence of the earth's location within the universe comes from the observation that there are approximately the same number of galaxies in all directions from the earth. This is far too coincidental, unless the earth is actually located near the center. Even more significant are the concentric rings of galaxies at equal increments of distance from our galaxy, the Milky Way. In other words, during the formation of the universe, distinct bands of galaxies formed at uniform distances from the starting point like waves spreading out from a rock thrown into a pond. **The Bible states that heavens were stretched out, and this is exactly what we observe if our galaxy is at the center of this expansion.** We could only observe the spherical pattern of galaxies if the earth is near the center. If the earth were anywhere else, we could not observe these galaxies in this concentric pattern.

No explanation other than the earth being at the center of the universe accounts for these known observations. Unless **God specifically placed the earth here**, the odds of the earth being at this special location are less than a trillion to one.

TJ: The In-depth Journal of Creation,
Vol. 16 (2) 2002, p.95-104

When I consider your heavens, the work of your fingers, the moon and the stars, which you have set in place, what is man that you are mindful of him, the son of man that you care for him?

Psalm 8:3-4

Evidence From
BIOLOGY

European blackbirds are able to live through the cold German winters because they are designed with God-given instincts and features. **To cope with the winter cold**, the birds **fluff** up their feathers. This creates more insulating dead air spaces between their warm bodies and the cold air. Then they **tuck** their heads inside their feathers, making their bodies into a ball. A round ball is the most heat-conserving shape possible. The ball also protects poorly insulated parts of their bodies like feet, legs, and beak. **The birds' need for energy is five times greater at 20°F below zero than it is during the summer.** So the blackbirds reduce their energy need by **lowering their body temperature** at night when they are curled into a ball. As a result, scientists have found that European blackbirds are in no danger of freezing, even during extremely cold winters.

The design of their feathers, the ability to change their metabolism, and the instincts which allow survival at low temperature all **point to the intelligent design** of birds.

Letting God Create Your Day, Vol. 3, p.157

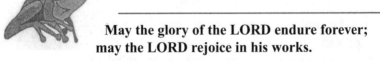

**May the glory of the LORD endure forever;
may the LORD rejoice in his works.**

Psalm 104:31

Evidence From ANATOMY

Babies naturally know how to nurse. Unborn children even practice by sometimes sucking their thumbs in the womb. **When a baby is placed at the nipple of his mother's breast, a fascinating chain reaction is set in motion.** The sucking sensation sends nerve impulses to the hypothalamus in the mother's brain. The hypothalamus sends a message to the pituitary gland, which secretes the hormone oxytocin into the bloodstream.

When oxytocin reaches the breast, cells are stimulated to contract, thus forcing milk into the ducts which carry a perfectly designed liquid to the nipple. Milk starts flowing out of the breast **within 30 seconds** of a baby beginning to nurse.

Is it reasonable to believe this precise sequence of events happened by chance?

THE HUMAN BODY: ACCIDENT OR DESIGN?, P.91-92

Let them give thanks to the LORD for his unfailing love and his wonderful deeds for men, for he satisfies the thirsty and fills the hungry with good things.

PSALM 107:8-9

Evidence From EARTH'S ECOLOGY

The hand of our Creator can be seen in the design of the giant fungus Armillaria. **This huge organism has been measured covering 38 acres and weighing as much as a blue whale.** Scientists estimate that some of these organisms have been alive for 1,500 years (based on their current rate of growth). Like most fungi, the Armillaria is made up of tiny tendrils growing almost invisibly underground. The tendrils push small fruiting honey mushrooms above ground as evidence of the larger organism alive below the surface.

Armillarias are usually found in the hardwood forests of North America. The giant fungus is territorial, which means that no two individuals will share the same area. Fungi are critically important components of forest ecology which decompose dead wood, releasing nutrients needed by other plants. In the decomposition process, the fungi also produce carbon dioxide, which is then used by plants to produce oxygen needed by humans.

It takes great faith to believe this organized system of maintaining forest ecology, each part dependant for life upon the other parts, could have evolved by chance random mutations over huge periods of time.

LETTING GOD CREATE YOUR DAY,
VOL. 3, P.171

"Has not my hand made all these things, and so they came into being?" declares the LORD....

ISAIAH 66:2

True Love

The *Love* of the Lord
   is so hard to conceive,
But He knows that,too;
   so He said, "Just Believe."

He gave us much *evidence,*
   this *world* and His *Book*;
And He simply tells us
   to *read it* and *look*.

He even came down
   from His throne up above
And lived as a human
   to *show* us His *Love*.

He could have come handsome
   and muscular, too;
Instead He came humbly,
   admired by few.

He gave an example—
   the life that He led.
He could have been rich,
   but served others instead.

He clearly explained
   that we *all* are in sin
And said He would save us,
   if we'd just *ask* Him.

Christ then *gave His life*
   as the ultimate test;.
To *prove* how He *Loved* us,
   He gave us His *best*.

Yes, He who was perfect
   has died in our place,
So He could stand with us
   when judgment we face.

Because of *this* act
   our sins are forgiven.
In deep thanks to Christ
   we all should be driven.

As we look around
   at God's world and His Word,
The truth of His *Love*
   to us is assured.

And *with* Christ's great *Love*
   there is much we can do
If we just live like Him
   and *Love others,*too!

Evidence From
CREATION FOUNDATION

There are *important reasons* for Christians *to study the factual* evidence supporting the Bible and Christianity.

1. It will confirm and **solidify your faith.**
2. It will **prepare you** to speak more knowledgeably and effectively to people that have been influenced by the attitudes of skepticism and unbelief.
3. It will **equip you** to maintain a clear and unwavering stand on the full integrity of God and His Word under all circumstances.
4. It will **encourage you** to know that God is in complete control and that you can trust Him 100%.

What was God's response when Job repeatedly asked the age-old question, "Why am I suffering?" He proceeded to give Job a lengthy creation lesson as assurance that Job could *trust* God and His purposes. When we truly understand that God is our Creator, has control over our circumstances, and His Word is trustworthy and verifiable, we no longer have to despair, even when circumstances seem hopeless.

MANY INFALLIBLE PROOFS, P.2

**How great you are, O Sovereign LORD!
There is no one like you, and there is no God
but you, as we have heard with our own ears.**

2 SAMUEL 7:22

Evidence From
BIOLOGY

When a predator comes close to a certain species of jellyfish, the jellyfish turns off the lights in its bell-shaped body and turns on the lights at the end of its tentacles. Then the jellyfish stretches its body as far as possible from its tentacles. As the predator approaches the lighted tentacles, the jellyfish switches off all its lights and scoots away as fast as it can. If the predator wasn't fooled and wants to continue the chase, the jellyfish switches to its backup plan. It now turns on both the blue lights in its body and the white lights in its tentacles. **When the attacker is very close, the jellyfish turns off the light in its body and takes off after detaching its still-glowing tentacles.** The tentacles continue to twist and turn in the water, distracting the predator. Jellyfish are among the most "primitive" multicelled animals, according to evolution. Yet this clever survival strategy clearly demonstrates that **jellyfish are neither simple nor primitive**.

Another kind of jellyfish collects in swimming colonies called siphonophores. These colonies can be up to 40 feet long and function in total darkness more than 1,500 feet beneath the ocean's surface. When they link up, some of the jellyfish act as mouths, while others act as stomachs. Some take care of the swimming, while others cast out their tentacles to gather food. **When joined, they act as one huge single creature!** How did creatures capable of independent survival evolve the ability to function as part of a complex colony? Does this not demonstrate planning and design?

LETTING GOD CREATE YOUR DAY, VOL. 3, P.7,9

Sing to the LORD a new song, for he has done marvelous things....

PSALM 98:1

Evidence From
PHYSICS

One of the primary evidences used to justify the belief in a five-billion-year-old earth is the fact that long-age radioactive isotopes have decayed into daughter elements which we find today within the crystals of rocks (like granite). During the decay of many radioactive isotopes, helium nuclei are given off (which almost instantaneously change to extremely stable helium atoms). At current decay rates, this process should have taken billions of years to reach the current level. This dating technique is presented as the premier proof that the earth is billions of years old. What follows is the *rest of the story.*

As radioactive elements decay, helium atoms are deposited into rock crystals. Helium atoms are so small that they easily leak through the rock structure and escape into the atmosphere. The rate at which helium leaks out of the rocks has been recently measured, and all of the helium produced by radioactive decay should have left the rocks if these formations were millions of years old. Yet the rock still contains much of the helium produced by this decay process. **This helium is still locked into the rocks because there hasn't been enough time for it to escape from the rocks.** This means that the radioactive decay could not have happened billions of years ago. Apparently there was a burst of radioactive decay within the last 10,000 years, possibly corresponding to when the earth was created, during the worldwide flood, or both. These are the types of scientific observations which make creation science so exciting.

ICR IMPACT ARTICLE #352, OCT. 2002

Prove all things; hold fast that which is good.

1 THESSALONIANS 5:21 KJV

Evidence From
ASTRONOMY

Light from the most distant stars in our universe would take billions of years to reach the earth. Is the universe really billions of years old, or did God create light en route to Earth with images of exploding stars at the same time He created the stars? Or is there a better explanation?

Ph.D. physicist Barry Setterfield has proposed that historical measurements of light indicated that its speed may be slowing down. The speed of light is different through various mediums. For instance, the speed of light through sodium atoms, near absolute zero, is only 38 miles per hour–20 million times slower than its speed in a vacuum. So what else could change the speed of light?

Modern physics tell us that even with every atom removed and cooled to absolute zero, each cubic centimeter of "empty" space contains the equivalent of 100 million years of energy output from our entire galaxy! This energy content of "empty space" is called the zero-point energy. If this energy content changed, so would the speed with which light travels through space. Did God create the entire universe starting with this zero-point energy by converting some of it to matter? If so, the speed of light could have been trillions of times faster as this energy was being converted to matter.

Although quite controversial, this theory is one of many possible explanations for how distant light could have reached Earth in a recently created universe. There is no scientific reason to assume the universe was not created quite recently.

"THE SETTERFIELD HYPOTHESIS"
WWW.SETTERFIELD.ORG

The day is thine, the night also is thine: thou hast prepared the light and the sun.

PSALM 74:16 KJV

Evidence From CREATION FOUNDATION

It has been said that all of modern science builds upon evolution. Yet in the century before evolution was taught as a fact in American schools, the United States won more Nobel prizes in science than the rest of the world combined. What great discovery has ever been made based on evolution? The world around us is far better explained as the creation of an intelligent designer followed by a recent global Flood.

Evolution has no adequate explanation for the following :
1. *The problem of order* - From the laws of thermodynamics to the information content of DNA, we see order everywhere. How did this arise from pure random chance?
2. *The problem of light* - What is light and energy? We give them names, but we really don't know what they are or why they exist.
3. *The problem of life* - It is absolutely statistically impossible that life could arise from random chemical reactions.
4. *The problem of conscious thought -* Why are humans self-aware? Do other creatures ask, "Where did I come from? Why am I here? What is the purpose of life?"
5. *The problem of reproduction* - How and why would a single-sex organism turn into two different sexes?
6. *The problem of decay* - All of life is dying. The entire universe is running down. Therefore, it must have been more perfect in the past. Evolution ignores this problem, because it cannot explain it.

Biblical creation has an explanation for all of these mysteries, so which model of our origin is more scientifically correct?

- BRUCE MALONE

We do, however, speak a message of wisdom among the mature, but not the wisdom of this age or of the rulers of this age, who are coming to nothing.

1 CORINTHIANS 2:6

Evidence From ANTHROPOLOGY

Museum dioramas commonly depict Neanderthal man as primitive and backward. **For over 100 years the world was led to believe that Neanderthal was a link between mankind and apelike creatures.** Instead of considering Adam as a perfect man falling from paradise, people started to believe mankind arose from brute beasts. Dr. Rudolf Virchow, the father of modern pathology, examined the original Neanderthal bones in 1872 and proclaimed that Neanderthal was fully human. However, **evolutionists ignored this expert opinion** and went on a highly successful 100-year road and museum show, implying and/or proclaiming that Neanderthal was an intermediate between man and some apelike creature.

Recent studies have shown that Virchow was totally correct in saying that **Neanderthals were completely human.** The only reason for the hunched appearance and thickened bones of the early specimens was their affliction with bone diseases such as arthritis and rickets. Neanderthal man, Heidelberg man, and Cro-Magnon man were all completely human. Artists' pictures of them, especially with wild long hair and brutish features, are pure imagination and designed to reinforce the belief in evolution.

In the Beginning, p.11-13
Unlocking the Mysteries of Creation, Prem. ed., p.135-136

For there are many rebellious people, mere talkers and deceivers...they are ruining whole households by teaching things they ought not to teach....

Titus 1:10,11

Evidence From ANATOMY

Atheists argue that we have "useless" organs which prove that we have evolved. Creationists respond that since the knowledge of the body is incomplete, we cannot know that an organ is useless. In the 1890s, scientists said that the human body had about 200 features that were useless leftovers of our evolutionary past. As a result of this evolutionary belief, doctors in the 1950s were quick to remove a child's tonsils. As our knowledge has increased, we have found that the organs on that list (such as tonsils, appendix, thyroid gland, and pituitary gland) have very important functions. Today we know our *tonsils* have several jobs and are a necessary part of our immune system. Our *appendix* has been found to serve as a backup system for other organs, such as taking over some of the spleen's functions when it is damaged. The *thyroid gland* is now known to be vital for body growth. Too much or too little of this gland's hormone, thyroxine, will cause all of our other organs to become over or underactive. We also know that the *pituitary gland* ensures proper growth of the skeleton and proper functioning of the thyroid, adrenal, and sex glands. When the pituitary gland does not work properly it can lead to Cushing's Syndrome (giantism).

True science has found useful functions for vitually all the so-called "leftover" organs. Yet if we evolved from some other life form, our bodies should be full of leftover nonfunctional features. Where are they all?

In the Minds of Men, p.264-274

This is what the LORD says–your Redeemer, who formed you in the womb: I am the LORD, who has made all things...who overthrows the learning of the wise and turns it into nonsense...."

Isaiah 44:24,25

Evidence From ARCHAEOLOGY

Archeologists and Bible critics claimed that the biblical account of King David's capture of Jerusalem by entering through water tunnels was in error, since these tunnels could not have existed this early in Jerusalem's history. The critics also implied that the existing water tunnels must have been built by unsophisticated people, because they are inefficient and poorly designed. These critics have been proven wrong on both accounts.

A more detailed study of the tunnels beneath Jerusalem has revealed that a cleverly designed dual water system served the ancient city. Nearly 3,000 years ago, engineers modified a natural network of channels and tunnels under Jerusalem to create this unique water supply system. New tunnels were dug to link existing natural tunnels so that it took the least amount of work to complete this ambitious engineering project. Two natural openings to the system were also found outside the walls of Jerusalem. It was through one of these natural openings that David conquered Jerusalem. As always, **the Bible has proven to be a 100% accurate account** of both history and science. Therefore, we can trust it to be a 100% accurate source of spiritual truth as well.

LETTING GOD CREATE YOUR DAY, VOL. 3, P.30

On that day, David said, "Anyone who conquers the Jebusites will have to use the water shaft...."

2 SAMUEL 5:8

Evidence From
THE FOSSIL RECORD

The famous "horse sequence" found in most textbooks has long been claimed to demonstrate the evolution of small multi-toed ancestors to large one-toed horses of today. Although it is still being paraded as a fact in textbooks, the sequence has been largely discredited as proof of evolution. The first animals in the sequence more closely resemble small rodents than horses, and many of the **later horses have been found in the same rock layers as their supposed ancestors.**

It is quite easy to arrange similar fossils from smallest to largest and then claim that this proves evolution. In the same way one could place the bones of a Chihuahua, beagle, boxer, and Great Dane in sequence and claim that this proves that dogs have evolved. This is essentially what has been done with the horse evolution series. The various breeds of dogs exist not because they have evolved, but because the **information** needed to breed the different varieties **was present from the beginning**. The same is true of horses–no evolution has been observed, only variation within a kind.

Tornado in the Junkyard: The Relentless Myth of Darwinism, p. 16-17

And God said, "Let the earth bring forth the living creature after his kind, cattle, and creeping thing, and beast of the earth after his kind:" and it was so.

Genesis 1:24 KJV

Evidence From CHEMISTRY

Even in the plant world, there is no such thing as "simple life." The voodoo lily, for example, was designed to raise its temperature by 25 degrees while it releases a scent that attracts beetles to pollinate it. There are many complex chemical reactions that take place within the lily. Some are specifically designed to raise the lily's temperature. The elevated temperature then increases the rate of evaporation of other chemicals designed to attract pollinating insects.

The chemicals which evaporate from the lily happen to be the same ones found in rotting meat. The smell of rotting meat is what attracts the pollinating beetles to the flowers. As the attracted beetles crawl around inside the flower looking for food, they get covered with pollen and spread the pollen to the next lily. How did the lily "learn" to make this exact scent? It could only have happened by design, possibly after the Fall of mankind, when radical changes occurred throughout the plant and animal kindgoms.

Specific chemical reactions with a specific purpose require careful **design and planning**. It does not make logical sense to assume the voodoo lily's complex chemical reactions evolved by chance.

LETTING GOD CREATE YOUR DAY,
VOL. 3, P.44

**For you are great and do marvelous deeds;
you alone are God.**

PSALM 86:10

Evidence From ASTRONOMY

When space probes passed Saturn late last century, they sent pictures of complex and intricately inner-woven rings made from billions of individual particles. Scientists are amazed at the appearance of turbulence and instability in Saturn's rings. The reason astronomers were surprised was the presupposition that the solar system is approximately five billion years old. **For Saturn's rings to have existed for billions of years, they would need to be in extremely stable orbits.** The rings of Saturn are assumed to be made from leftover debris after the formation of the planet. The instability of the orbits of these individual particles is extremely perplexing. Known laws of physics dictate that the particles should have disappeared long ago. **If, on the other hand, the rings are only a few thousand years old, what we see in Saturn's rings are consistent with known physical laws.**

As research continues, scientists are finding that most dating methods do not support the concept that our solar system is billions of years old. Primarily because evolution demands vast amounts of time to be considered feasible, only long-age dating methods are mentioned in schoolbooks and popular media. This indoctrination makes it very difficult for students and adults to even consider the evidence that the universe is not so old after all.

IT'S A YOUNG WORLD AFTER ALL, P.45

Behold, the heaven and the heaven of heavens is the LORD's thy God, the earth also, with all that therein is.

DEUTERONOMY 10:14 KJV

Evidence From COMPARING RELIGIONS

The final and greatest proof of Christ's absolute uniqueness is His resurrection. Not only did Christ die precisely at the time of His choosing, but He rose on the third day by His own power. Christ predicted this when He said that He had the power to lay His life down and He had the power to take it up again (John 10:17, 18). After three days Christ arose from the dead. **Christians worship a "living" Lord. All other religious founders and leaders (e.g., Muhammad, Shankara, and Budda) are dead.** In most cases their tombs are known and honored. Only the tomb of Christ was occupied for just three days, and thereafter it was empty forever!

Christ alone conquered death, which clearly shows that Christ is exactly who He said He was, "the resurrection and the life." It is Christ's resurrection that gives Christians hope in life, the realization that they have nothing to fear from death, and the assurance that they will see Christ again after their death.

MANY INFALLIBLE PROOFS, P.14

"He is not here; he has risen, just as he said. Come and see the place where he lay. Then go quickly and tell his disciples: 'He has risen from the dead and is going ahead of you into Galilee. There you will see him.'..."

MATTHEW 28:6,7

Evidence From BIBLICAL ACCURACY

The Bible records that Abraham traveled more than 1,000 miles from the city of Ur in Chaldea to Haram and then on to Canaan. **Some critics have rejected the Bible's accuracy because of its record of Abraham's travels.** They argued that travel could not have been so extensive such a long time ago.

Several years ago an ancient Babylon wagon rental contract was found on a clay tablet. The contract forbids the wagon renter from taking the wagon as far as the lands on the Mediterranean Coast. The implication from this find is that travel over such great distances was *so common* that mileage limitations had to be put on wagon rental contracts!

Time after time attacks on the Bible's straightforward proclamations of history and science have been proven totally inaccurate. God's Word can stand up to any and all criticism. God encourages and speaks highly of those who take time to study His Word and test its truths.

LETTING GOD CREATE OUR DAY, VOL. 3, P. 49

Now the Bereans were of more noble character than the Thessalonians, for they received the message with great eagerness and examined the Scriptures every day to see if what Paul said was true.

ACTS 17:11

Evidence From
BIOLOGY

Lungfish have been proposed as a link between sea and land animals because they have the ability to survive for long periods out of water. There are many varieties of lungfish found in Australia, Africa, and South America. In Australia they live in quiet pools of water which become stagnant in the summer. **Because there isn't much oxygen dissolved in the water, these fish need lungs in order to breathe air, just as we do.** Lungfish in South America live in swamps which often dry up during the dry season. They spend the dry season resting in burrows. The African lungfish also spends the dry season burrowed in the mud, but it builds a breathing tube through the mud to allow air to reach it.

Lungfish are not fish in the process of evolving into land animals–they are simply animals designed to survive for periods of time outside of water. Lungfish lack critical biological features such as bones and muscles for movement on land. This makes it impossible for them to ever become anything other than a fish. Furthermore, **the lungfish we find living today are exactly the same as those which are found in the fossil record.** There is absolutely no evidence that a lungfish has ever been, or ever will be, anything other than a lungfish.

LETTING GOD CREATE YOUR DAY,
VOL. 4, P.233

I will praise thee, O LORD, with my whole heart; I will show forth all thy marvelous works.

PSALM 9:1 KJV

Evidence From
HISTORY

According to the Bible, man and dinosaur lived on Earth at the same time. According to evolution, dinosaurs died out 65 million years ago and apelike creatures turned human "only" one to four million years ago. Yet virtually **every culture on Earth has stories about creatures which sound exactly like dinosaurs**, which range from cave drawings in the Grand Canyon to carvings found on Central American stone artifacts. Eyewitness accounts in Italy, Ireland, India, China, Arabia, Australian, etc. indicate that dinosaurs have been seen by humans around the world. As the Bible shows from this passage in the book of Job, **dinosaurs** were clearly known by mankind at the time this passage was written:

*Look at the behemoth, which I made along with you and feeds on grass like an ox. What strength he has in his loins, what power in the muscles of his belly! **His tail sways like a great cedar;** the sinews of his thighs are close-knit. His bones are tubes of bronze...Under the lotus plants he lies...When the river rages, he is not alarmed; he is secure, though the Jordan should surge against his mouth.*

Job 40:15-23

No known animal except the dinosaur had a huge "cedar-like" tail. If man had never seen those reptiles, why do ancient peoples all over the world have similar stories of enormous reptile-like creatures roaming and flying on the earth?

THE GREAT DINOSAUR MYSTERY AND THE BIBLE, P.36-49.

So God created the great creatures of the sea and every living and moving thing with which the water teems....And there was evening, and there was morning–the fifth day.... So God created man in his own image....And there was evening, and there was morning–the sixth day.

GENESIS 1:21-31

Evidence From
COMMON SENSE

There is a war of values raging in America today. Most of us are aware of the surface skirmishes (such as abortion, increasing violence, or euthanasia), but few are aware that the basis of this war is the question of man's relationship to God. **Either life's value is based on God's personal existence** (meaning absolute values do exist), *or* **man sets the standards**. There are no other possibilities.

The consequence of 150 years of indoctrination with evolutionary principles is the acceptance that man is part of the natural forces which shaped us. The inevitable result of this line of reasoning is the removal of an objective basis for determining the value of anything. Thus, mankind either arbitrarily assigns value to things (including people), or all life becomes of equal value. *In the case of the former*, atrocities such as human sacrifice, genocide, or passive acceptance of abortion occur. *In the case of the latter,* absurdities occur such as animal rights groups equating the murder and mutilation of humans with the slaughter of chickens. Both of these responses are inevitable outcomes of following the evolutionary humanist philosophy to its logical conclusion.

Christianity is rooted in the fact that a personal God exists and that people were made in God's image. Thus, human life is inherently valuable. There is something special about all humans. No one has the right to remove their value by murder, abortion, or euthanasia.

*SEARCH FOR THE TRUTH, P.*110

All of the words of my mouth are with righteousness; nothing crooked or perverse is in them. They are all plain to him who understands and right to those who find knowledge.

PROVERBS 8:8,9 NKJV

Evidence From
THE FOSSIL RECORD

Stories claiming that fossils of primitive apelike men have been found are extremely overstated. Consider the following sad and sordid history:

1. It is now universally accepted that **"Piltdown man"** was a hoax. After appearing in textbooks for over 40 years, it was a scientist outside the field of paleontology who exposed the fraud in 1953.
2. **"Nebraska man"** was based on a single tooth that turned out to be a pig's tooth.
3. **"Java man"** was based on a skull fragment and leg bone found 39 feet apart.
4. The evidence for **"Ramapithecus"** was a handful of teeth and jaw fragments that were pieced together incorrectly by Louis Leakey and others to resemble a human jaw. Ramapithicus was an ape.
5. A growing consensus is coming to acknowledge that **"Homo Habilis"** is really bits and pieces of many different creatures and never really existed.
6. **"Australopithecines"** have an even more apelike appearance. Detailed computer analysis has shown that their body proportions are not intermediate between man and ape.

It would seem that **the family tree of man** is a very slippery tree–whenever a supposed ancestor to man is placed there, it ultimately drops out as a fraud, mistake, or misinterpretation.

In the Beginning, 7th Ed., p. 11-12, 57-59
The Revised Answers Book, p.127

So God created man in his own image, in the image of God he created him; male and female he created them.

Genesis 1:27

Evidence From THE WORLDWIDE FLOOD

How could Noah's Ark have held two of every kind of animal? Many people assume that this is an impossibility and reject the Bible on other matters, as well. Unfortunately, these skeptics seldom take time to test the feasibility of the account.

Only air-breathing, land-dwelling animals needed to be rescued from the worldwide Flood aboard the Ark. There was no need for fish, insects, amphibians, or whales. Furthermore, a biblical "kind" (animals that could breed) is different than the modern species. Only one pair of dogs was needed and these would have had all of the genetic information needed to later breed different dog varieties, such as wolves, coyotes, foxes, dingoes, or domestic dogs. Taking this into account, at most 16,000 mammals, birds, and reptiles would have been on board, with an average size smaller than a sheep. The size of the Ark was approximately 1.4 million cubic feet. Modern railroad stock cars totaling a volume of 1.4 million cubic feet would be capable of housing 125,000 sheep-sized animals! **Only a small fraction of the huge vessel would be needed to house the required animal life; and plenty of room remained for people, food, and supplies.**

The enormous size of the Ark only makes sense if it was built to save every *kind* of land animal alive before the worldwide Flood. Every detail in the Bible is there for our benefit. The very dimensions of the Ark allow us to confirm the credibility of the account of Noah's Flood.

THE ANSWERS BOOK, P.179-188
NOAH'S ARK:
A FEASIBILITY STUDY

And of every living thing of all flesh, two of every sort shalt thou bring into the ark....Of every clean beast thou shalt take to thee by sevens....Of fowls also of the air by sevens....
GENESIS 6:19 AND 7:2,3 KJV

Evidence From LANGUAGE

Evidence continues to mount that human beings, unlike any other creature on Earth, are born with complex language ability. Research shows that children as young as two months have already learned to distinguish characteristic vowel and consonant sounds in the language spoken by their parents.

In one test, researchers rewarded babies who responded by turning their heads in the direction of the test sound. Sounds distinctive to English and Swedish were used. *American babies* responded to the English sounds two-thirds of the time, while Swedish babies ignored these sounds as gibberish. *Swedish babies* responded to the Swedish sounds two-thirds of the time, while American babies ignored them as gibberish!

Researchers have concluded that two-month-old children have already begun classifying the elements of language. This is the first step in organizing sounds into meaningful words. Other research shows that six-month-old infants already understand the basic emotional tones of language.

The human ability to learn language appears to be programmed into the baby's brain and goes to work immediately upon birth (if not before). Humans have been created uniquely different from any other creature on Earth.

LETTING GOD CREATE YOUR DAY, VOL. 3, P.90

Who endowed the heart with wisdom or gave understanding to the mind?

JOB 38:36

Evidence From MATHEMATICS

The coded instructions contained in the DNA of a human cell would fill 4,000 encyclopedia-sized books with meaningful information. Even if we assume life and matter evolved, there is zero probability that mutations and natural selection produced this tremendous amount of information.

Evolutionists assume that anything is possible with enough time. For instance, it has been stated that given enough time, even a monkey could type out the entire Encyclopedia Brittanica. However, it can be calculated that just getting the title "Encyclopedia Brittanica" by random trials would only happen one time in 10^{39} attempts. **One in 10^{39} is approximately the same as one monkey sitting on every square foot of the earth's surface, stacked 10 miles deep,** and making one attempt every second for 10 billion years. Yet all these attempts would only result in a correct title one time!

The odds of natural processes producing the information on a single strand of DNA vastly exceeds the total number of subatomic particles within the entire known universe. This intelligent information content of our cells could only have been produced by an inconceivably brilliant designer. How could anyone deny the existence of God in face of this evidence?

IN THE BEGINNING, 7TH ED., P.14, 62-63
SEARCH FOR THE TRUTH, P. I-9

$2 \times (3+4) =$

For you created my inmost being; you knit me together in my mother's womb. I praise you because I am fearfully and wonderfully made; your works are wonderful, I know that full well.

PSALM 139:13,14

Evidence From BIOLOGY

The largest known cooperative community of mammals spend their summers together inside Bracken Cave near San Antonio, Texas. During the day 20 million Mexican free-tailed bats raise their 20 million pups, while each night they gulp down an estimated 150 tons of insects! The bats winter in Mexico and mate in the spring. Then, for a reason unknown to scientists, only the females fly to Texas.

During their migration, the bats fly at 40 miles per hour at an altitude of eight to ten thousand feet. Once settled in at Bracken Cave, they become pregnant from the sperm of male bats which they have carried on the journey with them! Four months later each has a single pup. Although the cave's one-room **nursery has 20 million noisy pups, a mother bat released anywhere within the cave can find her own baby in as little as twelve seconds.**

How marvelous is our God who created such wonders!

Letting God Create Your Day, Vol. 3, p.91

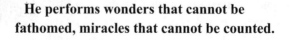

He performs wonders that cannot be fathomed, miracles that cannot be counted.

Job 5:9

Evidence From GREAT SCIENTISTS

Louis Pasteur was a dedicated Christian and brilliant scientist, yet if he lived today he would probably be an outcast in the scientific community for refusing to accept the theories of Charles Darwin. During Pasteur's lifetime, most biologists said that life arose from nonliving material. Pasteur believed that life was created by God. In spite of the opposition that Louis Pasteur received from colleagues, he conducted careful experiments showing life could only come from life. He effectively refuted the claim that life could come from nonliving chemicals. His research also showed that fermentation was caused by tiny yeast cells. This led him to discover that many diseases were caused by living organisms too small to see. As a result of his scientific work, **Louis Pasteur not only proved the claims of spontaneous generation of life to be false, but developed vaccines to fight diseases** like rabies, diphtheria, and anthrax in the process.

Pasteur once commented that the more he learned in science, the simpler his faith in the plain words of the Holy Scripture became. **There is no contradiction** between the belief in a supernatural *Creator* and *science*.

LETTING GOD CREATE YOUR DAY, VOL. 3, P.93

The fool says in his heart, "There is no God."...

PSALM 14:1

Evidence From
BIOLOGY

Every summer night female Mexican free-tailed bats leave the Bracken Cave in San Antonio, Texas, and fly as far as 60 miles, consuming as much as their total body weight in insects. After about five hours, the mothers return to the cave to nurse their pups and rest for about three hours. They then go out for another three hours of feeding. Even with this eating frenzy, the bat's diet normally would not provide enough fat for the mother bat to provide rich milk for her pups. Her nursing period, however, *"just happens"* to fall at exactly the same time that a particular local ant grows wings. It also *"just happens"* that this particular ant is a rich source of needed protein. These flying insects also *"just happen"* to be available in the bat's airspace, at just the right time! One wonders how this particular species of ant could have evolved at exactly the right time to ensure the survival of the Mexican free-tailed bat.

It is unknown whether the eating habits of this bat developed before or after creation's Fall. Either way, the bat's design clearly points to an intelligent Designer.

LETTING GOD CREATE YOUR DAY, VOL. 3, P.91

"You alone are the LORD. You made the heavens...the earth and all that is on it....You give life to everything...."

NEHEMIAH 9:6

Evidence From THE FOSSIL RECORD

Night-flying moths are designed with organs which enable them to hear the ultrasonic signals used by bats. Bats send out these signals to navigate and find food–including moths. Evolutionists believe that moths evolved the ability to hear ultrasonic bat sounds as a response to being eaten by the more recently evolved bats.

A number of years ago, a fossilized egg from a night-flying moth was discovered. Evolutionists said the egg was twice as old, according to their dating system, as any evidence of the first bat. The problem not usually disclosed is that the egg clearly belongs to a moth species that can hear bats. **Evolutionary scientists were quite puzzled by this discovery, because evolution would have no reason to evolve this species of moth before bats existed.** If all plant and animal life were created at essentially the same time, however, finds like this make perfect sense. Animals were either given or developed predatory abilities after the curse of creation. Both the bat and the moth were fully developed at this point.

The Bible says that God created all living things within days of each other. By studying nature, we can see how this statement proves itself true.

LETTING GOD CREATE YOUR DAY, VOL. 3, P.95

Thus the heavens and earth were completed in all their vast array. By the seventh day God had finished the work he had been doing; so on the seventh day he rested....

GENESIS 2:1-2

Evidence From
CHEMISTRY

Biologists have discovered a growing list of creatures which freeze solidly in the winter, only to thaw out and resume life in the spring. Three species of tree frogs have been added to this list. As cold fall weather approaches, these northern tree frogs burrow under the dead leaves in the forest. Scientists found that up to 35% of the frogs' body fluids freeze when they are cooled to several degrees below freezing. **How do these frogs survive death, when freezing even part of our bodies would result in the loss of skin, fingers, or limbs?**

Scientists have discovered that **these frogs produce glycerol,** which acts like antifreeze within their bodies. Even when it gets so cold that their blood freezes, this chemical prevents ice crystals from forming in a way that destroys cells. This ability indicates design and instantaneous creation, rather than evolution. The frogs could never have survived if the ability to resist freezing (and tolerate antifreeze chemicals) developed a step at a time, rather than the frog being created with all of these abilities in place.

LETTING GOD CREATE YOUR DAY, VOL. 3, P.76

"**But ask the animals, and they will teach you.... Which of all these does not know that the hand of the LORD has done this?**"

JOB 12:7,9

Evidence From
EARTH'S ECOLOGY

Science is learning how plants are designed to regulate carbon dioxide in the atmosphere.

First, when carbon dioxide levels go up, many plants increase their use of carbon dioxide, making more oxygen.

Second, at higher carbon dioxide levels, plants tend to make tissue that doesn't decay as easily. This ties up the extra carbon for longer periods of time.

Third, at higher carbon dioxide levels, plant tissues discourage insects from eating them, decreasing the re-release of the plants' carbon as carbon dioxide.

Our Creator expects us to take care of His creation. He knows, however, that we cannot control all of the possible changing conditions on planet Earth. For this reason He has built mechanisms into the creation that adjust to changing conditions and maintain a suitable habitat for human life.

LETTING GOD CREATE YOUR DAY, VOL. 3, P.77

The heaven, even the heavens, are the LORD's: but the earth hath he given to the children of men.

PSALM 115:16 KJV

Evidence From ANATOMY

Our kidneys are such extremely complex yet reliably designed organs that we can survive with a single kidney working at a fraction of its capacity. Each of these two dark red, bean-shaped organs is about the size of an adult fist and performs many absolutely critical functions within our bodies. The kidney's primary function is to filter impurities and toxins from our blood.

Each kidney has three layers, called the cortex, the medulla, and the pelvis. Blood flows into the cortex and medulla through the renal artery. The renal artery then branches into smaller vessels which connect to a blood filtration unit within the kidney called a nephron. **Two normal kidneys have about two million nephrons (60 miles in combined length), which purify all of the body's blood approximately every 50 minutes.** Over 400 gallons of blood are pumped through the kidneys each day. After being purified, about 99% of the blood's fluid is recycled back into the body for further use.

Many engineers over countless hours have worked to design artificial kidneys. Why would anyone accept that these comparatively huge and inefficient artificial kidneys have an intelligent designer, yet refuse to see God behind the infinitely more intricately designed kidneys within our bodies?

THE HUMAN BODY: ACCIDENT OR DESIGN?,
P.69-71

Consider what God has done...

ECCLESIASTES 7:13

Evidence From
ARCHAEOLOGY

In the late 1800s Sir William Ramsay, a scholar who was skeptical of the authenticity of the Book of Acts, went on an archaeological expedition in Asia Minor with the purpose of showing that Luke was not accurate in his historical account. After years of *research* and *literally digging up the evidence*, Ramsay had to admit that Acts was completely and totally accurate.

Luke mentions 32 countries, 54 cities, 9 Mediterranean islands, and 95 people groups (62 of which are not named anywhere else in the New Testament). **Every single reference which could be verified was found to be totally accurate.** This is truly remarkable, in view of the fact that the political and territorial situation of Luke's day was in a state of almost constant flux. Even modern historians with computer-aided research make some errors. How does one account for Luke's *precision*? **He could only have been guided by God.**

A STUDY COURSE IN CHRISTIAN EVIDENCES, P.115

"As for God, his way is perfect; the word of the LORD is flawless. He is a shield for all who take refuge in him."

2 SAMUEL 22:31

Evidence From
COMMON SENSE

Bird fossils found on the Hawaiian Islands show that many species became extinct before Western civilization arrived in 1778. **One-third of all known species on the islands have become extinct within the last 1,500 years. Yet no new species of Hawaiian birds have developed over the same time period.** There is no question that creatures are becoming extinct, whereas there is no evidence that completely different types of creatures are forming. These extinctions are from natural causes and have little to do with man's influence.

This evidence implies that the millions of different life forms on Earth could not have come from evolution, because **creatures become extinct far faster than they could possibly evolve into new types.**

LETTING GOD CHANGE YOUR DAY, VOL. 3, P.84

There is a time for everything, and a season for every activity under heaven: a time to be born and a time to die...

ECCLESIASTIES 3:1,2

Evidence From
CHEMISTRY

The bola spider doesn't weave a web, but catches insects by making a special silk thread with a sticky glob on the end (called a bola). **The *bola spider* then generates the same scent as the *female moth* in order to attract the male moth.** When a male moth comes close to investigate the scent, the resourceful spider casts its silken thread toward the unsuspecting prey and catches it on the sticky glob.

This spider's thread is so elastic it can stretch up to 600%, while sticky enough to snag a struggling moth. Chemists who have studied this spider's glue have yet to duplicate its adhesive properties. The spider allows the moth to struggle while it conserves its own energy. Once the moth has tired, it reels in its catch and wraps it in silk for storage until it is hungry. The bola spider is so efficient that it is not unusual for one spider to catch up to eight moths per night.

One species is normally not able to detect the scents of another species. One wonders how the bola spider could have evolved the ability to exactly duplicate the female moth's chemistry. This scent along with the ability to accurately produce and cast a bola must have evolved simultaneously. Otherwise this spider would have been extinct long before its unique abilities to catch its prey were perfected. The direct *creation* of these unique abilities, with their unique functions is the logical answer.

It is because of the fallen creation that each type of creature, just like mankind, must struggle for their existence.
Yet even in the struggle, God provides.

Letting God Create Your Day,
Vol. 3, p.89

These all look to you to give them their food at the proper time.

Psalm 104:27

Fully Rely On God

F.R.O.G. or Fully Rely On God
   Is a noteworthy acronym.
It really should make us take the time
   To *look to* and *trust* in Him.

We always seem to think we can
   Do everything on our own.
How easily, though, we do forget
   All we are and have is *on loan.*

The twentieth verse of *Romans 1*
   Again rings loud and true.
God said He'd show Himself to us
   In His creation, which we *should view.*

Take, for example, the little frog;
   God always meets its needs.
He gives it food, a mate, a home
   And watches its young in the weeds.

God carefully designed the frog's body, too,
   With a long tongue and powerful legs.
Its skin is perfectly camouflaged,
   And jelly protects its eggs.

Because of this, the frog never frets;
   There is much for it to do.
Since it only does what God planned out,
   It lives without worries, too.

The Bible says in *Job 12:9* and *10*
   Even the animals know
That Jesus has given them life and breath,
   So *full trust* in Him they show.

Lord, let us *learn* from what you've made
   To fully rely—*You know best.*
Then help us *do* what Your Word tells us to,
   So in Christ *we,* too, *can find rest.*

Evidence From CREATION FOUNDATION

According to the Bible, God created the heavens and Earth in six literal days. God carefully defined His terms. The very first time He used the word "day" (in Hebrew *yom*), He defined it as the period from "light" to "darkness." After separating the day from night, God completed His first day's work. God said in Genesis 1:5, "The evening and the morning were the first day." This same wording is used at the close of each of the six days. It is quite apparent that the length of each of the days, including the first, was the same. The context of each day's passage (evening, morning, "number" of the day) makes it very clear that a normal 24-hour day is intended.

To make the point even more concrete, one of the Ten Commandments, written by God Himself, commands man to rest on the seventh day, just as He rested from creation on the seventh day. This makes no sense if the creation period was millions or billions of years. **The days of creation can not be interpreted as long periods of time as needed by evolutionism.** The Bible must be ignored or denied to accept an old earth.

THE REVISED AND EXPANDED ANSWERS BOOK, P. 33-74
THE GENESIS RECORD, P.55-56

For in six days the LORD made the heavens and the earth, the sea, and all that is in them, and he rested on the seventh day....

EXODUS 20:11 KJV

Evidence From BIOLOGY

Hermit crabs are constantly on the lookout for a new home. Sometimes they will try on a new shell, return to their old one, and then try on the new shell again, just to see which one suits them best. Amazingly, God gave hermit crabs the ability to sense the calcium content in shells, because shells with the highest calcium content are the strongest. **Research shows that a hermit crab will always favor a correctly fitting shell with the highest calcium content.**

The ability to sense calcium involves many complicated organic reactions, sensors, internal communication systems, and instincts (to interpret for the crab what its sensors are saying). All of these processes would need to be operational before the first hermit crab could have sensed calcium. It is not possible that they could have evolved independently, nor is it conceivable they could have "just appeared" all at once.

The logical alternative is to acknowledge that the hermit crab was created fully functional, with all of its unique abilities and instincts. God knew exactly what the hermit crab would need.

LETTING GOD CREATE YOUR DAY, VOL. 3, P.75

...for your Father knows what you need before you ask him.

MATTHEW 6:8

Evidence From
COMMON SENSE

According to evolutionists, we exist because random mutations turned simple creatures into more complex creatures. If so, **where are the leftovers and mistakes?** Let's think about the process required to develop anything new.

When **Thomas Edison** worked to develop the electric light bulb, he tested over a thousand combinations of filaments and bulbs before discovering a combination that worked well. His laboratory was literally filled with failed attempts. The modern automobile is the result of 100 years of intelligent developments and improvements. Earlier versions were inefficient, less durable, and slower. These automobile *ancestors* did not improve by random changes, but by the intelligent design of engineers. Yet the earlier models are still around to see the developmental history. So where are mankind's evolutionary leftovers?

Evolutionists recognized this problem over 100 years ago. In the 1800s they listed almost 200 features of the human body believed to be rudimentary or vestigial (left over). **Today the list has shrunk to practically zero.** Virtually every feature of our body has been found to be designed for a useful purpose. Why aren't our bodies filled with useless leftover parts? Where are all the fossils showing evolution? Every fossil reveals a creature that is clearly identifiable and suited for survival in its environment.

Only design by someone of infinite intelligence can adequately explain the human body, which has been perfectly designed from the start with every feature serving a needed and useful function.

BRUCE MALONE

But God made the earth by his power;
He founded the world by his wisdom....

JEREMIAH 10:12

Evidence From
CREATION FOUNDATION

Many Christians consider creation irrelevant. They believe it makes no difference whether God used creation or evolution to create mankind and the Bible can be interpreted in many ways. Atheists have a much better understanding of the importance of this issue, as shown by the following quote from American Atheist Magazine, 2/78, p. 19,30:

> *"Christianity has fought, still fights, and will [always] fight to the desperate end over evolution, because evolution destroys utterly and finally the very reason Jesus' earthly life was supposedly made necessary...Destroy Adam and Eve and the original sin, and in the rubble you will find the sorry remains of the Son of God. [You will] take away the meaning of his death...If Jesus was not the redeemer who died for our sins, **and this is what evolution means**, then Christianity is nothing!"*

Logic allows no other alternatives. If God used evolution to create us, then we came from some sort of apelike creature. Therefore Adam and Eve must be a myth. Where is the Fall of man? At what point did the apes (ruled by instinct) rebel against their creator? **Why do we need a Savior if we were created from apes and are just doing what comes natural to us?** The Bible calls Jesus the "second Adam." Was the first Adam a man or an apelike creature? What does that make Christ? Did God create the current world (with all of its problems and suffering), or is this fallen state a result of man's rebellion? Acceptance of evolution is a poison which will destroy true Christianity. The evidence for this can be seen in the decline of the evangelical belief in Europe as the acceptance of evolution has increased.

BRUCE MALONE

The first man was of the earth, made of dust; the second Man is the Lord from heaven. *1 CORINTHIANS 15:47 NKJV*

...just as through one man sin entered the world, and death through sin... *ROMANS 5:12 NKJV*

Evidence From THE WORLDWIDE FLOOD

Story traditions of a mighty flood are worldwide. They come from Asia, Australia, North and South America, Europe and Africa. The parallels between many of the more than 230 stories scattered all over the world are amazing. They generally agree that:

1. An ark, barge, or some other floating vessel was involved.
2. Everything is destroyed by water.
3. Only a few chosen people were saved through divine intervention.
4. The Flood was judgment against the wickedness of mankind.
5. Because one person was warned beforehand, he was able to save himself and his family.
6. Animals were often saved with the few humans. Birds were sent out to determine the end of the Flood.
7. The vessel came to rest on the top of a mountain or people were saved at the top of a mountain.

These widespread cultural stories are exactly what you would expect to find after survivors from the Ark spread all over the world. The specific details of the Flood and the Ark would become distorted, but the event would be remembered. These story traditions **strongly support the reality** of the biblical account of this worldwide Flood.

The Creation, p.143-150
In The Beginning,
7th Ed., p.37

These were the three sons of Noah, and from them came the people who were scattered over the earth.

Genesis 9:19

Evidence From
BIOLOGY

Modern airplanes navigate electronically. They pick up radio or satellite signals, and complicated equipment translates the signal to tell the pilot his or her location. But for years we have known that **birds can navigate across great distances** without any mechanical aids. In one test of this incredible ability, a number of Manx Shearwaters, which nest off the coast of Wales, were tagged and released at different points far beyond their usual range. One was turned loose in Boston, some 3,200 miles from home. In just twelve and a half days the bird returned to its nest, having traveled 250 miles a day starting from a place thousands of miles from where it had never been before. What's more, based on the known speed of the bird, **it must have flown directly home across the open ocean**.

No one knows how it did this. **Could the incredible navigational system of birds have "just happened"?** Both the Bible and science indicate otherwise.

IT COULDN'T JUST HAPPEN, P.106-107

Two of every kind of bird, of every kind of animal and of every kind of creature that moves along the ground will come to you to be kept alive.

GENESIS 6:20

Evidence From ANATOMY

There are more than 600 muscles (containing about six billion muscle fibers) in the human body. They make up about 40% of the body's weight. Some muscles are voluntary, like the muscles of the arms and legs. One must "think" to move these types of muscles. Other muscles, like the heart and the intestines, are involuntary. The contraction and relaxation of these muscles cannot be consciously controlled.

Frequently, muscles work in pairs. For example, the biceps in the upper arm pulls the forearm up, whereas the triceps moves the forearm down. This perfect design allows one muscle to rest while the other muscle is being used. Each muscle has its own stored supply of high-grade fuel made from food which the body converts into usable sugars. **The muscle system also works together with other systems, like the nervous and skeletal systems.** The nerve connections are required to signal muscles as to when to contract or relax. Without a doubt, their cooperative nature was planned.

Webster's Dictionary defines *design* as "deliberate, purposeful planning." Just looking at the interaction between muscles and the rest of our body parts, how can anyone help but conclude that we have a Designer?

THE HUMAN BODY: ACCIDENT OR DESIGN?, P.22-24

Your hands made me and formed me....

PSALM 119:73

THE FOSSIL RECORD

Evidence From

Evolutionists use the presence of certain extinct animal remains to date rock layers that contain that particular fossil. For example, a certain type of mollusk (called *Pilina)* was believed to be extinct for some 400 million years, leaving no more recent remains in the fossil record. However, in 1952 a virtually identical mollusk was found alive and well living at ocean depths of 12,000 feet. This shows that this "living fossil," as it is called, hasn't evolved over the supposed "400 million year" period, because the modern specimens look exactly like their "400 million year old" ancestors. **How can an organism which is still alive be used to date rock layers?** Evolutionists just throw out this index fossil, but continue to use others. The contradictions to evolution compound themselves endlessly.

The *coelacanth* is another example of a fossilized animal which supposedly became extinct, leaving no fossils, for the past "60 million years." Yet many living coelacanths identical to the fossilized remains which are supposedly "60 million years" old have been caught in the Indian Ocean since 1938. Evolutionists have **no adequate explanation** for this. These types of "living fossils" were simply created similar to their present form and have never changed. The worldwide Flood is the event that created the majority of the fossil record, not billions of years of slow burial.

MYTHS AND MIRACLES, P.29

And God said, "Let the water teem with living creatures...." So God created the great creatures of the sea and every living and moving thing with which the water teems, according to their kinds...

GENESIS 1:20,21

Evidence From BIOLOGY

The protective hand of God is clearly displayed in the unique parenting habits of the emperor penguins of Antarctica. The female emperor penguin lays one egg on bare ice and then jumps into the water, apparently not giving her egg another thought for the next two months. It is up to the male penguin to keep the egg warm during this two-month period by continuously standing over it and holding the egg between his feet and stomach. **He does this without eating during the worst part of the Antarctic winter.**

When the chick hatches, the male feeds it with a milky substance from its throat. Eventually the female returns, fattened from eating, and takes over the care of her baby. The father then goes to sea for about three weeks before returning with food for his family. Does this "shared parenthood" happen by chance? **It is obvious that every penguin chick would have died long ago if its parents had not been designed to do things correctly from the start.**

MYTHS AND MIRACLES, P.36-37

So God created...every winged bird according to its kind. And God saw that it was good.

GENESIS 1:21

Evidence From GENETICS

Mutations (chance errors in genes) are the only proposed mechanism whereby new genetic information for evolution can emerge. It is common knowledge that rarely, if ever, does a mutation improve an organism in its natural environment. Almost all observable mutations are harmful; some are meaningless; many are lethal. **No known mutation has ever produced a form of life having greater complexity** and viability than its ancestors.

"There is no reason to believe that mutations or any natural process could ever produce any new organs—especially those as complex as our eye, ear, or brain. For example, an adult **human brain contains over 10^{14} (a hundred thousand billion) electrical connections**, more than all the electrical connections in all the electrical appliances in the entire world. Just the **human heart, a ten-ounce pump that will operate without maintenance or lubrication for over 75 years,** is an engineering marvel. To this day the heart is unparalleled by any man-made pump."

How could random mistakes to the genetic code produce improvements? How could random changes have produced these marvels in the first place?

In the Beginning, 7ᵀᴴ Ed., p.6-7

God's voice thunders in marvelous ways; He does great things beyond our understanding.

Job 37:5

Evidence From
EARTH'S ECOLOGY

What keeps the animal world from becoming overpopulated? Why don't particularly aggressive animals totally dominate worldwide? **There is significant evidence from the study of animal populations that when the optimum number of animals in a given area is reached, the population stabilizes.** This is not caused by a struggle-for-existence conflict, but by built-in physiological or psychological mechanisms which somehow slow down the reproductive activity.

The check-and-balance systems built into animal populations are so intricate that they can only point to a Designer. The Bible says that in the beginning God built a perfect and balanced system and saw that it was very good (Genesis 1:31). When sin entered, it brought with it cruelty, selfishness, and violence. What is truly amazing is that God maintains such a balance in spite of Satan's attempt to destroy His plan. One truly begins to better comprehend the character of God by studying the earth and observing the intricate design and delicate balance of nature.

THE GENESIS RECORD, P.76

"You are worthy, our Lord and God, to receive glory and honor and power, for you created all things, and by your will they were created and have their being."

REVELATION 4:11

Evidence From
BIBLICAL UNIQUENESS

The Bible consists of 66 separate books written by about 40 different authors living on three different continents. They used three different languages over a time span of at least 1,500 years. It contains history, poetry, prophecy, science, geography, and philosophy, yet contains no errors or internal discrepancies. **In spite of this diversity, the Bible presents a marvelous unity** within the development of its great themes.

For over 2,000 years it has been the world's top-selling book. Our understanding of both history and morality is based on what the Bible has to say. The Bible is also the foundation for both Western civilization and much technology (such as the printing press, which was invented due to the need to share God's Word).

From beginning to end there is one over-arching and unfolding story: God's redemption of man. **There is nothing remotely comparable among all of the millions of books written by man.**

MANY INFALLIBLE PROOFS, P.14

For ever, O LORD, thy word is settled in heaven. Thy faithfulness is unto all generations: thou hast established the earth, and it abideth.

PSALM 119:89-90 KJV

Evidence From
ANATOMY

The stomach is a remarkable organ. It is a baglike structure that serves as a temporary holding tank for food. The average adult stomach can hold about one and one-half quarts of food for three to four hours. During this time, the food is bathed with gastric juices which flow from three types of glands in the wall of the stomach. Amazingly, the stomach digests foods made of materials much tougher than itself. Scientists found we would have to boil much of our food in strong acids at 212° F to do what our stomach and intestines do at the normal body temperature of 98.6° F.

One of the most amazing things about the stomach is that it does not digest itself! Some of our stomach acids are strong enough to dissolve metal, yet they do not harm our stomach. The primary mechanism which keeps us from dissolving our own stomach is a thin gastric lining which continuously oozes a mucus coating. This coating forms a barrier between the acid and stomach wall. The mucus, somewhat alkaline, neutralizes the acid at the stomach wall and helps keep the stomach from digesting itself. The lining of the stomach **sheds one-half million cells every minute** and replaces them so quickly that we have what amounts to a new lining every three days. The stomach truly shows evidence of design.

*The **Human Body:** **Accident or Design?***, P.35-36

Know that the LORD is God. It is he who made us, and we are his....

Psalm 100:3

Evidence From ASTRONOMY

Every subject addressed by the Bible reveals absolute accuracy which could only have been divinely inspired. Even 500 years ago many people thought the earth was flat. **Yet the prophet Isaiah spoke of the earth being a "circle."** The Hebrew word for circle was *khug,* which means something with "roundness or sphericity." **How did Isaiah know this?**

Jeremiah the prophet declared that the stars in the sky were countless. In Jeremiah's time (600 B.C.) only about 3,000 stars could be seen on a clear night with the naked eye. Twenty-two centuries later, Galileo caught a glimpse of the vastly greater number of stars with his telescope. For the first time, humans were able to see how numerous the stars are and admit that what God said about the stars being countless (by human beings) is literally true. It was not until the last century, however, that Sir James Jean (1930) wrote in his book *Mysterious Universe* that the "total number of stars is roughly equal to the total number of grains of sand on all the seashores of all the world." **This scientific truth was revealed by God 2,500 years before it was discovered by man.**

A STUDY COURSE IN CHRISTIAN EVIDENCES, P.132
MYTHS AND MIRACLES, P.26

He sits enthroned above the circle of the earth.... *ISAIAH 40:22*

" '...as countless as the stars of the sky and as measureless as the sand on the seashore.' "
JEREMIAH 33:22

Evidence From
HISTORY

Man has always treasured his ability to see. As far back as records allow, we find that mankind has practiced eye surgery. **The oldest record of eye surgery dates back 4,000 years.** The Code of Hammurabi said that a surgeon who saved a man's eye was to be paid the same fee that was given to a doctor who saved a man's life. On the other hand, **if the eye was lost during surgery, the law required the surgeon's fingers to be cut off!** Not only were men intelligent enough to do eye surgery, but the consequences for failure indicate that they were apparently very skillful.

The Bible says Adam was created in God's image. It is only the false preconceptions of evolution, clouding people's minds with images of "ape-men," that have caused people to believe that ancient man was any less intelligent than modern man. Our technology has built upon the discoveries of the past, and there is every indication that ancient mankind was as intelligent as modern man.

LETTING GOD CREATE YOUR DAY, VOL. 3, P.173

Is there anything of which one can say, "Look! This is something new"? It was here already, long ago; it was here before our time.

ECCLESIASTES 1:10

Evidence From BIOLOGY

The lacewing larvae enter termite-infested tree branches in order to finish their growth cycle within the termite tunnels. Amazingly, the larvae don't wait for the termites to vacate the tunnels before entering. California termites are 30 times larger than the larvae and normally destroy any invader to their tunnels. The larvae boldly enter the termite tunnel waving their abdomen in the air. As the termites race forward to kill the larvae, the termites suddenly stop and topple over. Biologists discovered that this strange behavior is due to a paralyzing chemical which the larvae release. Even more amazing is the discovery that this chemical only paralyzes *this specific* California termite. The relationship between the beaded lacewing larva and the California termite poses a real problem for those who believe there is no Creator.

If this were all a matter of chance rather than intelligent design, **one wonders how the lacewings evolved the perfect chemical protection to work on the specific termite that makes safe tunnels for them to grow in.** Even though this conflict is quite likely a result of the fall of creation from perfection, this unique relationship between these insects gives us all the more reason to acknowledge God as Designer. God preserves even the smallest creeping things in His creation.

LETTING GOD CREATE YOUR DAY, VOL.4, P.23

The LORD is righteous in all his ways and loving toward all he has made.

PSALM 145:17

Evidence From
BIOLOGY

A study of the **monarch butterfly** should convince anyone of God's amazing design. Consider just a few of the monarch's abilities:

1. The female butterfly uses six sharp needles on her forelegs to test for food's chemical composition.
2. The caterpillar increases in weight 2,700 percent in 20 days.
3. The female butterfly can smell a male butterfly two miles away.
4. The female butterfly can store sperm and delay egg-laying for months if she is impregnated too close to migration time.
5. The butterfly navigates alone to a never-before-seen location over 2,000 miles away.
6. As a caterpillar, it digests only one type of plant, the milkweed, which is poisonous to other animals that eat it, but not to this caterpillar.
7. The monarch butterfly chemically reconstructs itself from a **caterpillar** with six simple eyes which can only see in black and white, a chewing mouthpiece, sixteen legs, and the ability to crawl. It becomes a **butterfly** with two eyes that can see in color (each with 6,000 lenses), a sucking mouthpiece, six legs, four wings, and the ability to fly.

The probability of random-chance mutations evolving this perfectly timed, chemically miraculous metamorphosis from caterpillar to monarch butterfly is far beyond the realm of reason.

FROM DARKNESS TO LIGHT TO FLIGHT

...I will meditate on your wonderful works. They will tell of the power of your awesome works, and I will proclaim your great deeds.

PSALM 145:5-6

Evidence From GENETICS

Biologists have discovered that certain living cells come with a built-in self-destruct mechanism. A certain gene within these cells triggers a sequence of events which cause the death of that cell. This is God's way of renewing, recycling, reshaping, or repairing different parts of an organism.

For example, as a tadpole turns into a toad, it no longer needs its tail. When the special gene gives the order, the tail cells begin to die. In other words, some living cells contain a gene that signals the death of the cell at its appointed time. **Why would evolution develop genes that order death?** By definition, such a gene would not aid survival.

LETTING GOD CREATE YOUR DAY, VOL. 3, P.141

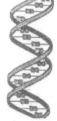

Just as man is destined to die once...

HEBREWS 9:27

Evidence From
ASTRONOMY

The Bible says, **"There is nothing new under the sun."**
(Eccl. 1:9) A good example of this is the knowledge of
astronomy which the ancient Mayans of Central America
had. These people built numerous observatories, like the one
found at Chichen Itza in the Yucatan Peninsula. The Mayan
people seem to have been focused on charting the paths of
the stars and planets. Their ancient astronomers devised an
accurate cosmic clock to predict the solstices and equinoxes
(first day of each of the four seasons). Their **mathematics and
astronomical calculations were so precise;** they were able
to figure the length of a solar year to within 2/10,000 of a day.
The Mayans calculated the length of each year at 365.2420
days. Only recently have astronomers been able to calculate
the solar year with any greater accuracy at 365.2422 days.

Every ancient civilization seems to have suddenly popped into
existence about 5,000 years ago–exactly when the Bible states
that the worldwide Flood ended and people spread across the face
of the earth. **Ancient civilizations such as the Mayan showed
amazing intelligence and ingenuity from the very onset.** The
words of the Bible prove to be true time and time again.

UNLOCKING THE MYSTERIES OF CREATION,
PREMIER ED., P.216

**What has been will be again, what has been
done will be done again; there is nothing new
under the sun....There is no remembrance of
men of old, and even those who are yet to come
will not be remembered by those who follow.**

ECCLESIASTES 1:9,11

Evidence From
CHEMISTRY

God said He used the "dust of the ground" to make man. This is a remarkable statement, because it is not at all obvious. Rocks seem to be composed of totally different substances than human flesh. The biblical statement "dust of the ground" actually conveys the thought of the smallest particles of the earth. In modern terminology, the thought would mean the most basic chemical substances such as nitrogen, oxygen, carbon, calcium, etc. In reality, both human flesh and dust are indeed made from a few dozen basic chemical elements. Modern science has verified this straightforward statement of the Bible.

How could this information have been known and recorded by the ancient writers of the Bible unless it was revealed to them by God?

THE GENESIS RECORD, P.85

...the LORD God formed the man from the dust of the ground....

GENESIS 2:7

Evidence From THE FOSSIL RECORD

The most commonly repeated theory for why dinosaurs went extinct is the idea that a large meteorite impacted the earth 65 million years ago. This supposedly resulted in massive extinctions and climatic changes, ending the age of the dinosaurs. **However, problems with this theory are seldom addressed or shared.** For instance:

1. The extinction was not sudden (using evolutionary interpretations of the geologic record). The spread of these fossilized bones through the rock layers does make sense if much of the sedimentary rock formed in Noah's flood.
2. Light-sensitive species did not go extinct. Why not, if the impact caused a worldwide cloud layer to form?
3. Extinctions don't correlate to known crater dates.
4. Huge modern volcanic eruptions do not cause massive extinctions, even if they are large enough to cause documented worldwide temperature changes.
5. The iridium enrichment, supposedly a clear proof of the impact, is not nearly as conclusive as presented.
6. Drill cores of the apparent crater in the Yucatan Peninsula in Mexico do not support that this is an impact crater.

There very well may have been multiple meteorite impacts during the worldwide Flood; but *the Flood*, not the meteorite, caused the demise of the dinosaurs.

EVOLUTION REFUTED 2, P.146-147

It is the glory of God to conceal a matter; to search out a matter is the glory of kings.

PROVERBS 25:2

Evidence From BIBLICAL ACCURACY

Within the oldest book of the Bible is **the story of Job**. This book is the account of a righteous man who is allowed to suffer enormous loss, grief, and difficulty. Job pleaded for God to reveal why he was suffering, but God did not answer Job's questions. Instead, God pointed to His own creation, power, and knowledge. In this way Job was reminded to trust God and His purposes.

As part of this dialogue, God asked Job if he had ever entered the *springs* of the sea. **We now know there are such springs off the coasts of Greece, Italy, Israel, Syria, and Australia.** In 1976 the U.S. Geological Survey also found fresh water in the Atlantic Ocean along the seacoast from New England to Georgia. How could the writer of the book of Job, which was written thousands of years before ocean exploration, have known that there were fresh water springs in the sea?

A STUDY COURSE IN CHRISTIAN EVIDENCES, p.128

"Have you journeyed to the springs of the sea or walked in the recesses of the deep?"

JOB 38:16

MAY 23

Evidence From ANTHROPOLOGY

Both ethnologists and anthropologists have presented abundant evidence that a monogamous [one partner], permanent marriage has everywhere and in all ages been the ideal form of family life. True happiness, true fulfillment, and true accomplishment of God's purposes involve obeying God's command that a man be united to his wife and become one with her. What woman wouldn't want the man to whom she is willing to give her life, to dedicate himself to her alone with a *lifelong* and *permanent* commitment?

Monogamy can hardly be a product of evolution, since it is not commonly found with primates or most other animals. If evolution were true, then it would be a major advantage to any animal to have multiple offspring by multiple mates in order to more successfully propagate its genes. Thus, why shouldn't the preferred human relationship be for each man to randomly impregnate as many women as possible? Although this arrangement is *common in degenerating civilizations*, it has always been considered abhorrent behavior and drives the downfall of a society.

Following evolutionary principles to their logical conclusion always results in disaster.

THE GENESIS RECORD, P.102

"Haven't you read," he replied, "that at the beginning the Creator 'made them male and female,'...'For this reason a man will leave his father and mother and be united to his wife, and the two will become one flesh'?...''Therefore what God has joined together, let man not separate."

MATTHEW 19:4-6

Evidence From
THE WORLDWIDE FLOOD

The existence of salt lakes and inland seas provides strong evidence that there has been a global Flood. The huge salty Caspian Sea is completely landlocked and during the past several centuries has been shrinking in size. **How did sea water get so far inland? Why did it not dry up millions of years ago?** A gigantic flood within the last 5,000 years would seem to be a very good answer.

Lake Van (5,900 feet in elevation) to the southwest of Ararat and Lake Urmia (4,300 feet in elevation) are excellent examples of high-elevation, landlocked, salty lakes. The huge Gobi Desert in Central Asia has tiny leftover lakes which are only a small fraction of the size they once were. In America, the Great Salt Lake and its nearby desert tell the same story–it is the leftover remains of a much larger body of isolated salt water. Lake Titicaca in the Andes, 12,500 feet above sea level, and covering more than 300 square miles, was also apparently much larger in the past.

It is the worldwide *extent and rate* at which these isolated bodies of water are *currently shrinking* that testifies they were much larger in the relatively recent past. This is exactly what would be expected as the continents lifted up at the end of the one-year-long global Flood, leaving pockets of stranded water to slowly recede over the subsequent millennia.

MYTHS AND MIRACLES, P.100

For forty days the flood kept coming on the earth, and as the waters increased they lifted the ark high above the earth. The waters rose and increased greatly on the earth....
GENESIS 7:17-18

Evidence From PHYSICS

God said in His Word that "He imparted weight to the wind." Man did not discover that air had weight until 1643. Evangelista Torricelli, Galileo's student, built the first barometer to measure the pressure and weight of air.

The pressure exerted by the movement of individual air molecules is quite small; but our atmosphere is over 100 miles thick, and the total pressure of gravity pulling all of this air downward is quite significant. Although we cannot feel the pressure (except when the air is moving), air is pressing in on us with a force of 14.7 pounds per square inch. **The total air pressure pushing onto the outside surface of a typical human body exceeds 20,000 pounds of force!** The only reason we are not instantly squashed is that the same pressure exists inside each of our cells pushing outward.

How could the author of Job have known that air has weight 3,000 years before modern science proved this fact?

MYTHS AND MIRACLES, P.10

For he looketh to the ends of the earth, and seeth under the whole heaven; To make the weight for the winds; and he weigheth the waters by measure.

JOB 28:24-25 KJV

Evidence From
BIOLOGY

The peppered moth of England is often used as an example of evolution in action. We're told that the light variety of Biston betularia (the peppered moth) evolved into the dark variety during the industrial revolution as a result of factory soot coating the trees. It is a known fact that both light and dark varieties of the peppered moth lived in England prior to the industrial revolution, but the dark ones were rare. As the light-colored trees darkened with soot, the prevalent white moths landing on the trees became more visible to bird predators. The rarer dark moths were now better camouflaged, and their population began to flourish. This is presented in textbooks as an example of evolution. The implication is that this shift in moth population proves that one type of animal can change into another type.

However, before the industrial revolution *there were light and dark-colored moths.* **After the industrial revolution** *there were light and dark-colored moths.* What a wonderful system (called *natural selection)*, God has built into animals so that they can adapt to environmental changes! But this example does nothing to show how one kind of animal could change into another kind of animal.

The fact that the peppered moth is still in textbooks is an example of how evolutionists misuse simple shifts in population to support their belief that new animals evolve. No new information is added and no completely new type of animal ever results.

Unlocking the Mysteries of Creation, p.85
The Icons of Evolution, p.137-158

There is a way that seems right to a man, but in the end it leads to death.

Proverbs 14:12

Evidence From
ARCHAEOLOGY

Some biblical critics feel the Ark was too large of a project for early man to have attempted. A survey of the ancient world shows this is not true. *The Great Pyramid*, for example, is thought to be the work of Egypt's 4th Dynasty, which was long before Abraham. This pyramid contains over two million blocks of stone, each weighing about 2 1/2 tons. Its vast sides, which are 756 feet long, are set to the points of a compass to an accuracy of a small fraction of one degree! Another example is the *Colossi of Memnon* built during the 18th Dynasty of Egypt. This wonder was made from blocks of sandstone that weigh 400 tons each and were brought 600 miles to their present position.

The Ark's dimensions, given in the Bible, are well within the realm of reason. Given the 120 years that Noah had to complete the construction of the Ark, there is no reason to doubt this accomplishment.

THE CREATION, P.150

"So make yourself an ark of cypress wood; make rooms in it and coat it with pitch inside and out. This is how you are to build it...." Noah did everything just as God commanded him.

GENESIS 6:14,15,22

Evidence From
BIOLOGY

Every feather is a marvel of engineering design. A single pigeon feather is composed of more than a million individual parts. *Barbs* extend from each side of a center shaft. Smaller *barbules* grow out of both sides of these barbs, which in turn are made with tiny microscopic *barbicels*. These *barbicels* are tiny hooks which interlock with *barbules*, weaving each feather together like the teeth on a zipper. If the barbs are pulled apart, the bird hooks them back together by simply running its beak through the feathers. For their weight, feathers are stronger than any man-made structures.

If the design itself were not miraculous enough, the functions of the feather are even more astounding. This extremely lightweight, durable, and complex design enables the bird's wing to flare and hold air as it flies. The trapped air within the feathers serve as extremely efficient insulators against both hot and cold temperatures. A minute coating of oil makes feathers waterproof, keeping birds dry and warm.

Evolutionists claim that reptile scales evolved into feathers. Could this have happened? **There is virtually no similarity between scales and feathers, nor is there any fossil evidence showing the transition from scale to feather.**
A scale could only become a feather as specific information is added to the DNA molecule. The feather has a much more complex DNA code than a reptile scale. Random mistakes could not produce this complex information.

It couldn't Just Happen, p.106
CEA Update Newsletter, 6/95

How awesome is the LORD Most High, the great King over all the earth!

Psalm 47:2

Evidence From CHEMISTRY

The earth's air is made up of about 21% oxygen, 78% nitrogen, 0.03% carbon dioxide, and trace amounts of other gases. Chemical reactions within plants and in our upper atmosphere maintain this exact balance of 21% oxygen to 0.03% carbon dioxide. For life to exist, ***this balance must have been maintained from the beginning!*** If oxygen levels were lower by only 4%, animals could not breathe. If oxygen levels were higher by as little as 4%, increased fires and extensive oxidation reactions would make life on Earth difficult–if not impossible. With even a slight change of the carbon dioxide level, the earth's temperature and plant growth rates would be radically affected.

It would seem that the very composition of the air we breathe has been designed specifically for our benefit. It takes incredible faith to believe this could have happened by chance.

IT COULDN'T JUST HAPPEN, P.32

Come and see what God has done, how awesome his works in man's behalf!

PSALM 66:5

Evidence From
ARCHAEOLOGY

The sun, moon, and stars were created for signs, seasons, days, and years. From the beginning, God wanted man to be a chronologer (someone who measures time) in order for us to live orderly lives. Studies of ancient civilizations show early man understood this purpose and tried to fulfill it. We know, for example, that **eclipses of the sun and moon have been used for at least 4,000 years to measure time.** This has enabled modern historians to check dates in ancient history with perfect accuracy. Ancient civilizations also knew how to measure a year by the stars. The position of the stars changes slightly every night. At the earth's current rate of rotation around the sun (which we know is slowing down at a known rate), the stars now return to their exact position after 365 days 6 hours 9 minutes and 9.6 seconds.

Even our geometry and mathematics are tied to the solar year. **Almost all ancient civilizations used a 360-day year,** which accounts for the change over the years. This 360-day year is the basis of our 360-degree circle and 360-degree compass. The Egyptians measured the passing of a year by the position of the rising of the bright star Sirius over the Nile at dawn. This is called the "Sidereal (star) Year," and atomic clocks are still adjusted in reference to it.

Much of the world's population still lives by farming, and many have no calendar except the one God has provided in the stars. God truly provides for all of our needs, just as He promises in His Word.

MYTHS AND MIRACLES, P.18-21

And God said, "Let there be lights in the expanse of the sky to separate the day from the night, and let them serve as signs to mark seasons and days and years..."

GENESIS 1:14

Evidence From ASTRONOMY

As astronomers look far out into the universe with increasingly more powerful telescopes, they observe that rapidly moving galaxies often cluster tightly together. **If these galaxies started out as a single point of matter (as we have been taught by the big bang theory), they should be evenly dispersed by now.** For galaxies to remain tightly clustered is analogous to throwing a handful of rocks at a target 20 feet away and having every one of the rocks hit the exact center of the target. This never happens, because the individual rocks spread out as they travel different trajectories at different speeds. It is only right after they leave your hand that they will all be in close proximity.

The same is true of these clusters. If they have been moving through space for billions of years, they should not be in tight clusters, but widely spread apart. This is one of the huge problems which have many scientists doubting the validity of the big bang theory. **The galaxies within clusters are so close together, they could not have been flying apart for very long.** The visible mass of these clusters is much too small to hold the galaxies together by gravity. Based on observable evidence, they are in close proximity because they were recently created.

IN THE BEGINNING, 7TH ED., P.35
CREATION EX NIHILO MAGAZINE, VOL.20, NO.3,
JUNE–AUGUST 1998, P.42-44

"Do you know the laws of the heavens? Can you set up God's dominion over the earth?"

JOB 38:33

June JUNE

God Cares for You

When you see a bug around you,
  Think of Jesus up above.
He even cares for little things
  And showers them with love.

Just open up your Bible
  And take a real good look.
You'll see He talks of animals
  Throughout His awesome Book.

In Matthew 6, verse 26,
  You'll read about the birds
And how our Lord takes care of them;
  It says so in His Word.

Now look at Job, in chapter 12;
  You'll see God makes it clear.
We are to ask the animals
  And make sure that we hear.

It says in verses 9 and 10
  That even the *creatures* know
That God gives us our life and breath
  And all to Him must go.

So when you see the earth and stars,
  Plants, bugs, and creatures, too,
Remember Jesus loves you *more*
  And that His love is *true*.

Evidence From
COMPARING RELIGIONS

Only the Bible starts with the special creation of all things by an eternal, all-powerful, personal God. **The Bible has a unique and reasonable solution to the origin problem**–"In the beginning, God created...." Other religious books reveal ignorance on this point. They all propose ideas for the evolution of the universe from existing matter, but do not explain how the matter originated.

For example, the *Babylonians stated* in their "Enuma Elish," that the universe began with a primeval chaotic mixture of three kinds of water. The *Greek myths* proposed an initial state of matter randomly coming together. *Roman writers*, like Lucretius, assumed that there was a universal blind interplay of atoms. The *Orphic myths* supposed the universe developed out of a primeval world-egg. Similarly, *the modern theory of evolution* begins with eternal matter in one form or another. No other book (including modern evolutionary "science" books) is able to go beyond the present order of things to a real first cause.

Only the Bible explains the origin of matter by the existence of God. He is outside of matter, time, and space. He brought matter into existence and can take matter out of existence.

MANY INFALLIBLE PROOFS, P.11

And God said unto Moses, I AM THAT I AM: and he said, Thus shalt thou say unto the children of Israel, I AM hath sent me unto you.

EXODUS 3:14 KJV

Evidence From
LANGUAGE

If humans have evolved from less intelligent creatures, one would expect the earliest written languages to be the least complex. The exact opposite is true. The oldest written languages are the most complex. Ancient Chinese and Greek were far more complicated than modern Chinese and Greek. One of the most difficult of all written languages is Sanskrit, which goes back to 1500 B.C. **Each verb had up to 500 variations!** Compare this with English, in which most verbs have only five forms (do, does, did, done, doing). Ancient Chinese, which originated before 2000 B.C. had 6,000 "characters" or letters. Modern English has only 26.

There is no group of humans anywhere in the world that does not have a fully developed, highly complex descriptive language. Even people groups using "Stone Age" tools for survival had highly developed languages. These facts sharply contradict the theory that language has evolved from grunts to grammar, from simple to complex, from primitive to civilized.

MYTHS AND MIRACLES, p.109-110

...you are familiar with all my ways.
Before a word is on my tongue you know it completely, O LORD.

PSALM 139:3-4

Evidence From
HISTORY

If a great flood did indeed wipe out everything on the earth about 5,000 years ago, then the oldest human records should only date back that far. This is exactly what we find. **All civilized cultures on Earth seem to have appeared suddenly approximately 5,000 years ago.**

Even more revealing is the fact that most ancient cultures began in an advanced state. There is no trace of "primitive" generations leading up to the sudden explosion of advanced civilizations across the world. Take, for example, the great Pyramid of Cheops near Cairo, Egypt. The intricacy and stability of this monument of human engineering is unbelievable. The detailed planning necessary to construct this massive monument is phenomenal. Legends from surrounding people insist that the forefathers of the Egyptians (before the Flood) were even *more* knowledgeable! It has been widely reported that the Egyptian culture extends back 9,000 years or more, but the current trend among Egyptolgists is to revise these dates to a more recent date. This agrees well with the biblical timetable.

The sudden appearance of advanced civilizations supports what the Bible states: **man was made in God's image** (Genesis 1:26). From the beginning, man was a rational, creative, and very intelligent being. Anthropology, the science of origin, culture, and the development of human beings, confirms this fact.

UNLOCKING THE MYSTERIES OF CREATION,
p.182

From one man he made every nation
of men, that they should inhabit the
whole earth; and he determined the times set
for them and the exact places where they should live.

ACTS 17:26

Evidence From
ANTHROPOLOGY

Every culture in the world organizes their schedule around a seven-day week. Historians who reject the Bible have always been puzzled concerning the origin of this system. The seven-day week does not fit into the 365 1/4 days of the solar year nor the lunar month of 29 days. The seven-day week could only have come from the pattern set by God as a reminder of the seven-day creation period. **Throughout documented history, experience has proven the seven-day week to be the most satisfactory way of organizing man's life.**

For example, both the French and Russian revolutionaries tried to abolish it, as did the government of Sri Lanka (Ceylon) in the 1960s. In each case it was a disaster. One rest day out of eight or ten days is too long an interval–one day in six is too short–one day in seven is just right. All three governments had to revert back to a seven-day week. How interesting that **even communist and atheistic cultures are forced to acknowledge the Creator in how they organize their calendars!**

MYTHS AND MIRACLES, P.48-49

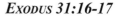

The Israelites are to observe the Sabbath, celebrating it for the generations to come as a lasting covenant. It will be a sign between me and the Israelites forever, for in six days the LORD made the heavens and the earth, and on the seventh day he abstained from work and rested.

EXODUS 31:16-17

Evidence From
ASTRONOMY

The perfection of God's design can be seen when we study our planet. The **earth's distance from the sun is exactly right** for maintaining the delicate balance of the earth's temperature. If the average temperature of the earth were raised only two or three degrees, the ice sheets and glaciers would melt, putting London and New York under 200 feet of water.

The size of the earth is also crucial. If it were too small, the earth's weakened gravitational field could hold neither air nor water. If the earth were twice as large, the atmosphere would be pulled closer to its surface and everything would weigh eight times more. Even the total volume of gas in our atmosphere is critical. If the air were thinner, it would not provide adequate protection from the 20,000 or so meteorites that rush toward the earth daily. With thinner air the earth's temperature would also drop, making life impossible. The 23.5° tilt of the earth's axis is perfect for enabling us to have our seasons and double the amount of arable (crop-growing) land on our planet.

Which is the more logical belief:
1. The precise balance of conditions necessary to maintain life upon earth *just happened* by chance.
2. An *intelligent designer* (God) created this planet with the perfect conditions to sustain life.

MYTHS AND MIRACLES, P.24
IT COULDN'T JUST HAPPEN, P.27

For by him all things were created: things in heaven and on earth, visible and invisible....He is before all things, and in him all things hold together.

COLOSSIANS 1:16,17

Evidence From
BIOLOGY

There is astounding variety of very different mammals living in the oceans. **These sea mammals (whales, seals, walruses, dolphins, sea elephants, etc.) are highly specialized,** with each species perfectly designed for its own particular nitch. For example, the mother whale has an ingenious device for giving milk to her baby. The baby's mouth fits snuggly into his mother's body so that sea water cannot get mixed with the milk. The baby whale's windpipe is also elongated above the gullet so milk cannot flow into its lungs.

This design had to be perfect in both the mother and the baby whale from the very first time a baby whale was born and needed to nurse underwater. It could not have evolved by gradual changes. These are the types of specifically designed features which have led many biologists to reject evolution in favor of creation as the best explanation for our existence.

MYTHS AND MIRACLES, P.27-28

The LORD Almighty has sworn, "Surely, as I have planned, so it will be, and as I have purposed, so it will stand."

ISAIAH 14:24

Evidence From
COMMON SENSE

Evolutionists say that human beings "evolved" from simple cells entirely by random-chance processes. Man's understanding and use of technology (tool-making, electronics, aeronautics, and the principles of science) are also said to be "evolving."

When the word "evolving" is used with *technology*, **it means improvements that are planned, carefully worked out, and implemented using intelligent guidance.** When the word "evolution" is used in *biology*, **however, it shifts meaning in order to deny any planning or intelligent design.** Common sense shows that life simply does not form or advance in this way. In reality, it is deceiving to use the same word to mean something which is perfectly logical and then, with no warning or disclaimer, shift the meaning to support something based on faith that actually contradicts the observations.

MYTHS AND MIRACLES, P.40

REASON EMOTION

Stay away from a foolish man, for you will not find knowledge on his lips. The wisdom of the prudent is to give thought to their ways, but the folly of fools is deception.

PROVERBS 14:7-8

Evidence From
BIOLOGY

The Bible states that God created Eve, the first female, in a special way—out of Adam—to be Adam's helper and companion. **Science has no adequate explanation for how gender developed.** The process of reproduction is marvelously complex and must have been perfect from the beginning to be successful.

The August 18, 1997, issue of U.S. News and World Report was dedicated to great scientific mysteries. The origin of gender was listed as one of the most mysterious. This is because evolution has no answer for how a single-sex organism could possibly have turned into two completely different sexes. Both sexes would have **had to appear simultaneously**, yet the reproductive organs and functions of each are completely different.

Evolutionists believe that sexual separation must have happened numerous times throughout evolutionary history as completely different types of plants and animals developed different sexes at different times. Yet no adequate cause or mechanism has been proposed which can explain how opposite sexes could have developed even once!

SEARCH FOR THE TRUTH, P.61
MYTHS AND MIRACLES, P.42

Then the LORD God made a woman from the rib he had taken out of the man, and he brought her to the man.

GENESIS 2:22

Evidence From
BIOLOGY

Many textbooks have a series of pictures showing how the horse is supposed to have "evolved" from a small creature about the size of a terrier. What these books *do not tell you* is that **nowhere on earth has anyone found these "horse ancestor" fossils lying on top of one another in regular order.** It is just as reasonable to believe that all these animals lived on Earth at the same time, either as different species or as larger and smaller members of the same species (compare Great Danes and dachshunds).

One modern breed of horse in Argentina averages only 43 centimeters (17 inches) in height. Shire horses weigh up to a ton, while Shetland ponies weigh only 400 pounds. If all three types were to be found fossilized, they could easily be arranged to claim that they have evolved over millions of years to show gradually increasing size. Whereas in fact, all three types are alive today.

No one has shown why small horses should become steadily larger by natural selection. Just the opposite seems to have happened in the past: modern bears, tigers, turtles, and many other animals are considerably smaller than their prehistoric relations. The horse evolution sequence is simply a persistent myth which hangs on because no better evidence for evolution has surfaced.

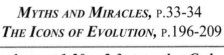

Myths and Miracles, p.33-34
The Icons of Evolution, p.196-209

Genesis chapters 1:20 to 2:3 states that God created all the animals on the fifth and sixth days. Nothing was created after the sixth day.

Genesis Ch.1:20 to 2:3

Evidence From ANATOMY

The human nervous system is the most remarkable communication center ever designed. It *regulates* the actions of organs; *monitors* the senses; and *controls* one's thinking, learning, and memory capacity all at the same time. The specialized nerve receptors in the sensory organs (eyes, ears, nose) receive millions of bits of information from the environment. They are constantly **sending the data to the brain at a rate of 300 miles per hour by way of nerve fibers.** The brain then analyzes the data and determines the right action to take.

Scientists have found that even the nervous system of simple animals such as a starfish is extremely complex. **A single starfish's nerve ganglia and fibers have been described as more complex than London's entire telephone exchange system.** If it took intelligence to design the sophisticated communication systems of the earth, why would we believe that blind chance devised the infinitely more intricate human nervous system?

The Human Body: Accident or Design?, p.48-49

"This is what the LORD says–your Redeemer, who formed you in the womb: I am the LORD, who has made all things..."

Isaiah 44:24

Evidence From BIOLOGY

Every feature and function of a bird's body **testifies to design.** From the moment they lay their eggs to their yearly migrations across the globe, birds provide eloquent testimony to their Creator.

While most birds have been given instincts to build strong nests to protect their eggs, the *guillemot* does not build any nest. Instead, guillemots simply lay their eggs on bare windswept rocks. **Their eggs are shaped in such a way, however, that when the wind blows, they spin in place, instead of rolling off the rocks.** Who programmed the guillemots to form their eggs in exactly the right shape in order to survive in their harsh environment, whereas other sea birds produce ordinary shaped eggs and build nests to protect these eggs?

How do hundreds of species of birds migrate thousands of miles every year at the right time and to the right place? Every fall the *American golden plover* youngsters make an astounding **3,000 mile flight across the Pacific Ocean from Alaska to the island of Hawaii, with no parent to guide them.** They fly through the darkness, clouds and storms, and land at the correct destination. Their bodies are so efficient that they only burn two ounces of body weight on this incredible 3,000 mile flight. Who designed their bodies with this extraordinary efficiency, taught these birds to navigate, and gave them the desire to make this journey?

MYTHS AND MIRACLES, P.32
CEA UPDATE NEWSLETTER (Summer/95)

I know every bird in the mountains, and the creatures of the field are mine.

PSALM 50:11

Evidence From GENETICS

One of the often repeated statements in support of evolution is the *claim* that **chimp DNA is 97% similar to human DNA.** This is considered by many as proof of our evolutionary origin. Yet textbooks omit the following perspectives as they lead students toward only evolutionary conclusions:

1. **A Corvette and a Volkswagen could be considered 97% similar depending on the features selected. Yet one did not evolve from the other, but both exist because they were designed and built by intelligent people.**
2. **DNA similarity is required for survival in similar environments. If humans were totally different than other forms of life, what would they eat and how could they process food?**
3. **Consider the following 97% similar sentences:**
   a. "Many scientists reject evolution because it lacks evidence, contradicts laws of science, and is the foundation of atheism."
   b. "Not many scientists reject evolution because it lacks evidence, contradicts laws of science, and is the foundation of atheism."

This mere 3% difference (3 out of 102 letters) totally changes the meaning, function, and purpose of the sentence. **Furthermore, the amount of information contained within 3% of our total DNA code is equivalent to thousands of pages of specific instructions.** A 3% difference is not a small change, but an enormous amount of information which could never have arisen by chance mutational changes.

CREATION MAGAZINE, FEB. 1997, P.21-22

Every word of God is flawless; he is a shield to those who take refuge in him. Do not add to his words, or he will rebuke you and prove you a liar.

PROVERBS 30:5-6

Evidence From
THE FOSSIL RECORD

One needs to be very careful about accepting the conclusions of paleontologists who claim to have found fossil links between man and apelike creatures. In the past, bones from pigs, monkeys, alligators, horses and even an elephant have been reconstructed into missing links between humans and some imaginary apelike creatures. In 1979 a piece of bone discovered in Northern Africa was said to be the clavicle of an apelike creature that was evolving into a man. Its discoverer said the bone indicated the creature had possibly walked upright, like modern humans. It was later shown that the fossil was the rib bone from a Pacific white-sided dolphin!

This repeated misinterpretation of fossils by paleontologists is a result of the assumption that evolution is a fact–therefore some apelike creature must have turned into a man. The possibility of creation is never considered. Therefore, **almost any bone that is even slightly outside of the norm is assumed to be proof of this transformation.** Since instant fame awaits the discovery of each subsequent find, the objectivity of the researcher is very suspect.

Jesus stated that man and woman were created as uniquely different *"from the beginning."* This couldn't be more clearly stated, and the fossil evidence supports this factual statement.

LETTING GOD CREATE YOUR DAY,
VOL. 3, P.103

And Jesus answered and said unto them, "... from the beginning of creation, God made them male and female."

MARK 10:5,6 KJV

Evidence From
COMMON SENSE

It takes a mind to build a house. A home electrical system requires the skilled labor of an electrician who has spent many years learning his trade. The plumbing requires the work of a plumber who has worked for years as an apprentice. The structure of the house requires the skilled labor of a team of carpenters. The heating system, insulation, drywall, roofing, siding, finishing, carpeting, and landscaping all require planning, skill, and intelligence before a finished home results.

Each part of the human body has corresponding components. Our nervous system is far more complex than the electrical system of a house. Our blood vessels, heart, and lungs are infinitely more complex than any home heating and ventilation system. Our digestive track is more intricately designed than any plumbing system. Our body fat insulates far more efficiently than any home insulation. Our skin is far more durable and complex than drywall, siding, paint, or carpeting.

It takes a mind to conceive, design, and build a house. How can we believe that it did not take **a far superior creative intelligence to conceive and create the human body?**

RICH AND TINA KLEISS

For every house is built by someone, but God is the builder of everything.

HEBREWS 3:4

Evidence From
THE WORLDWIDE FLOOD

Hundreds of giant fossils have been discovered over the years. These include ten-foot turtles, dragonflies with a two-foot wingspan, and 50-foot-long crocodiles. Could the size of these creatures be the result of long lives and/or a more protective atmosphere? **It is interesting to note that some reptiles today never stop growing, but continue to get larger as long as they live.** The large size for prehistoric (i.e., pre-flood) reptiles, including dinosaurs, probably indicates very long lives. Even today, scientists do not fully understand what causes us to age and die. Given more ideal conditions and fewer genetic problems before the Flood, it is not hard to believe that pre-flood man could have lived 10 times longer than modern man.

Most likely the cause of the longer life expectancy before the flood was fewer genetic problems. Contrary to what evolutionists would have us believe, with every passing century the number of mistakes and problems on our genes increases. There is also an intriguing possibility that the original earth was protected by a water-canopy above the atmosphere. This protective canopy would have shielded living things from the harmful radiation which shortens life. This may help account for both early man's long life span and larger animals. Josephus (a Jewish historian in 100 A.D.) records that the historians from *nine* other nations report people living up to 1,000 years old before the great Flood.

MYTHS AND MIRACLES,
P.76 *TJ JOURNAL,*
8(2):138-141, 1994

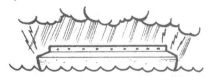

Altogether, Adam lived 930 years, and then he died.

GENESIS 5:5

Evidence From
BIBLICAL ACCURACY

For many years academics have taught that the Bible, especially the book of Genesis, came to us as a result of traditions and story telling. **The implication is that the Bible is not the literal word of God** which was guided by the Holy Spirit to be believed in a straightforward manner. We are taught that it contains exaggerations and should not be trusted to reveal true history.

According to these experts, the historical accounts in the Bible are fanciful stories written down by some unknown scribes, compiled by an unknown editor, and combined to form the Book of Genesis. **Genesis is not even in story form.** Genesis 5, for example, is a record of the chronological geneology of the ancestry from Adam to Noah. There is absolutely no evidence for the idea that Genesis is merely a collection of ancient stories. It is clearly written as the account of factual historical events.

The biblical experts who teach that the Bible is a collection of ancient myths are not basing their theories on facts. Rather, their ideas are based on the mistaken theory of evolution, which includes the idea that early man could not write. Wherever we find civilized mankind, we find writing–as early as 3000 B.C.

MYTHS AND MIRACLES, P.74-75

For the word of the LORD is right; and all his works are done in truth.

PSALM 33:4 KJV

Evidence From
BOTANY

Researchers at the University of Edinburgh in Scotland have shown that plants can react to their environment as quickly as animals. It is known that plants respond to movement by adding calcium. **Whenever stressed by high winds, plants add calcium to their cell walls.** The calcium acts as an internal skeleton, giving strength to the plant. However, until recently it was not known how quickly this increase in calcium occurred. Botanists used a novel method to study the speed at which calcium is added to cells; they added jellyfish genes to the plants. These genes bind to the calcium in the plants and emit a blue glow as the calcium level increases.

What the researchers found absolutely astounded them. When they squirted these genetically modified plants with puffs of air, the plants increased their bluish glow. There was an almost instantaneous reaction to air movement as the plants added calcium to their cells.

When God created plants, He gave them abilities that defy the evolutionary idea that they are simple forms of life.

LETTING GOD CREATE YOUR DAY, VOL. 3, P. 187

Then God said, "Let the land produce vegetation....And God saw that it was good."

GENESIS 1:11,12

Evidence From BIOLOGY

Man has only recently learned the danger of overexposure to ultraviolet radiation. It is now commonly known that excessive exposure to sunlight causes skin cancer and many other problems. Melanin is the pigment that turns human skin brown when it is exposed to the sun. Melanin protects skin from the damage caused by the sun's ultraviolet radiation. **Mankind can adapt and stay out of the sun, but what about animals which don't know about this hazard?**

Unlike most mice which are nocturnal, the African four-striped grass mouse operates in the fierce equatorial sun and is exposed to powerful doses of ultraviolet radiation. **Because this creature spends most of its life in the sun, the mouse not only has melanin-pigmented skin, but an *additional* melanin-pigmented layer between its skull and outer skin to provide additional protection.** It was also discovered that white tent-making bats have similar protection on their skulls. These bats sleep during the day in a curled position that exposes their heads to the South American sun.

If God protects and cares for the animals so meticulously, how much more **He must care for mankind** whom He created in His own image.

LETTING GOD CREATE YOUR DAY,
VOL. 3, P.189

Every good and perfect gift is from above, coming down from the Father of heavenly lights, who does not change like shifting shadows.

JAMES 1:17

Evidence From
BIBLICAL ACCURACY

The Mississippi River dumps an average of about six million gallons of water into the Gulf of Mexico every second. **Where does all that water go?** The vast surface of the ocean allows enormous amounts of evaporation to take place. High in the atmosphere this invisible water vapor condenses into clouds, which produce rain or snow, which in turn fall onto land surfaces. The water then completes the circuit by flowing into rivers and then back into the ocean again.

No one really understood or accepted the idea of the complete water cycle until the late 16th and early 17th centuries. Pierre Perrault, Edme Mariotte, and astronomer Edmund Halley all contributed valuable data to the concept of the water cycle. Yet Solomon and Isaiah both wrote about it in the Bible.

In Ecclesiaties 1:7 King Soloman describes the water cycle as follows, *"All streams flow into the sea, yet the sea is never full. To the place the streams come from, there they return again."* This hydrologic cycle was quite accurately described in the Bible thousands of years before it was understood scientifically.

A STUDY COURSE IN CHRISTIAN EVIDENCES, P.129

As the rain and the snow come down from heaven, and do not return to it without watering the earth and making it bud and flourish...

ISAIAH 55:10

Evidence From
BIOLOGY

The *mosquito* begins life as a tiny larva crawling out of an egg laid on water. The wiggler breathes through a microscopic breathing tube at the tip of its abdomen which has five flaps that open to draw in air and then close whenever it goes under water. As the mosquito grows from wiggler to pupa to adult, it goes through a total chemical rearrangement, emerging as an adult capable of flying through the air.

The male mosquito has no bite and lives only a little over a week during which time it must mate. His antennae have been specifically equipped with whirls of long hair having special sensory cells at their base. The female's wings are designed to beat with such intensity that they move these hairs from up to 10 inches away. The movement stimulates a mating instinct, which takes place in the air. The female stores the male's reproductive cells in a special sac for immediate *or* later use.

The female mosquito needs a supply of blood before fertilizing her eggs. As soon as she lands on her victim, she goes to work with a **special set of tools** tucked inside her proboscis (mouthpiece). This mouthpiece has a *syringe* for injecting numbing and anti-thickening chemicals, two tiny *spears* to start the drilling operation, both a coarse and fine-toothed *saw* for cutting through different skin thicknesses, and a *syringe* connected to a *pump* in her head through which she can suck up to 4 times her body weight in blood.

A careful study of its many parts reveal that even the irritating mosquito is a creature uniquely designed for its specific function, not the result of evolution by random changes.

CHARACTER SKETCHES, Vol.II, P.212-213

And there are also many other things that Jesus did, which if they were written one by one, I suppose that even the world itself could not contain the books that would be written.

JOHN 21:25 NKJV

Evidence From
BIOLOGY

Many humans and even some animals will endanger or sacrifice their lives to save the life of another–sometimes even the life of a completely different species. This type of behavior, known as *altruistic*, is universally considered the most praiseworthy form of character. According to the theory of evolution, natural selection explains all individual characteristics. How could altruistic behavior have evolved by natural selection or mutational change? **This type of selfless behavior, by definition, reduces the chances of survival** for the individual creature who exhibits it. The only rational explanation for altruistic behavior is that it was programmed into animals.

Stealing and *aggressiveness* produce immediate benefits to an individual, whereas *cooperation* produces longer term benefits for an entire group. If macroevolution has happened, selfish behavior would tend to eliminate unselfish behavior. **How could individuals know that self-sacrificing behavior has greater long-term benefits?** Although it can be demonstrated that altruism benefits the whole once it is established, it has never been explained how it could have developed in the first place. Altruism contradicts evolution and has the fingerprints of God all over it!

In The Beginning, 7ᵀᴴ Ed., p.7

Greater love has no one than this, that he lay down his life for his friends.

John 15:13

Evidence From
COMMON SENSE

Even in the simplest of things, such as snow, the character of God is revealed.

Snow forms from water within clouds as the water vapor condenses on small particles of dust, pollen, salts, or even bacteria. Thus, each snowfall serves to clear our atmosphere of contaminants. Every individual snowflake is unique and different–forming a starlike, six-pointed crystal at perfect 60-degree angles. See how many different starlike patterns you can develop–you are likely to exhaust your creativity after 100. **Yet it is estimated that an ordinary snowstorm contains 1,000 billion uniquely individual flakes.**

Snow works as an important insulator by trapping air between the individual insulating flakes. Eskimos must frequently rebuild their igloos when the snow compacts, loses it air space, and turns to ice. The insulating characteristic of snow protects plants and roots from freezing in the winter. Snow also adds nitrogen to the soil and waters farmland in the spring, producing a promise of improved crops.

Is it reasonable to look at the combined beauty and usefulness of snow and believe it "just happened that way"? **In snow, God reveals His infinite wisdom and His profound sense of beauty**—to those who acknowledge Him as Creator.

CEA Update Newsletter

As the rain and the snow come down from heaven, and do not return to it without watering the earth and making it bud and flourish... so is my word that goes out from my mouth: It will not return to me empty, but will accompish what I desire and achieve the purpose for which I sent it.

Isaiah 55:10-11

Evidence From
BIOLOGY

Animals communicate with each other using a wide variety of methods. It has long been recognized that bees use an intricate dance which conveys the direction and distance to food sources. It has recently been discovered that bees also communicate using *scents*. Beehives are full of scents, yet honeybees are constantly alert to bees who are not members of the hive. Invaders to a hive are killed if they do not have exactly the same scent as the rest of the hive.

Entomologists (scientists that study insects) have discovered that all members of an individual hive learn to produce exactly the same chemical password. Amazingly, all honeybees use a specific combination of only two chemicals to make the scent distinctive to their hive. Bees from each hive can instantly tell whether a bee carries that hive's specific chemical password. When bees start a new hive, they develop a new distinctive chemical password!

This complex method of defence, possibly created within the bees after the Fall, is strong evidence of a wise and powerful Creator.

LETTING GOD CREATE YOUR DAY, VOL. 3, P.209

All thy works shall give thanks to thee, O LORD...

PSALM 145:10 RSV

Evidence From BIBLICAL UNIQUENESS

The Bible is unique in how it deals very openly with the sins of people. Biographies are generally biased and tend to exaggerate the character traits, depending upon the viewpoint of the writer. For example, if we look at the prominent men and women in history, we see that most are portrayed as great with few personal flaws. Examples abound, from Washington to Lincoln, Mother Teresa to Voltaire, Freud to Darwin; we hear about great accomplishments, but little about personal failures.

The Bible does not follow this pattern. It shows people as they are: sinful, lost, and in need of a Savior. Moses, David, and the apostle Paul were all murderers. Abraham, Isaac, and Jacob were all liars. The disciples were cowards. The genealogy leading directly to Jesus included prostitutes, liars, thieves, idolators, cowards, and murderers. **This is hardly a ringing endorsement of the goodness of mankind nor a book likely to have been written by the deceitful human heart.**

THIS INFORMATION IS CONDENSED FROM
EVIDENCE THAT DEMANDS A VERDICT, P.23.
THIS BOOK IS AN EXCELLENT RESOURCE ON BIBLICAL ACCURACY.

And God saw that the wickedness of man was great in the earth, and that every imagination of the thoughts of his heart was only evil continually.

GENESIS 6:5 KJV

Evidence From
EARTH'S ECOLOGY

There are several thousand species of wasps that help control crop pests by using them for food. These wasps are a popular form of pest control among farmers and gardeners. Biologists have found that the wasps do more than just eat the pests. **The wasps also wage an incredibly complicated form of biological warfare**.

Wasps inject their eggs directly into wormlike pest larvae. These eggs are coated with a virus that keeps the larvae from maturing until the young wasps hatch. The virus then seems to move to the larva's liverlike organ and affects the insect's immune system. The virus also acts on the larva's endocrine system to take away its appetite. As a result, the larva destroys less crop, and being starved for food, does not develop into an adult. This gives the wasp eggs more time to develop into young wasps, who will then finish off the pests.

God created this earth with careful balance. Unfortunately this balance was upset by man's actions in the Garden of Eden. The world we now live in groans with the pain of sin–resulting in warfare at all levels of the plant and animal kingdom. Yet God still designed and maintains a balance in the fallen creation. When mankind takes the time to study this finely balanced and intricately designed world, he can't help but see God's hand everywhere he looks.

LETTING GOD CREATE YOUR DAY, VOL. 3, P.216

It is my pleasure to tell you about the miraculous signs and wonders that the Most High God has performed for me. How great are his signs, how mighty his wonders!...

DANIEL 4:2-3

Evidence From BOTANY

It has been known for many years that tea can help fight cavities. A chemical in the tea helps keep the bacteria that cause cavities from attaching onto the surface of our teeth. Scientists have found, however, there is more to the tea than just this. Isao Kubo, a chemist from the University of California, discovered that **certain molecules found in abundance in green tea actually kill bacteria that cause cavities.** His tests have shown that natural chemicals in tea are also able to kill at least two different kinds of molds, three classes of yeasts, and eight kinds of bacteria. In addition, green tea is effective against some bacteria responsible for gastrointestinal disease and acne. These chemicals are also found in coriander, sage, and thyme.

Just as the Bible says, God gave us plants to study, tend, use, and eat. One wonders how much more is yet to be discovered in plants!

LETTING GOD CREATE YOUR DAY, VOL. 3, P.153

The LORD God took the man and put him in the Garden of Eden to work it and take care of it.

GENESIS 2:15

Evidence From BIOLOGY

Every square mile of our planet contains some form of life. Did these life forms evolve to fit into harsh environmental nitches, or were they designed with the potential to adapt and survive in extreme conditions?

Unlike most reptiles that lay eggs, Yarrow's spiny lizards bear live young in arid desert enviroments. A hot desert is a tough environment for a newborn lizard to survive, so the **baby lizards are born with a built-in canteen of water**. At birth this full canteen of water makes up 10% of the lizard's weight. After the first month of life, the canteen shrivels up and disappears. Because older lizards have a greater need for speed, a bulky water reservoir would inhibit them.

The lizard is also designed without a urinary bladder. Its waste water is recycled within the lizard's body since water is a precious resource in the desert. The spiny lizard is designed to remove essentially every usable molecule of water from its waste.

The probability of all of these complex systems evolving by chance is essentially nil. They all had to work perfectly from the first moment to insure the Yarrow's spiny lizard's survival. This **testifies to design,** not chance mutations (random changes in genetic material).

Letting God Create Your Day,
Vol. 3, p.218

"**The wild animals honor me, the jackals and the owls, because I provide water in the desert and streams in the wasteland....**"

Isaiah 43:20

Evidence From GEOLOGY

In 1961 the bones of three dinosaur species and two tropical reptiles were reported on the Alaskan tundra near Prudhoe Bay. Today, this area is far too cold to support such life. The remains of many other warm weather species have also been discovered in the far North. Were these organisms carried there by the worldwide Flood, or was the climate on the earth vastly different in the past?

The most recent creation research indicates that the climate around the Artic Ocean would have been quite mild for centuries after the worldwide flood. **This area would have remained relatively warm until the oceans cooled off from the tectonic and volcanic flood activity.** Once this body of water permanently froze over the climate rapidly changed, trapping temporate animals and vegitation into a permanently frozen state.

This theory may someday prove to be wrong. Other Earth characteristics such as the *worldwide Flood*, the *roundness of the globe*, the *paths of water in the ocean*, the *weight of air*, the *hydraulic water cycle*, and many other recent discoveries of Earth science are specifically mentioned in the Bible. Modern science has confirmed the total accuracy of these statements.

While we don't depend on science to prove the Bible accurate, **scientific findings have never disagreed with the clear and straightforward statements which the Bible makes** about science and Earth history.

LETTING GOD CREATE YOUR DAY,
VOL. 3, P.219

And God made the firmament [atmosphere] and separated the waters which were under the firmament from the waters which were above the firmament. And it was so.

GENESIS 1:7 RSV

Evidence From
EARTH'S ECOLOGY

The Bible says God put man in the garden of Eden and told him to tend and keep it. Where man does this properly, nature flourishes. **Innumerable problems develop whenever man neglects his environment** by *overusing* natural resources or *polluting* the air, ground, or water. This results in resources being used up, plants and animals becoming extinct, sickness abounding, and nature's beauty being destroyed.

God has given perfect examples in nature to show us how He takes care of His earth. For example, water is purified by the water cycle, seeds are spread and fertilized by animals, animals live in symbiosis by helping each other, and plants provide medicine. It is only when man "works and takes care" of the earth as God intended that ecology is not a problem.

RICH AND TINA KLEISS

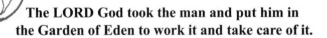

The LORD God took the man and put him in the Garden of Eden to work it and take care of it.

GENESIS 2:15

Evidence From
BIOLOGY

Animals are primarily controlled by instinct, but they have not been left without the ability to use rather complex forms of communication. It is known that sperm whales can echolocate (use high-frequency sounds to orient themselves) in the same way as bats. Sperm whales send out a series of clicks from a special organ in their head. Scientists believe that even though other whales lack this specific organ, they can communicate by means of a less precise method of echolocation which uses low-pitched calls.

The haunting mating melodies of the humpback whale can last 30 minutes. A humpback song will be the same within a single population of whales, and sometimes within an entire ocean basin. Some whales are even believed to **carry on conversations over thousands of miles.** Could these intricate forms of communication have developed by chance?

LETTING GOD CREATE YOUR DAY, VOL. 3, P.230

Those living far away fear your wonders; where morning dawns and evening fades you call forth songs of joy.

PSALM 65:8

The Book
Above All Books

JULY
July

The Bible, it was written,
  fifteen hundred years, the span.
Aramaic, Greek, and Hebrew
  are the tongues which wrote God's plan.

From different walks of life,
  God drew some 40 men.
He sent His Holy Spirit
  to guide each author's pen.

From general to doctor,
  from herdsman to king,
These writers wrote with purpose,
  so God His Word could bring.

Their mood sometimes showed sorrow
  or joy or sometimes wrath.
No matter what their feelings,
  toward God they'd point the path.

Upon 3 different continents
  is where these authors wrote.
Could unity be likely
  without each other's notes?

Such controversial subjects,
  so much the authors said,
Would not perfect agreement,
  point out that God had led?

Just think of all the prophecy,
  one fourth of the good Book.
You'd think since it's so accurate,
  it'd make us take a look.

And then there's all the science
  in God's Word we can find.
If we'd just look around us,
  we'd see God's Master Mind.

The history that's recorded
  is always accurate, too.
Geography and health
  will also prove God true.

So as man searches Scripture
  and tries to find mistakes,
If we'd just look more closely,
  God proves His Word — not fake.

The Bible is the *treasure*
  that stands out all alone.
For it tells things so awesome
  that man could *not* have known.

Evidence From CREATION FOUNDATION

Creation implies responsibility and accountability to a Creator. In Romans 1:20 **God says that by the observation of creation He makes Himself known to everyone and that no one has an excuse for not believing in Him.** Yet if evolution is true, there is no evidence for God's existence or character from the observation of creation, because evolution means that random processes (such as mutations) created us. Where is the evidence for the existence and nature of God in random mutations and natural selection? Either the Bible is wrong or evolution is wrong–they can't both be true.

The Bible says that it is the Word of God. This claim should be verified since it holds us accountable for our words, thoughts, and actions. The Bible contains enough scientific, historical, and prophetical evidence to make its verification possible. Each of us has the choice to accept or reject its clear statements. Rejection of the Bible leaves mankind with no source of truth and reality other than what he himself chooses to believe or invent. It should be no surprise that any society where evolution is taught and believed is also a society where immorality, selfishness, violence, and hatred inevitably increase.

RICH AND TINA KLEISS

For since the creation of the world God's invisible qualities–his eternal power and divine nature–have been clearly seen, being understood from what has been made, so that men are without excuse. For although they knew God, they neither glorified him as God nor gave thanks to him, but their thinking became futile and their foolish hearts were darkened. *ROMANS 1:20-21*

Evidence From EARTH'S ECOLOGY

Hazardous materials are not just man-made phenomenon, but also a natural part of creation. For example, uranium and other **radioactive elements occur naturally** in the environment and can be dissolved in ground water. Chlorofluorocarbons are spewed from volcanoes. Dioxins occur naturally with every forest fire. **One might expect a well-designed creation to have the ability to process hazardous materials into harmless substances. Scientists are learning that this is exactly the case with several types of bacteria** which decontaminate water containing dissolved uranium. One species of bacteria makes uranium phosphate crystals by combining the phosphate in the water with the uranium. The crystals are stored harmlessly within the bacteria. Another species uses enzymes to make a uranium ore, which settles harmlessly out of the water. Scientists have also discovered a type of bacteria that breaks down chlorofluorocarbons.

The hazardous chemicals in the enviroment are a reminder that we no longer live in a perfect enviroment, but that our world has been affected by the curse of the Fall. Yet the earth is still full of abundant evidence that it is a well-designed system. By studying nature, scientists are learning how to clean up mankind's messes.

LETTING GOD CREATE YOUR DAY,
VOL. 3, P.242

You made him [man] ruler over the works of your hands; you put everything under his feet: all flocks and herds, and the beasts of the field, the birds of the air, and the fish of the sea....

PSALM 8: 6-8

Evidence From ANTHROPOLOGY

Although claims of ape-to-man links frequently make headlines, rarely is it even mentioned, as these claims invariably are proven false. One of many examples of the poor quality of evidence used to support evolution is the single tooth commonly known as *Nebraska Man*. This tooth was publicized a genuine "missing link" and was used as evidence during the famous 1925 Scopes "Monkey Trial" in Dayton, Tennessee. A vivid reconstruction was commissioned, based on the only evidence–a single tooth found in Nebraska and a few supposed tools. This was one of the main pieces of hard evidence used to swing public opinion in favor of evolution and ridicule the biblical account of creation. Later excavations uncovered the rest of the remains and found that it was not the tooth of a man, an ape, or an ape-man. **This single tooth, used mightily to shake the public's confidence in the Word of God, actually turned out to be the tooth of an extinct wild pig.** The new discovery did not receive the publicity it had received when it was presented as a missing link, leaving most people with the impression that an ape-to-man link had been found.

Interestingly, every ape-to-man link used to support evolution during the Scopes Monkey Trial has since been debunked or withdrawn. Despite this lack of evidence, the dogma of evolution continues to be taught as if it were a fact of science.

The Illustrated Origins Answer Book, p.36

...So turn away from godless chatter and the opposing ideas of what is falsely called knowledge.

1 Timothy 6:20

Evidence From
BOTANY

The more scientists study plants, the more evident the complexity of their design becomes. Plants control their rate of photosynthesis with pores called stomata. Stomata allow carbon dioxide to enter the plant and oxygen to exit as the process of photosynthesis takes place. However, water can also exit when the stomata are open, so the stomata stay closed when there is little light or when water needs to be conserved. The wider the stomata open, the faster photosynthesis takes place and the faster the plant grows. Thus, **plants must balance the need to grow with the need to conserve water**.

While blue and red light can both be useful for photosynthesis, **scientists have found that the plant's mechanism which opens and closes the stomata only responds to blue light.** This blue wavelength of light causes certain cells within a plant to swell and open the stomata. Since red wavelengths heat the plants and tend to dry them out, designing plant stomata to open primarily for blue wavelengths is pure genius.

Using this information, scientists tried an experiment using orchids. By providing extra blue light to open the stomata, they more than doubled the growth rate without drying out the orchids.

Even plants have complex mechanisms that point to their Designer.

LETTING GOD CREATE YOUR DAY,
VOL. 3, P.246

The LORD is good to all; he has compassion on all he has made.

PSALM 145:9

Evidence From
THE FOSSIL RECORD

There are only two possible explanations for life:

1. **Evolution**–*which states that life has evolved from simple forms of plants and animals into the more complex forms we find today.*
2. **Creation**–*which states that God created the entire universe and all of the creatures on Earth fully formed and completely functional.*

Paleontologists have found a greater variety of creatures in the fossil record than now exist, including soft-bodied creatures such as worms and jellyfish. **However, even in the lowest rock layers, these worms and jellyfish are fully formed and easily categorized into the same kinds of animals alive today.**

If *evolution* is the correct explanation, then there should be thousands of intermediate forms as one type of creature slowly turned into another type. If *creation* is true, then the classifications of distinctly different types of animals, both living and in the fossil record, should remain essentially the same.

The fossil evidence clearly supports creation. True science progresses when all of the evidence is presented.

Letting God Create Your Day,
Vol. 3, p.247

Casting down imaginations, and every high thing that exalteth itself against the knowledge of God, and bringing into captivity every thought to the obedience of Christ....

2 Corinthians 10:5 KJV

Evidence From ANATOMY

Any organism's reproductive system must be fully functional in order for the organism to reproduce itself. A closer look at one small aspect of the male's reproductive system reveals incredible complexity which could never have developed by mutational changes from some "simpler" system.

Human sperm cells, for example, are about 1/600th of an inch in length with three basic parts–the "head" (which holds the genetic information of the father), the "body" (which supplies the energy for movement), and the "tail" (which propels it). **Human sperm can only survive within the narrow temperature range of 95°F (plus or minus 2°F.)** Yet the average human body temperature is 98.6°F. For this reason, a muscle within the walls of the male's scrotum adjusts the testicle location, closer or farther from the body, in order to maintain exactly the right temperature.

About 200 million sperm are made every 24 hours within the 750 feet of tiny twisted tubules. Inside of these coils are special cells called sertoli cells, which have an elaborate "communication network" allowing each cell to protect and care for about 150 sperm. Other small cells secrete testosterone (a male hormone), which must be exactly balanced with estrogen (a female hormone) in order to develop specific sexual characteristics. The production of these hormones is controlled by the pituitary gland in the brain. **Every part of this complex system (plus much, much more) are required for the reproductive process to succeed. This clearly points to a masterful Designer.**

THE HUMAN BODY: ACCIDENT OR DESIGN?,
P.79-83

My frame was not hidden from you when I was made in the secret place...your eyes saw my unformed body. All the days ordained for me were written in your book before one of them came to be.

PSALM 139:15,16

Evidence From
HISTORY

Skeptics are forever trying to discredit the Bible. In the 1800s an interesting puzzle was proposed as proof that the Bible could not be trusted. The book of Luke states that Quirinius was governor of Syria when Christ was born. Other passages would indicate that this birth took place in the year 4 B.C. Nonreligious historical records, however, show that Quirinius governed Syria after 6 A.D. This ten-year discrepancy was used by Bible critics in the nineteenth century as proof that the Bible could not be divinely inspired.

The puzzle was solved with further archeological evidence which confirmed the Bible. In 1912 an inscription was discovered which said that Quirinius was governor in Syria and Cilicia around 10 B.C. Apparently Quirinius ruled Syria and Cilicia twice. He was ruler at the time of Christ's birth, exactly as reported in the Bible. **How much damage was done to people's faith based on partial evidence and false assumptions?**

Through in-depth study, every so-called contradiction in the Bible invariably proves false. Throughout all of human history there is no book which comes close to the Bible in accuracy or influence.

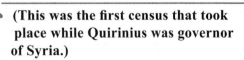

Letting God Create Your Day, Vol. 3, p.261

(This was the first census that took place while Quirinius was governor of Syria.)

Luke 2:2

Evidence From ARCHAEOLOGY

Dr. Nelson Glueck, President of the Hebrew Union College and one of the greatest modern Palestinian archaeologists, said that, **"absolutely no archaeological discovery has ever controverted a biblical reference."** He also writes, "Scores of archaeological findings have been made which confirm in a clear outline or exact detail historical statements in the Bible."

One of the most controversial narratives from the Bible is the **"long day"** in Joshua 10. To modern man it seems impossible and unbelievable that a day could have actually been extended. It is noteworthy that the Bible is not the only ancient record of this extended day. **Ancient traditions of a long day (or a long night in the case of Native Americans and South Sea Islanders) are quite common.** There is much documentation on this fact. The only reason to disbelieve the account of the long day is the preference for naturalism over God's Word.

THE BIBLE HAS THE ANSWER, P.71-72

...**So the sun stood still in the midst of heaven, and did not hasten to go down for about a whole day. And there has been no day like that, before it or after it....**

JOSHUA 10:13,14 NKJV

Evidence From MICROBIOLOGY

Almost all plants survive by a remarkable process which converts sunlight, water, and air into food. This incredibly complex process is called photosynthesis and is only found in living plants. **Biologists have recently discovered a type of lake algae that not only feeds itself through photosynthesis, but also eats bacteria.**

The average alga will consume an incredible one-third of its weight (or 36 bacteria) every hour. **This would be equivalent to a 150-pound person eating 1,200 pounds of food per day!** The cells of the alga were designed to share a fibrous casing with flagella (whiplike tails) coming out of the top of the casing. These flagella force water into the casing, allowing the cells to consume the bacteria contained within the water.

The entire process of an alga plant capturing and digesting living bacteria is extremely complicated and could not have happened by any step-by-step process of random mutational changes. In addition to keeping the algae alive, this process keeps the bacteria population in check and makes the lake water safe for other creatures. The existence of this unique lake algae points to God's design in the balance of nature.

LETTING GOD CREATE YOUR DAY, VOL. 3, P.258

For the LORD is the great God....The sea is his, for he made it....

PSALM 95:3,5

THE FOSSIL RECORD
Evidence From

An ancient termite nest discovered in fossilized wood from the Big Bend National Park in Texas was buried in the same sedimentary rock layers found to contain dinosaur bones. **Examination of the fossilized wood has provided the following information:**

1. **Small hexagonal grainlike particles** have been found within the petrified wood. The distinctive hexagonal shapes are believed to be termite droppings, since termites are the only insects that make hexagonal droppings. The ancient droppings are identical to those made by modern termites.
2. **The wood had been tunneled** in the same way that modern termites tunnel wood.
3. **The nest was placed in the center of the wood,** exactly where modern termites build their nest.
4. These ancient termites had also placed their **droppings around the edge of the nest** (just like modern termites) to plug any air leaks and prevent   drafts.

This evidence indicates that termites, from the supposed "time of the dinosaurs"–built homes and behaved exactly the same as termites do today. **There is absolutely no evidence of any termite evolution.** This agrees with the Bible's claim that creation was "completed" on the sixth day.

LETTING GOD CREATE YOUR DAY,
VOL. 3, P. 260

God saw all that he had made, and it was very good. And there was evening, and there was morning—the sixth day. Thus the heavens and the earth were completed in all their vast array.

GENESIS 1:31, 2:1

Evidence From
BIOLOGY

After a long process of detailed study and testing, scientists discovered one of the most bizarre methods of hearing in the animal kingdom. **The preying mantis has only one hearing organ, which is located in a groove underneath its thorax (the middle section of its body).** A teardrop-shaped groove in the thorax has a thinner covering than other parts of the mantis body, and under this covering is a relatively large air sac connected to the insect's respiratory system. Nerves near the top of this sac carry the sensation of sound to the nervous system.

Scientists discovered that this hearing organ senses not only audible sounds, but ultrasonic frequencies. When researchers sent a bat-like ultrasonic frequency toward a preying mantis in flight, it immediately took an evasive flight path to escape the sound of the bat. One truly has to question how anyone could believe that this intricately designed organ could have evolved by a chance process, one mutation at a time.

LETTING GOD CREATE YOUR DAY, VOL. 3, P.265

"...Great and marvelous are your deeds,
Lord God Almighty...."

REVELATION 15:3

Evidence From COMMON SENSE

If human *similarity* to apes is evidence that an apelike creature evolved into man, why aren't the *vast differences* between man and ape accepted as evidence that man did not descend from apes? The human nose is totally different from that of primates; man's lips are formed differently; apes have thumbs on their feet, while men do not; man's head is located at a different position on the spinal column; and human babies are far more dependent upon their mothers at birth than apes.

Even more physically perplexing is the fact that apes have a bone in the male's reproductive organ, while the human male makes use of an incredibly complicated hydraulic system. How could anyone reasonably conclude that the bone in an ape's reproductive organ slowly evolved into mankind's complex hormonal/hydraulic mechanism by some step-at-a-time mutational process? If the bone disappeared before the human system was completely in place, the apelike creature would not be able to reproduce and survive. Since apes have no difficulty reproducing, why would the human hydraulic reproduction system have ever evolved?

Dr. John C. Whitcomb observed that *"While the physical differences between man and primates are quite great, the spiritual/mental/linguistical/cultural differences are little short of infinite."* It is extremely poor and superficial science to conclude that some apelike creature evolved into mankind.

IN THE MINDS OF MAN, P.254
TORNADO IN THE JUNKYARD, P.107

REASON EMOTION

And if you call out for insight and cry aloud for understanding, and if you look for it as for silver and search for it as for hidden treasure, then you will understand the fear of the Lord and find the knowledge of God.

PROVERBS 2:3-5

Evidence From
ANATOMY

The eye is an incredibly complex organ that moves 100,000 times in an average day. Numerous muscles and tear ducts are in place to keep the eye constantly moist, protected, and functional. Our eyes process 1.5 million bits of information simultaneously and provide 80% of the sensory stimulation sent to the brain. They receive light images traveling at 186,000 miles per second through the iris, which opens or closes to let in just the right amount of light. These images travel through a lens, made of transparent cells, which focuses them on the retina at the back of the eyeball. The retina covers less than one square inch of surface, yet this square inch contains approximately 137 million light-sensitive receptor cells. Approximately 130 million are rod cells (designed specifically to see in black and white), and 7 million are cone cells (allowing color vision). Finally, the image is sent at a rate of 300 miles per hour to the brain for processing. How could all of this have come about by some step-by-step, random-chance evolutionary process?

Mankind has designed and patterned the camera after the eye. It is only reasonable to acknowledge that the eye, which is an infinitely more complex instrument, was also designed by intelligence.

THE HUMAN BODY: ACCIDENT OR DESIGN?,
P.56-58

Ears that hear and eyes that see—the LORD has made them both.

PROVERBS 20:12

Evidence From BIOLOGY

One of the most fascinating and unique creatures of all creation is the common hummingbird. What is the probability that all of the unique characteristics of the ruby-throated hummingbird, each of which are needed for its survival, developed by some step-by-step evolutionary process? A few of the hummingbird's incredible abilities are listed below:

1. **The unique ability to fly forward,** backward, upside-down, and straight up like a helicopter as no other bird can.
2. **The use of a special fringed tongue** to sweep insects out from the inside of flowers. It cannot survive on nectar alone, but also needs the protein from eating insects. Without its special tongue it could never catch the insects.
3. **The ability to fly 500 miles nonstop** over the gulf waters to Mexico. The hummingbird can conserve its strength for long flights by taking a prolonged rest just prior to the flight and making every motion count in flight.
4. **The ability to go into a "torpid" condition** at night by almost shutting down its metabolism. Because of its incredibly high energy activity, gram for gram the hummingbird has the greatest energy output of any warm-blooded animal. Yet at night it uses only about one-fifth of its normal energy.

The hummingbird is truly a marvel of God's creativity.

CHARACTER SKETCHES, VOL. II, P. 42-48

Look to the LORD and his strength; seek his face always. Remember the wonders he has done, his miracles, and the judgments he pronounced.

PSALM 105:4-5

Evidence From GENETICS

Not only does your genetic code store far more information in a microscopic space than our largest computers, it also has a built-in error correction system. Errors are constantly creeping into the DNA code because of radiation, chemical exposure, and other outside forces. **Scientists have discovered a number of key enzymes within the cell whose only job is to find and correct errors in the genetic code.** These enzymes faithfully correct mistakes, thereby preventing mutations. Yet we are expected to believe that these mistakes and mutations are what cause evolution to happen. Why would a system evolve whose sole function is to prevent the very mechanism which supposedly drives evolution (mutations)?

Life could not accurately reproduce without this genetic proofreading. Scientists have no adequate explanation for how these specific enzymes could have evolved by random processes. Everywhere we hear that things have "evolved," yet no explanation is given for how specific biological functions, such as this mistake-correcting mechanism, could have evolved.

"Only our Creator could have been wise enough to design an information system which can correct its own errors."

LETTING GOD CREATE YOUR DAY, VOL. 4, P.214

"...stop and consider God's wonders."

JOB 37:14

Evidence From
CREATION FOUNDATION

Evolution cannot be combined with Christianity for the following reasons:

1. **The Bible states 10 times that life reproduces only "after its own kind."** This is certainly true as we observe the biological world around us. Dogs stay dogs, and people stay people. Yet evolution preaches that all life is a blurred continuum.
2. **The God of the Bible demands unselfish sacrifice for the good of others. "...whosoever will be chief among you, let him be your servant" (Matthew 20:27).** Would this same God use a method of dead ends, extinctions, and survival of the fittest to make us?
3. **Belief in evolution justified the excesses of the industrial revolution, the Nazi elimination of the Jews, and the rise of Marxism and Communism.** It also serves as the justification for disbelief in God. If we are a product of biological forces, why not extend these forces into our dealing with other humans? Animal groups do not lament wiping each another out in order to survive. Why shouldn't we do the same if we are just part of an evolutionary process which formed us?
4. **There is abundant scientific evidence that macro-evolution has never taken place.** The fossil record shows no credible links between major groups of plants and animals; the chemical structure of DNA contains useful information which could not have developed by natural processes; and there is abundant evidence for a worldwide flood, which contradicts evolution.

Evolution is a philosophy unsupported by the majority of scientific observations.

***SEARCH FOR THE TRUTH,* P.113**

There is a way that seems right to a man, but in the end it leads to death.

PROVERBS 14:12

Evidence From MATHEMATICS

At one time living cells were considered no more complex than empty table tennis balls. As biochemists have learned more about the complexity of life, it has become increasingly apparent that thousands of specific and complex chemicals are required for any form of life to survive. **Evolutionist Harold Morowitz estimated the probability for chance formation of even the simplest form of living organism at $1/10^{340,000,000}$.** By comparison, only 10^{20} grains of sand could fit within a cubic mile, and 10 billion times more (10^{30}) would fit inside the entire earth. So the probability of forming a simple cell by chance processes is infinitely less likely than having a blind person select one specifically marked grain of sand out of an entire earth filled with sand.

There is nowhere near enough time nor matter in the entire universe for even the simplest cell to have formed by chance combinations. Even if all the correct chemicals somehow came together in the correct place, **you still wouldn't have life**. This is exactly the situation every time a living organism dies. Immediately after death, all the right chemicals exist, in the right proportions, and in the right place–yet the creature is still dead!

Five billion years is nowhere near long enough for evolution to have taken place. In reality, all of eternity would not provide enough time for random processes to form the enormous complexity of life.

ENERGY FLOW IN BIOLOGY, ACADEMIC PRESS, NY, 1968, P.99

I will proclaim the name of the LORD. Oh, praise the greatness of our God! He is the Rock, his works are perfect, and all his ways are just....

DEUTERONOMY 32:3,4

Evidence From
BIOLOGY

Bats have the extraordinary ability to close their ears as they send sonar signals and reopen them in time to hear returning echos. They do this at the incredible rate of 50 to 60 times per second. **Studying the bat's unique method of detecting objects has allowed scientists to discover the principles of sonar.** Using these principles, mankind has produced sensitive detection instruments of his own.

As complex and sensitive as our sonar detection systems are, they still lack the precision of the bat's. **It is estimated that the bat's sonar system is still many times more sensitive than anything man has yet designed.** We know it took man's intelligence to design his detection systems. Isn't it foolish to assume a bat's sonar system, which is much more complex and sensitive, happened by accidental mutational changes?

CHARACTER SKETCHES, VOL. II, P.95

You are good, and what you do is good; teach me your decrees.

PSALM 119:68

Evidence From
ANATOMY

Animals are much better prepared for physical survival at birth than humans. A newborn wildebeest stands and runs with its mother five minutes after birth. The baby elephant can follow its mother all day long within twenty-four hours after birth. Yet the newborn human is a completely helpless creature.

This is the exact reverse of what one would expect if the Darwinian scenario were factual. According to evolutionary theory, those characteristics which aid in survival and reproduction will be most likely propagated. How would infant vulnerability and lack of strength contribute to evolutionary survival and development? The physical helplessness of humans at birth is a vivid illustration of how dependent we are on God for our spiritual existence. It is also yet another of the countless evidences that evolution is not the method God used to bring us into existence. Instead, God designed humans to have adequate time to train their children to love and obey the One who created them and knows what is best for them.

THE HUMAN BODY: ACCIDENT OR DESIGN?, P.92-93

Train a child in the way he should go, and when he is old he will not turn from it.

PROVERBS 22:6

Evidence From PROPHECY

Psalm 22 is an amazing prophecy that describes the crucifixion of Christ. This Psalm was written approximately 1,000 years before its fulfillment. It describes in graphic detail the sufferings of Christ long before death by crucifixion was known or practiced by the Romans or Jews. This Psalm predicts how Christ's hands and feet would be pierced, His bones would be pulled out of joint, and He would experience extreme thirst. It also describes how men would gamble for His clothes and how the crowd would mock Him. Even the exact words Christ would speak from the cross were recorded in this Psalm. **Is it logical to conclude that all of these prophecies, predicted in precise detail almost 1,000 years before they happened, could have been fulfilled by mere chance?**

The science of probability (a mathematical method for calculating the likelihood with which an event is going to happen) can clearly reveal that guesses could not have produced this passage of Scripture. It could only have been written by inspiration from someone outside of time. Only God, who created mass, energy, and time could fulfill this qualification.

THE DEFENDER'S STUDY BIBLE, P.608

...My God, my God, why hast thou forsaken me?(v.1)...All they that see me laugh me to scorn(v.7)...all my bones are out of joint (v.14)...they pierced my hands and my feet. (v.16)...they look and stare upon me (v.17)...and cast lots upon my vesture....(v.18)

PSALM 22, KJV

Evidence From
BIBLICAL UNIQUENESS

How can we know if the original manuscripts of the Bible have been accurately transmitted to us? One method for determining the reliability of any ancient manuscript is to note the total number and the agreement between the various copies. There are over 24,000 ancient manuscripts containing various portions of the New Testament. Except for extremely minor variations, these copies agree word for word. **No other ancient document even begins to approach such massive authentication.** By comparison, the *Iliad* by Homer has the second highest number of surviving manuscript copies– totalling only 643! No one doubts the authenticity or accuracy of the Iliad; yet the Bible, with far more evidence in its favor, is under constant attack. One wonders, why the hostility?

God said in the Bible that His Word would never pass away. His Word has far more supporting evidence than any other book in history. **God gives us overwhelming evidence (which archaeology continues to verify) that Scripture has been accurately maintained, reproduced, and passed down through the ages.** Only the Bible can make this claim.

THIS INFORMATION IS CONDENSED FROM
EVIDENCE THAT DEMANDS A VERDICT, P. 39
THE NEW EVIDENCE THAT DEMANDS A VERDICT, P. 33-116
THESE BOOKS ARE EXCELLENT RESOURCES ON BIBLICAL ACCURACY.

Heaven and earth will pass away, but my words will never pass away.

MATTHEW 24:35

Evidence From
PHYSICS

In the Bible, God says that He "upholds" all things. The New Testament Greek word which is commonly translated as uphold means to *support* or to *maintain*. The implication of this word being in the present tense is that it is happening continuously. In other words, **at this very moment, God is sustaining everything in the universe.** If He would cease to sustain, we would cease to exist.

If the negatively charged electron were not kept moving, it would drop toward the positively charged nucleus and every atom in the universe would be destroyed. What keeps these electrons moving? We can model and describe the movement, but really don't know what keeps them moving.

All matter is made up of tiny particles called atoms. If the force holding the nucleus of these atoms together were reduced, the positively charged protons in the nucleus (which strongly repel each other) would instantaneously fly apart. Positively charged particles repel each other in the same way the positive ends of two bar magnets repel each other. It is still not completely understood why positively charged protons in the nucleus stay close together. **Although scientists have called the force which holds the protons in the nucleus by various names, including "gluons" and "the strong nuclear force," they really don't understand what it is or how it operates.**

Things do not just happen in our universe by accident. **God holds the universe together**, just like He stated in His Word.

GOD: COMING FACE TO FACE WITH HIS MAJESTY, P.78

...[He] upholds all things by the word of His power...

HEBREWS 1:3 NAS

Evidence From PROPHECY

In Ezekiel 26:3-21, specific predictions were made against the city of Tyre. The prophecy stated that this city would be destroyed as many nations came against it. **It was predicted that Tyre would be made bare as the top of a flat rock and that fishermen would spread their nets over the site.** The walls and the towers would be destroyed, the debris would be scraped clean, and Tyre would be left barren. This very specific prediction was made at the height of Tyre's power and importance.

Three years after the prophecy was given, Nebuchadnezzar laid a 13-year siege on mainland Tyre. When he finally entered the city, he found that most of the people had moved to an island ½ mile off the coast. They had fortified a city on this island with powerful walls reaching to the very edge of the sea. Over 200 years later, Alexander the Great laid siege to the island city of Tyre. Since he had no fleet, he demolished the old city of Tyre, cast the debris into the sea, and built a 200 foot wide causeway out to the island. By doing this, Alexander was able to move his army across the land bridge and destroy the island city. Tyre's history doesn't end here. Many subsequent attempts were made to rebuild Tyre, but sieges always destroyed the city. **Today both the original city and the island city are bare rocks where fishermen can be seen drying their nets.** The accuracy of biblical prophecy is undeniable evidence for the Bible's authenticity.

WHY I BELIEVE, P.18-22

"...I will bring many nations against you (v.3)....They will destroy the walls of Tyre... I will scrape away her rubble and make her a bare rock (v.4)....I am goingbring...Nebuchadnessar (v.7)....they will throw...your stones...and rubble into the sea(v.12)....I will make you a bare rock...a place to spread fishnets. You will never be rebuilt, for I the LORD have spoken....(v.14)"

EZEKIEL 26: 3-14

Evidence From
ASTRONOMY

Evolutionary scientists believe that matter spewed from exploding stars was used to form planets. They teach that the solar system and the sun formed from this great cloud of compacting gas. Yet they have no undisputed explanation for why **Mars, Earth, Venus, and Mercury do not have the same high percentage of hydrogen and helium as our sun and the rest of the visible universe.** Less than 1% of these planets are composed of hydrogen and helium.

How could this be, given the current prevalent theory that our solar system is the result of a condensing cloud of hydrogen gas? **How could 99.86% of the mass within our solar system (our sun) be made of hydrogen and helium, while the four planets closest to the sun are composed almost entirely of heavier elements?**

Something is seriously wrong with the theory of solar system evolution, which is being taught to our children as if it were a fact.

IN THE BEGINNING, 7ᵀᴴ ED., P.19

Praise him, you highest heavens and you waters above the skies. Let them praise the name of the LORD, for he commanded and they were created.

PSALM 148:4-5

Evidence From
BIOLOGY

The sidewinder, a desert snake, is too slow to catch one of its favorite foods, the gecko lizard. It improvises for this shortcoming by burying its entire body in the sand except for the tip of its tail. **The tail sticks out of the sand, imitating a lone blade of grass.** When ants discover this potential source of food in the barren desert, they begin to explore it. This draws the gecko, tempted by its favorite food, the ant. While the gecko dines on ants, the sidewinder grabs the gecko from beneath the sand and eats the lizard!

Could the sidewinder have perfected this neat little trick by evolution? How did the snake learn that its tail could attract ants which would, in turn, attract geckos? How did the snake manage to pass this instinct along to its young? Both the skill and the instinct must have been imparted before birth, because snakes raised in captivity also know how to hunt this way. **This intelligently designed interrelationship between three different desert creatures gives witness to the fact that there is one all-wise Creator** who provides for His creation even after the Fall (when bloodshed and competition replaced the originally created harmony among creatures).

LETTING GOD CREATE YOUR DAY, VOL. 4, P.7

Sing to the LORD with thanksgiving...He gives to the beast its food...

PSALM 147:7, 9 NKJV

Evidence From GEOLOGY

The soil which sustains life covers the earth's bedrock at an average depth of less than 12 inches. Without this layer of life-producing dirt, the earth would be as dead and sterile as the moon. This thin film of soil stands between man and extinction. **Scientists estimate that it takes 5,000 to 20,000 years for plant growth, bacterial decay, and erosion to produce six inches of top soil.** If the earth is billions of years old, why is there not more top soil? If it has been washed into the ocean by erosion, the ocean floor should be covered with soil and sediment hundreds of feet thick. This is not what oceanographers have found.

In places where there is a local accumulation of eroded soil, such as river deltas, the evidence also indicates a young earth. The Mississippi River carries tremendous amounts of soil and silt into the Gulf of Mexico each year. This material settles into the gulf, forming an ever-growing river delta. **By measuring the rate at which silt is carried into the gulf and the size of the current delta, it is possible to calculate how long the Mississippi River has been in existence.** The result of this calculation is *far less* than the millions of years that geologists tell us the Mississippi River has been around, but is exactly what would be expected if the river was formed following a relatively recent worldwide Flood. **Why is evidence like this left out of textbooks?**

UNLOCKING THE MYSTERIES OF CREATION,
PREMIER EDITION, P.52

"This is what the LORD says, he who made the earth, the LORD who formed it and established it—the LORD is his name..."

JEREMIAH 33:2

Evidence From
BIOLOGY

The cheetah is truly a remarkable creature. It is the world's fastest land animal, capable of accelerating from 0 to 40 miles per hour in 2 seconds. The cheetah can reach a speed of 70 miles per hour. **How does the cheetah reach these phenomenal speeds?** It is designed with a high-performance body containing a uniquely powerful heart, strong large-diameter arteries, and extra-large nostrils for breathing large volumes of air. The cheetah also has hip and shoulder girdles that swivel on its spine. As it runs, the cheetah's spine curves up and down as its legs contract and extend. When moving at high speed, the cheetah may only touch the ground once every 23 feet.

Evolutionists would claim that some unknown pre-cheetah creature turned into the cheetah by chance mutations of its heart, liver, arteries, nostrils, hips, shoulders, spinal column, and muscles. **Yet the oldest known cheetah fossils reveal an animal that is essentially identical to the cheetahs alive today.** Once again, the actual physical evidence supports creation, rather than evolution. The cheetah's unique characteristics are a result of design. All of the information necessary for the cheetah's speed was programmed into the first large "cat-type" creature. No series of random modifications could have produced this fast, sleek animal.

Letting God Create Your Day,
Vol. 4, p.19

...The LORD is faithful to all his promises
and loving toward all he has made.

Psalm 145:13

Evidence From
COMPARING RELIGIONS

Historian Philip Schaff wrote the following about Christ:

> **"This Jesus of Nazareth, without money or arms, conquered more millions than Alexander, Caesar, Muhammad, and Napoleon; without science and learning, He shed more light on things human and divine than all the philosophers and scholars combined; without the eloquence from schooling, He spoke such words of life as were never spoken before or since and produced effects which lie beyond the reach of orator or poet; without writing a single line, He set more pens in motion and furnished more sermons, orations, discussions, learned volumes, works of art, and songs of praise than the whole army of great men in both ancient and modern times."**

THE PERSON OF CHRIST,
THE AMERICAN TRACT SOCIETY, 1913

For great is the LORD and most worthy of praise; he is to be feared above all gods. For all the gods of the nations are idols, but the LORD made the heavens.

1 CHRONICLES 16:25-26

Evidence From
BIBLICAL ACCURACY

Sheep, cattle, and deer chew their cud by regurgitating partially digested vegetable matter and regrinding it with their molars before swallowing it a second time. The hare does not do this. **Why then, ask Bible critics, does the Bible call the hare a "cud-chewing animal"?**

It has been discovered that the hare does indeed re-eat and re-digest its food. The answer was found within one of the two types of pellets which the hare passes. One pellet is large, dry, hard, has little food value, and is eliminated as waste. The second pellet is soft and encased in a moist membrane. This pellet is also passed from the hare's body, but it is not permitted to touch the ground. Instead, **the animal reaches underneath with its mouth and swallows this pellet—a process called reingestion.** The reprocessed pellet provides nourishment and aids digestion by providing lactic acid, potassium, sodium, and phosphorus. This reinjestion allows the hare to extract and to utilize nutrients missed the first time.

The discovery of this unique ability points to a Master Designer and once again proves the Bible totally accurate.

CHARACTER SKETCHES, VOL. II , P.72

Nevertheless these ye shall not eat of them that chew the cud...as the...hare....

DEUTERONOMY 14:7 KJV

Evidence From MICROBIOLOGY

DNA is the master code which directs cells to produce proteins. Each cell in our body is made from thousands of different and very specific types of protein. This master code also directs the production of special proteins which make more DNA in order to reproduce an exact copy of the cell. In other words, **to *make* DNA, you have to *have* DNA in the first place!** How could DNA have developed when the existence of coded information on the DNA molecule is required to produce DNA from the start? This leads to the conclusion that cells could never have evolved, they simply had to have been created with the DNA code already in them!

Everywhere we look, from the microscopic molecules within every cell to the most complex plants and animals, **we see undeniable evidence for our Creator**.

It Couldn't Just Happen, P.68

But in fact God has arranged the parts in the body, every one of them, just as he wanted them to be.

I Corinthians 12:18

Evidence From
ASTRONOMY

By studying any basic astronomy textbook, one can see some obvious problems with the big bang theory. For example:

- **Where did everything come from that supposedly expanded to form the entire universe?**
- **How could an explosion have created the incredible order which we find throughout the universe?**
- **We see stars periodically exploding, but have never seen a new one form. Why aren't stars coming into existence?**

Even more intriguing, **why is there so much diversity in the various structures we see in the universe?** One would logically expect that the matter in space would be of relatively similar random composition if formed by the big bang. This is not the case. *Comets*, *asteroids*, and *meteoroids* are all composed of different substances, as are each of the planets in our solar system.

The *moons* which orbit our planets present a problem to evolutionary scientists, as well. Their composition is not only different from each other, but also from the very planets they orbit. Where did all this diversity come from? All of the beauty, complexity, and diversity of the universe point to our Creator God.

ANY BASIC HIGH SCHOOL EARTH SCIENCE OR ASTRONOMY TEXTBOOK

The heavens proclaim his righteousness, and all the peoples see his glory.

PSALM 97:6

Character: A Wish from God's Heart

Character, what does it mean?
  The word itself sounds strong.
It rings of truth and honesty,
  which chooses *right,* not wrong.

It speaks of dedication to
  a world that does not care.
It takes a stand for what is good
  when others would not dare.

It gives to people of itself,
  with no thoughts of return.
When others choose to waste their time,
  it seeks to grow and learn.

It also shows deep loyalty,
  not just to any cause.
But first takes time to think things through
  and search for hidden flaws.

It's diligent, resourceful too;
  commitment is its strength.
When others quit or just give up,
  it always goes the length.

It sees the need to give a hand
  to others who are weak,
But shuns all arrogance and pride
  and works on being meek.

It seeks to show a thankful heart,
  in spite of all life's woes,
And looks at life realistically,
  yet cheerfulness it shows.

It strives to be responsible,
  and orderly it lives.
It's flexible, decisive, too;
  and gentle words it gives.

It never seeks the big applause;
  in quietness it moves.
Its good effect on all of us
  with time it always proves.

Now as you look around, you'll see,
  true character is rare.
How desperately we need it, though,
  to keep us from despair.

This hope for all is one that's deep,
  a wish made from God's heart,
That as we choose our way in life,
  Christlike character is where we start!

Evidence From CREATION FOUNDATION

Neither creation nor evolution can be scientifically proven, since neither is repeatable. **Evolution and creation are both belief systems.** As thinking people, we should look at all the facts and put our faith in the one which is best supported by the the majority of the evidence. For example, it is interesting to note that of the hundreds **of possible dating methods, over 90% indicate an earth far younger than would be needed for any evolutionary process to have taken place.** Yet it is presented as a fact that the earth is billions of years old, and children are only exposed to those few evidences that support this belief. We are not following the principles and methods of true science when we consider only the few methods which seem to indicate an old earth, while ignoring the majority of the evidence which indicates that the earth is young.

One cannot help but wonder why so many scientists insist on believing in an old earth in light of so much evidence to the contrary. Could it be because a young earth totally eliminates the possibility of evolution, which means there must be a Creator to whom we are ultimately accountable?

RICH AND TINA KLEISS

O Timothy, keep that which is committed to thy trust, avoiding profane and vain babblings, and oppositions of science falsely so called...

1 TIMOTHY 6:20 KJV

Evidence From GENETICS

In order to find the effects of mutations, **fruit flies have been irradiated to simulate millions of years of evolutionary "progress."** There have been over ninety years of fruit fly experiments involving over 3,000 consecutive generations. The mutation rate within fruit flies has been greatly accelerated, and the results have been carefully documented. The result has been the rearrangement and corruption of genetic information already contained within the fruit fly's DNA, but nothing other than a modified fruit fly has ever developed. The loss of genetic information has produced organs which are deformed, but no new organs as required by evolution.

Scientific experimentation has confirmed that there is no basis for believing that any natural or artificial evolutionary process will ever transform a fruit fly into anything other than another fruit fly. Mutational changes never cause the fruit fly to increase in complexity. **Experimentation confirms that mutations could never produce a genetic improvement in any creature.**

In the Beginning, 7ᵀᴴ Ed., p.6-7

I know that everything God does will endure forever; nothing can be added to it and nothing taken from it. God does it so men will revere him.

Ecclesiastes 3:14

Evidence From BIOLOGY

Some animals, such as the duckbilled platypus, have organs that completely confound any evolutionary explanation. The platypus has a mixture of features from animals completely unrelated to its supposed ancestry. For instance:

1. **The warm-blooded platypus feeds its babies milk like other mammals.**
2. **It lays leathery eggs, has a single ventral opening (for eliminating its waste, mating, and birth), and has claws and a shoulder girdle like most reptiles.**
3. **It can detect electrical currents like some fish.**
4. **It has webbed feet like an otter, a flat tail like a beaver, and the male can inject poison into its predators like a snake.**
5. **It has a bill like a duck.**

It would seem that animals such as the platypus are God's reminder of His unfathomable creativity. These animals combine features from many unrelated creatures and have **no logical place on the "evolutionary tree."** There is no direct evidence that any major group of animals (or plants) arose from any other group. Completely different types of animals are only observed going out of existence (extinctions), never coming into existence.

IN THE BEGINNING, 7ᵀᴴ ED., P.7

Great is the LORD and most worthy of praise; his greatness no one can fathom....I will meditate on your wonderful works. They will tell of the power of your awesome works, and I will proclaim your great deeds.
PSALM 145:3,5,6

Evidence From
HISTORY

The Bible claims that Adam and Eve were the first humans and that three of Adam's sons were named Cain, Abel, and Seth. In the first recorded murder, Cain killed Abel. Since these were the first people on Earth, this question is often asked, **"Where did Cain find a wife?"** This question puzzles most people, not because the answer is complicated, but because they have been trained to think based on evolutionary assumptions.

Evolution begins with the assumption that nature has always functioned similar to how it is operating today. Evolution also teaches that things are increasing in complexity and improving over time. The *Bible* teaches the opposite–Adam and Eve as originally created would have been perfect with no genetic mistakes in their DNA. Genetic mistakes started to occur after the Fall and have quite rapidly built up over time. Today, whenever both parents have the same genetic mistake, their children develop the resulting genetic problem. This is why brothers and sisters cannot marry. It was mankind's disobedience that brought this imperfection into God's creation.

The biblical law against brothers and sisters intermarrying did not exist until 2,000 years after creation (approximately 4,000 years ago). Abraham (alive approximately 3,000 years ago) was married to his half sister. The Bible states that Adam and Eve had other sons and daughters. Jewish tradition even suggests that they had 46 children. **Cain merely married one of his sisters.**

Search for the Truth, p.32

After Seth was born, Adam lived 800 years and he had other sons and daughters.

Genesis 5:4

Evidence From BIOLOGY

In His Word, God tells us that He cares for His creatures. One can observe repeated examples of this in nature. Every creature on Earth has been preprogrammed to take care of itself. An example is the female red-cockaded woodpecker, which changes her diet to include more calcium at egg-laying time. **Scientists have found that the woodpecker starts gathering, storing, and eating *bone fragments* a few days before laying her eggs.** Bones contain an extremely high concentration of calcium, which is needed for the shells of the woodpecker's eggs. After her eggs are laid and her body requires less calcium, the woodpecker shows little interest in pieces of bone.

Where did this instinct to eat bones originate? How does the woodpecker know when she can stop eating bone fragments? Would this process have taken place before the Fall, when the world was a perfect paradise? No one knows, but it is apparent that this instinct had to be programmed into the woodpecker for it to survive in the current fallen world. What a leap of faith to believe that the woodpecker's ability to meet her need for increased calcium just "evolved" by chance!

LETTING GOD CREATE YOUR DAY, VOL. 3, P.22

Look at the birds of the air; they do not sow or reap or store away in barns, and yet your heavenly Father feeds them. Are you not much more valuable than they?

MATTHEW 6:26

Evidence From BIOLOGY

God tells us in Exodus 8 of a devastating swarm of flies sent into Egypt. **We can see how this could happen by considering the life cycle of flies and the delicate balance by which they are kept in check.** A female fly can lay as many as 1,000 eggs during her 30-day summertime life span. She lays between 100 to 250 eggs at a time, which hatch within 24 hours. It has been calculated that **if all the offspring of an individual pair of flies lived, their population (starting in April and ending in August) would reach a total of 190,000,000,000,000,000,000!**

We can start to appreciate how critical it is that the fly populations be controlled when we understand that flies are one of the most dangerous insects to man. They live on filth. They enjoy decaying flesh, garbage, and manure. Then they walk around in the sugar bowl on your table. A single fly can hold up to 30 million organisms or bacteria in its internal tract and 500 million on its body surface. The common housefly is capable of transmitting about 40 serious diseases. Birds, toads, spiders, and other predators keep the fly populations from growing to plague proportions.

Developing a better understanding of nature and its complex system of interactions gives us reason to praise God. His attentiveness to details is truly astounding.

CHARACTER SKETCHES, VOL.II, P.116-122

...and there came a grievous swarm of flies... into all the land of Egypt: the land was corrupted by reason of the swarm of flies.

EXODUS 8:24 KJV

Evidence From
MATHEMATICS

The simplest conceivable form of life (e.g., bacteria) contains at least 600 different protein molecules. Each of these molecules performs specific functions by fitting into other molecules shaped in exact three-dimensional spacial arrangements. These proteins work like a key fitting into a lock–only a specifically shaped protein will fit. **Yet there are multiple trillions of possible combinations of protein molecules and shapes.** How could the exactly required shape find the exactly correct corresponding protein in order to perform the required cellular function?

The mathematical probability that the precisely designed molecules needed for the "simplest" bacteria could form by chance arrangement of amino acids (these are the chemicals that link up to form proteins) is far less than 1 in 10^{450}. Most scientists acknowledge that any probability less than 1 in 10^{50} is considered an impossibility. **One wonders why this "impossibility" is being taught as a "fact of science" to millions of schoolchildren each year.**

In the Beginning, 7ᵀᴴ Ed., p.14

"As the heavens are higher than the earth, so are my ways higher than your ways and my thoughts than your thoughts."

Isaiah 55:9

Evidence From THE FOSSIL RECORD

As soon as a plant or animal dies, its DNA begins to decompose. The oldest accurately known DNA samples are from a 4000-year-old mummy. Based on the deterioration of the molecule from samples of this age, **it is estimated that essentially no DNA could survive longer than 10,000 years.** However, DNA segments have been found in magnolia leaves (dated by evolutionists at 17 million years), dinosaur bones (dated at 80 million years), scales of a fossilized fish (dated at 200 million years), and amber-encased insects and plants (dated at 25-120 million years). Evolutionary scientists should be asking how DNA could still be contained in samples this old when more recent samples indicate that the DNA molecule is far too sensitive to have lasted this long. Perhaps there is something wrong with the old-earth dating methods and these fossils still contain DNA fragments simply because they are not as old as believed. These samples have been simply been dated wrong due to faulty assumptions of radiometric dating methods.

Evolutionists have a similar problem with *protein* preserved in dinosaur bones. **As with DNA, no protein should last 75 to 150 million years;** yet protein has been found in dinosaur bones. These plant and animal remains are simply not as old as evolutionists need to accept in order to continue to believe in the story of evolution.

In The Beginning, 7ᵀᴴ Ed., p.29-30

"...I am He; I am the first and I am the last. My own hand laid the foundations of the earth...."

Isaiah 48:12,13

Evidence From
PHYSICS

Radiohalos are rings of color which form in rock crystals when bits of radioactive elements decay. These discolored rings give very specific patterns which are indicative of the radioactive decay sequence happening within the rock crystal. Radiohalos have been found in granite, biotite, fluorite, diamond and other minerals and gems. They also provide undisputable evidence that enormous layers of rock which form the lowest crust of our planet formed and cooled almost instantaneously.

Polonium is a radioactive element which decays within seconds to months of its formation. It leaves very distinctive discolored rings when this decay happens inside of granite and other materials. These discolorations had to have formed after the granite was cool, because temperatures higher than 140°C destroy the discoloration. In some cases the polonium decays in less than a second, and in others it is gone within months. **The only way that radiohalos could exist within granite is if these massive rock layers, as much as a mile thick, also formed and cooled almost instantly.**

Critics claim that the polonium came from other radioactive elements which were deposited millions of years after the rock crystals formed and cooled. There is no evidence, however, that the tiny bits of radioactive polonium came from any previous form of radioactive material. Nor is there evidence to show how the radioactive material could have entered the rock. The polonium had to be present as the rock formed.

The existence of polonium radiohalos in granite indicate that the granite was created as a solid, just as we see it now, and did not form from molten material.

CREATION'S TINY MYSTERY, P.11-37

"**Where were you when I laid the foundations of the earth? Tell Me, if you have understanding.**"

JOB 38:4   NKJV

Evidence From
ANATOMY

The human ear is an engineering marvel. **This tiny organ has the intricate workings of the most sophisticated microphone, telephone wiring system, and balancing mechanism known to man.** Sound waves enter the ear and pass along a tube to the middle ear. Stretched across this tube is a thin membrane called the eardrum. As the sound waves vibrate this thin tissue, the vibrations move into the middle ear, where they move three small bones. Tiny muscles attached to the bones amplify the movement and allow the bones to pass the vibrations to another membrane called the oval window. This generates movement within a small liquid-filled spiral passage called the cochlea. The cochlea is filled with 25,000 auditory receptors that pick up the vibrations and transform them into electrical impulses. These impulses are sent by way of the auditory nerve to the brain. **The brain receives up to 25,000 auditory signals per second and interprets them as voices, thunder, music, or a million other sounds.**

Besides hearing, the ear also gives us our sense of balance. The cochlea is connected to three tubes called the semicircular canals. They are partially filled with fluids that move whenever the head moves. Nerve endings from these canals are also connected to the brain; and this, in cooperation with our muscles, allows us to balance properly. The ear's **marvelously designed and coordinated workings** demonstrate the incredible planning of a Master Designer.

THE HUMAN BODY: ACCIDENT OR DESIGN?, P.58-60

The hearing ear, and the seeing eye, the LORD hath made even both of them.

PROVERBS 20:12 KJV

Evidence From MICROBIOLOGY

Biological immune systems can recognize bacteria, viruses, and toxins that invade the body. Each system can quickly mobilize just the right type of defenders to search and destroy these invaders. Each system also has a memory that learns from every attack so that the defense is quicker and more effective the next time.

If the extensive instructions that direct the immune system of a plant or animal were not already programmed into the organism's genetic system when the organism first appeared on the earth, any infection would have quickly destroyed the organism. This would have nullified any genetic changes that might have accumulated. The genetic information governing the immune system could not have accumulated in a slow evolutionary way.

Immune systems became critical for survival after the Fall, when sin and death changed the order of things. Yet the very existence of these systems testifies to a mastermind Designer. How could the immune system of animals and plants have evolved? This very basic question still has no answer.

IN THE BEGINNING, 7ᵀᴴ ED., P.16-17

I will tell of the kindnesses of the LORD, the deeds for which he is to be praised, according to all the LORD has done for us....

ISAIAH 63:7

Evidence From HISTORY

Thomas Huxley, arguably history's most influential proponent of evolution, stated that,

> *"It is clear that the doctrine of evolution is directly antagonistic to that of creation...if consistently accepted, it makes it impossible to believe the Bible."*

This statement could not be more true. Creation requires accountability to a greater power. Evolution ultimtely implies that we are accountable to no one but ourselves.

The straightforward application of the principles of evolution has resulted in some of the greatest atrocities in history. For example, **Hitler** accepted the evolutionary platitudes of Nietzsche: the idea of a super race. *Preservation of Favoured Races in the Struggle for Life* is the subtitle of Darwin's book on evolution. Hitler's master-race mentality was merely a natural consequence of evolutionary thinking. **Mussolini** frequently quoted the Darwinian catch phases and carried the survival-of-the-fittest mentality to its logical conclusion– believing war was essential for progress. **Karl Marx** asked Darwin to write an introduction to *Das Kapital*, since he believed that Darwinism provided a scientific foundation for communism. **Communist governments** worldwide push evolution in an effort to remove God and accountability to Him. This conveniently leaves government as the only source of authority and provides the justification for the murder of millions. Truly, **evolution is a poor trade** for the truth of the creation.

WHY I BELIEVE, P.52-53

Have nothing to do with godless myths and old wives' tales; rather train yourself to be godly.

1 TIMOTHY 4:7

Evidence From ANATOMY

It has been said that the human brain is the most complex structure in the universe. During intense concentration, your brain can burn as many calories as your muscles use during exercise. Intense thinking can be as physically exhausting as a physical workout. More than 100,000 chemical reactions per second can occur within your brain.

Our brains act as far more than a motor control center or place to capture memories. Along with these functions, the brain also acts as a chemical factory. Our brains produce over 50 different drugs needed to control our body, emotions, and thoughts. Some of these chemicals affect memory, others intelligence, while still others are sedatives. For example, *endorphin*, the brain's pain-killer, is three times more potent than morphine. *Sertonin* is produced by the brain to moderate our moods. *Dopamine* seems to affect how talkative and excitable people become. Another hormone regulates hunger.

The brain is also a radio transmitter, sending out measurable electromagnetic signals. In fact, the brain has been shown to continue sending these signals for as long as 37 hours after death!

We only understand a small part of how the brain operates. Yet our growing knowledge of the brain is sufficient to conclude that the design of this incredible organ is no accident.

Letting God Create Your Day, Vol. 2, p. 59

Can you fathom the mysteries of God? Can you probe the limits of the Almighty?

Job 11:7

Evidence From BIOLOGY

The rattlesnake has been marvelously designed to have pits under its eyes that serve as a second pair of eyes.

"Researchers have learned that there is a membrane stretched over the back of each pit, a thousandth of an inch thick, which is crammed with sensors which pick up the infrared radiation or heat, given off by all warm-blooded creatures. These sensors are hooked up to a second vision center in the brain so that the rattlesnake can see the image of its warm-blooded victim even in complete darkness."

A snake has also been designed with a sense organ in the roof of its mouth. When it flicks out its tongue, it is actually smelling by picking up scent molecules from the air and rubbing these molecules on this sense organ. The snake's uniquely designed sense of smell can only point to the Master Designer.

After the Fall, God provided for the snake's survival by designing methods by which it could find food which would otherwise be invisible to it.

LETTING GOD CREATE YOUR DAY, VOL. 4, P.22

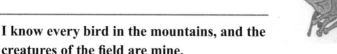

I know every bird in the mountains, and the creatures of the field are mine.

PSALM 50:11

Evidence From BIOLOGY

Bee bread is a highly nutritional food made by bees from the pollen they gather. Young worker bees must eat bee bread in order for their glands to properly produce food needed by the queen and developing larvae. Older worker bees can live on honey alone.

Scientists have discovered that even as bees collect pollen, they begin to work on the bee bread recipe. First they mix secretions from special glands with specific microorganisms, which in turn make enzymes known to release a number of important nutrients from the pollen. Other microbes are added to make antibiotics and fatty acids which keep the "bread" from spoiling. At the same time unwanted microbes are being removed, the bees are adding honey as a binder to hold it all together.

The bees' recipe for bee bread involves the sophisticated use of three areas of science–microbiology, nutritional chemistry, and biochemistry. Does logic allow the conclusion that bees evolved by blind chance and all of these independent processes just fell into place?

LETTING GOD CREATE YOUR DAY, VOL. 4, P. 23

Great are the works of the LORD; they are pondered by all who delight in them.

PSALM 111:2

Evidence From BOTANY

The *skunk cabbage* is a uniquely designed plant. **It generates enough heat to melt the snow around itself so that it can begin to grow and flower.** Even if the air temperature drops as low as 10°F, the skunk cabbage produces the heat it needs to maintain a temperature of between 72°F and 74°F. However, if the temperature stays extremely low for more than 24 hours, the hooded flower exhausts its heating ability and the flower dies. The skunk cabbage then prepares more flowers and repeats the process.

This amazing plant also has a built-in thermostat. If the flower becomes too cold, more heat is summoned. If the flower becomes too warm, the heat is withdrawn. Because of its amazing abilities, the skunk cabbage is one of the first plants to break through the snow in early spring. Normally, honeybees are unable to fly in temperatures below 65°F. However, when the skunk cabbages are in bloom, honeybees can fly when temperatures drop as low as 45°F. Inside the flower's hood, the bees warm up enough to travel to the next cabbage flower. In cold weather the bees fly from one skunk cabbage to another, warming themselves as they travel back to their hive. Could this intricately designed flower be the result of random-chance mutational changes?

CHARACTER SKETCHES, VOL.III, p.209-212

I will meditate on all your works and consider all your mighty deeds. Your ways, O God, are holy. What god is so great as our God?

PSALM 77:12-13

Evidence From
CHEMISTRY

Living organisms survive by using thousands of chemicals, each involved in a long series of complex chemical reactions. For example, **the clotting of blood involves over twenty distinct individual reactions, each of which is absolutely vital to heal a wound.** However, clotting could be fatal if it happens too soon or too late. Omitting even one of these twenty sequential chemical reactions, inserting an unwanted step, or altering the timing of a step would result in death. If even one reaction is missing, all of the other marvelous steps that had previously performed flawlessly would be in vain.

In Michael Behe's excellent book *Darwin's Black Box: The Biochemical Challenge to Evolution*, this long sequence of reactions is called an irreducibly complex process. **If even one step or one chemical reaction is out of place, the whole complex system doesn't work and the organism bleeds to death.** These complex chemicals and reactions had to have been created as an intricate, highly integrated unit from the very beginning.

DARWIN'S BLACK BOX: THE BIOCHEMICAL CHALLENGE TO EVOLUTION, P.74-97

Yet for us there is but one God, the Father, from whom all things came and for whom we live; and there is but one Lord, Jesus Christ, through whom all things came and through whom we live.

1 CORINTHIANS 8:6

Evidence From THE FOSSIL RECORD

After Darwin published *The Origin of Species* in 1859, many people began thinking that all forms of life had a common ancestor. **Scientists came to believe that over long periods of time molecules had turned into man.** Although they admitted that there were gaps in this "evolutionary tree," they believed that these gaps would be filled as scientific knowledge increased.

Instead, just the opposite has happened. **As scientific knowledge has progressed, the obvious "missing links" (in-between steps as one type of plant or animal becomes another) in this hypothetical tree have multiplied enormously.** Furthermore, the difficulties in "bridging" these gaps have become even more apparent. For example, in Darwin's day, all life was classified into two categories (or kingdoms): animals and plants. Today it has been necessary to divide life into at least **five radically different kingdoms,** only two of which are animals and plants. This does not even include viruses, which are complex and unique in their own way. In the 1800s the animal kingdom was divided into 4 animal phyla (basic body designs); today there are about 40. **Yet all of these different kingdoms and phyla appear suddenly in the fossil record with no intermediate forms,** exactly what one would expect to find according to the Genesis account.

IN THE BEGINNING, 7ᵀᴴ ED., P.18-19

The fool says in his heart, "There is no God."...

PSALM 53:1

Evidence From ANATOMY

Healing is a remarkable process. There is intelligent design involved in both the order of the steps which our bodies use to repair wounds and the advanced biochemistry needed to make those steps happen. The process of healing a wound proceeds as follows:

1. **As soon as you cut yourself**, the bleeding must be stopped While the scab is forming over the surface of the wound, the blood below is making a completely different kind of clot out of blood platelets and protein.
2. **Once the bleeding has stopped**, your body increases the flow of blood enriched with white blood cells. These cells not only search out and kill germs, but clean the wound of damaged cellular tissues.
3. **Skin cells start to increase** the rate at which they make new cells in order to bridge the cut with new skin.
4. **Underneath this new skin,** cells called fibroblasts fill the wound to strengthen the tender new tissue, and then contract to pull the wound closed.
5. **Finally, blood vessels and nerves complete their repairs** as the fibroblasts position themselves along the lines of stress to prevent future damage.

The human body is an incredible engineering marvel!

Letting God Create Your Day, Vol. 4, p.77

**Your compassion is great, O LORD;
preserve my life according to your laws.**

Psalm 119:156

Evidence From
BIOLOGY

For years it was thought that sunlight provided the energy for all forms of life. We have recently found other forms of life living at widely separated locations on the dark ocean floor which use only chemical and thermal energy. **For one energy-conversion system to evolve into another would be like changing a home's heating system from gas to electricity by thousands of random accidents that happened slowly, one accident each year.** The occupants would risk freezing each winter. Survival on the ocean floor without solar energy–a totally unexplained capability–would need to have evolved at different times in different oceans.

Many other giant leaps must have happened for life to exist. Here are just a few of the numerous unexplained problems:

- How did the incredibly complex process of *photosynthesis* (changing sunlight into usable energy within a cell) develop?
- How did *warm-blooded* animals change into *cold-blooded* animals?
- How did *floating marine plants* (such as plankton) change into *rooted vasular plants*?
- How did *egg-laying* animals change into animals which bear *live young*?
- How did *land mammals* change into *sea mammals*?
- How could *insect metamorphosis* have developed?

These problems are unsolvable for evolution because **an all-powerful Creator made all life,** not random evolutionary processes such as mutations.

In the Beginning, 7ᵀᴴ Ed., p.19

Yours, O LORD, is the greatness and the power and the glory and the majesty and the splendor, for everything in heaven and earth is yours....

1 Chronicles 29:11

THE FOSSIL RECORD
Evidence From

What happens when a fossil is found that does not fit the standard evolutionary time sequence? Evolutionists never throw out the theory of evolution, because to do so they would cease to be evolutionists. **To an evolutionist, evolution is a fact.** Any "out-of-place" fossil is either disputed or evolution is modified to absorb the find. An example of this is the appearance of fish with backbones (vertebrates).

Vertebrates were once the only major animal group that were not found at the lowest level of rock in which all other life forms suddenly appear (Cambrian rocks). These rocks are said to be 545 million years old by evolutionists. When fish with backbones were found above the Cambrian layer and "dated" at 420 million years, it was assumed that it had taken 125 million years for a fish without a backbone to "evolve" a backbone.

By the 1990s, fish with backbones had been found even closer to the Cambrian layer and "dated" at 530 million years. It is now taught that *backbones developed rapidly* or that they *evolved during the Cambrian explosion of life.* No matter what is found in the rock layers, it is fit into the "theory" of evolution; because evolution is actually a belief sytem that is readily modified, but never abandoned. Evolution is used to explain everything–regardless of how the evidence changes. There is no such thing as an *out-of-place fossil.* Evolution is assumed to be a fact and any evidence is forced into a modified evolutionary sequence.

CREATION EX NIHILO *22*(3), P.38-39
"SLOW FISH IN CHINA" BY DR. TAS WALKER

...**"Teacher, rebuke your disciples!" "I tell you," he replied, "if they keep quiet, the stones will cry out."**
LUKE 19:39-40

Evidence From ASTRONOMY

Evolutionists have no adequate explanation for why, if our solar system evolved, the planets do not all spin in the same direction. Most planets rotate in the same direction as their orbits; but Venus, Uranus, and Pluto rotate backwards.

In the nebula model of solar system evolution, the 72 known moons should orbit planets in the same direction. Instead, at least eight moons have backward orbits. The planets Jupiter, Saturn, Uranus, and Neptune have moons orbiting in *both* directions!

These types of undisputed observations contradict the current theories of how the solar system evolved. They are, however, exactly what an all-powerful Creator, who wanted to reveal His hand in creation, would place in the universe for our enjoyment.

What grand diversity we see exhibited by our Creator!

IN THE BEGINNING, 7ᵀᴴ ED., p.21

Dominion and awe belong to God; he establishes order in the heights of heaven. Can his forces be numbered?...

JOB 25:2-3

Evidence From
BIOLOGY

The *mongoose* is a mammal about 18 inches long, weighing only a few pounds. Its short legs provide great running speed while keeping it close to the ground, making it perfectly designed to feed on snakes. Mongooses keep the snake population in check while dining on some of the most poisonous snakes in the world. With their slender bodies they can run up to a wall or corner at full speed and turn without slowing down. They can stand on their hind legs, make small leaps into the air, and roll into a ball.

Scientists have found that a mongoose raised in captivity instinctively knows how to kill a snake, even if it has never seen a parent do so. **Its amazing ability to avoid snakebites and its internal programming which allows it to act as an effective snake killer had to have worked perfectly from the beginning of its existence.** Imagine an animal born with the desire to kill poisonous snakes, but no instincts directing it how to do so. It certainly wouldn't have survived long.

Did God originally create a world with this deadly competition between various forms of life? Or are these abilities the result of random changes over time? The Bible has another answer—God was involved from the beginning in the design and creation of all things. The current world, with its bloodshed and competition, is a result of man's sin and the Fall, not the way things were orginally created.

LETTING GOD CREATE YOUR DAY,
VOL. 4, P.171

I will meditate on all your works and consider all your mighty deeds.

PSALM 77:12

Evidence From ASTRONOMY

Contrary to popular opinion, planets should not form from the mutual gravitational attraction of particles orbiting the sun. **Orbiting particles are much more likely to be scattered or expelled by their gravitational interactions than they are to be pulled together.** Experiments have shown that colliding particles almost always fragment rather than stick together. Similar difficulties relate to a moon forming from particles orbiting a planet.

Despite these problems, let us assume that pebble-size to moon-size particles somehow evolved. *Growing a planet* by many small collisions will produce an almost nonspinning planet, because a spin imparted by impacts will be largely self-canceling. Yet all planets spin, some much more than others.

The more we explore and understand our solar system, the more reasons we have to acknowledge that it did not evolve, but was created.

IN THE BEGINNING, 7ᵀᴴ ED., P.22

By the word of the LORD the heavens were made, and by the breath of His mouth all their host.

PSALM 33:6 NASV

Evidence From PHYSICS

The first law of thermodynamics states that the total amount of mass and energy in the universe is fixed and although it can change form, it cannot be created or destroyed. Countless experiments have always found this to be true.

A conclusion of this first law is that natural processes cannot create energy. "Consequently, energy must have been created by some agency or power outside and independent of the natural universe. Furthermore, if natural processes cannot produce mass and energy–the relatively simple inorganic portion of the universe–then it is even less likely that natural processes can explain the much more complex organic (or living) portion of the universe."

The only other alternative to the first law of thermodynamics is to assume that the universe itself is eternal and has always existed. Yet this contradicts the second law of thermodynamics that says the universe is "winding down." Countless experiments have also always found this to be true. If the universe is winding down, who wound it up?

It is only because the naturalistic redefinition of science starts with the assumption that God did not create all matter and energy that evolutionary scientists are **forced to ignore** these basic laws of observable science.

IN THE BEGINNING, 7ᵀᴴ ED., P.24

I know that everything God does will endure forever; nothing can be added to it and nothing taken from it. God does it so that men will revere him. *ECCLESIASTES 3:14*

Evidence From ASTRONOMY

Many stars end their lives with a bright explosion called a supernova. These deaths have been recorded throughout history. Similarly, star births should be accompanied by the appearance of new starlight in an area of the sky where no star has previously been seen. Yet no new light has ever appeared in any area of the sky photographed decades earlier. If stars evolve, star births should about equal star deaths.

It is widely reported that stars are forming in various parts of the universe. What is actually seen are great dust clouds surrounding existing or former stars. **We have never seen a star born, but we have seen hundreds of stars die.**

Scientific observation of the heavens has revealed **absolutely no evidence** that stars have ever evolved. Although there is much speculation, there is also no sound scientific explanation for how stars could ever evolve from clouds of dispersed gas.

In the Beginning, 7ᵀᴴ Ed., p.27

The Bible clearly states God made the stars
and set them in the sky on the 4th day of
creation and that He completed His creation on
the 6th day. ***Genesis 1:16-19, 2:1-4 (summarized)***

Evidence From HISTORY

There is extensive evidence for an Ice Ige with glaciers covering much of our planet and altering landscapes. **But where does the Ice Age fit into biblical history?**

Earth science textbooks state that there have been numerous ice ages over millions of years. But all of the evidence for multiple events and the long time period between the ices ages is circumstantial. The Ice Age is best explained as the result of changes to the earth's environment after Noah's Flood. No other model adequately explains the cause of this drastic climatic change.

In order for the earth to experience any ice age, enormous amounts of water would need to evaporate from the oceans and fall as snow onto the continents. This would form huge sheets of ice spreading toward the equator. The oceans after Noah's Flood would have been considerably warmer due to extensive volcanic activity. Warmer oceans would result in increased evaporation. **Increased evaporation in combination with volcanic dust high in the skies would have resulted in massive snowfall at the polar regions which would not have melted during the summer.** This build-up of ice, year by year, would have continued for centuries.

The Bible does not mention the Ice Age, even though it is a direct consequence of the worldwide Flood. Nevertheless, no model of Earth history explains the cause of the Ice Age as well as the worldwide flood of the Bible.

PROCEEDINGS OF THE SECOND INTERNATIONAL CONFERENCE ON CREATIONISM, "THE EVIDENCE FOR ONLY ONE ICE AGE," P.191-200

Have you entered the storehouses of the snow or seen the storehouses of the hail?... From whose womb comes the ice? Who gives birth to the frost from the heavens when the waters become hard as a stone, when the surface of the deep is frozen? *JOB 38:22, 29-30*

Evidence From COMMON SENSE

"Old" Earth age estimates are based on "clocks" that today are moving at extremely slow rates. For example, for many years coral growth rates were thought to be very slow, implying that coral reefs are hundreds of thousands of years old. More accurate measurements under ideal growth conditions reveal that even the largest coral formation could be as young as 3,400 years old. **In fact, most straightforward dating methods also indicate a very young earth.** Here are a few examples:

1. The development of the total **population** of our planet could be reached in less than 4,000 years based on all known historical population growth rates.
2. The known rate of decay for the earth's **magnetic field** indicates that it could not possibly be older than 10,000 years.
3. The rim of **Niagra Falls** is wearing back at a known rate so that it could not be much older than 5,000 years.
4. The entire **Mississippi River Delta** can easily be accounted for in 5,000 years.
5. **Volcanism** alone is spewing out so much lava and water that all the water in the oceans and the entire crust of the earth would have been created in 1/10 the time given by evolution for the age of the earth.

In addition to these, there are **many more examples** which clearly indicate that the earth has not been here as long as we have been led to believe.

In the Beginning, 7ᵀᴴ Ed., p.28
The Young Earth, p. *45-118*

The Bible implies that the age of the earth is about 6,000 years. God included precise genealogies in both the Old and the New Testaments to give us the approximate age of the earth all the way back to Adam.

Evidence From
ANATOMY

God created our bodies with features suited for their required functions. By starting with this truth it becomes apparent that back problems are the result of poorly maintained muscles or abuse–rather than inadequate design. The curve of our lumbar (lower) spine is toward the front–the opposite of apes. This is thought by evolutionists to be the result of mankind adapting to upright posture. Yet this forward curvature serves a beautiful purpose. Like the arch of a bridge, it adds strength, allowing a person to lift more weight (proportionally) than an ape with its opposite spine. The vertebrae of the human spine also increase in size toward the bottom. Four-legged animals have uniform-sized bones all along their spinal column. If we evolved from four-legged creatures, why are our spinal columns designed so differently?

There is much we can learn from the design of the human spine. Mankind has only recently learned to produce strong yet lightweight building structures by sandwiching foam materials between solid plates. Yet the bones of the spinal column have been "foam-filled" with canceleous bone (an open, latticed, or porous structure) surrounded by harder cortical bone. Our spinal bones are also designed like radial-ply tires, with each disc having radial-ply fibers. This construction makes a healthy disc stronger than solid bone.

When one examines the way the human body is formed and how it works, one can't help but be in awe of the Master Designer. **It's like looking at a beautiful painting and seeing the artist's signature.**

CREATION MAGAZINE, 25:1, 2/03, p.25-27

Give unto the LORD the glory due unto his name; worship the LORD in the beauty of holiness.

PSALM 29:2 KJV

Evidence From GEOLOGY

In the early 1800s it was noticed that certain fossils are usually preserved in sedimentary rock layers that lie above other types of fossils. After the theory of evolution was proposed, it was concluded that the upper organisms must have evolved after the lower organisms. Next, geologic ages were associated with layers containing certain extinct "index fossils." Those ages were extended to similar animals and plants based on the assumption that evolution is a fact. Fossil animals found in the same layers were assumed to have evolved about the same time. These early geologists did not realize that there were alternative explanations for how these fossils or rocks formed.

Noah's Flood also explains the general tendency for sea creatures to be found in the lowest rock layers and more "complex" land animals to be found in higher layers. Even on a worldwide scale it is reasonable to expect that marine animals would be buried first, followed by amphibians, with land mammals last due to their mobility and environment. Evolutionists simply interpret the data incorrectly because they deny the reality of the worldwide Flood.

Geological formations are almost always dated by their fossil content–which, as stated above, assumes evolution. Yet, evolution is supposedly shown by the sequence of fossils. This circular reasoning does not prove evolution but shows the poor logic and faulty reasoning inherent in evolution.

IN THE BEGINNING, 7ᵀᴴ ED., p.28-29

" 'This is what the Sovereign LORD says: Woe to the foolish prophets who follow their own spirit and have seen nothing!' "

EZEKIEL 13:3

Evidence From COMMON SENSE

It is not uncommon for students to complete 12 years of schooling without being exposed to any of the evidence for creation. Thus, many adults are either totally opposed to creation or consider the subject completely irrelevant. Yet there are thousands of well-documented books, videos, and periodicals available on the evidence for creation. **Why are more people not being exposed to this evidence?** Primarily because there is a strong form of censorship on this issue.

Libraries seldom carry technical books dealing with the scientific evidence for creation, because these books are not on the approved library resource lists. A recent survey of the Midland, MI, public library revealed over 200 books on cosmic, chemical, and biological evolution but only two books on intelligent design. **Not a single technical volume** was available showing the evidence for a worldwide flood or young Earth.

Most public schools do not deal with the evidence, because they do not want the controversy. It is a common practice in school systems to discourage discussion on controversial subjects such as abortion, homosexuality, and evolution. Even in debate class, when the students can choose the topics, the creation/evolution discussion is often taboo.

Given this supression of the evidence for creation, is it any surprise that the subject is considered irrelevant to so many people? It is not a lack of evidence supporting creation which prevents its being accepted, but a subtle form of censorship which keeps most people from seeing the evidence.

- Bruce Malone

For the wrath of God is revealed from heaven against all ungodliness and unrighteousness of men, who suppress the truth in unrighteousness.

Romans 1:18 NKJV

SEPTEMBER

September

God Cares For You

As a creature of the Lord's,
God shows He loves me,too.
And I am just a bird—
Much more He cares for *you!*

The Bible says God guides us,
He tells us where to feed.
Now if God cares for animals,
He'll *surely* meet *your* need!

So *don't get scared and worry*
About things of this earth.
God says He will protect you;
To *Him,* you have *great worth.*

And when a worry tempts you,
Quick, *lay it at God's feet.*
Allow the Lord to show you
That *trusting* Him is sweet.

But you must take that first step;
Refuse to fret and fear.
Fill up your mind with Scripture,
And *let Christ draw you near.*

Look at the birds of the air; they do not sow or reap or
store away in barns, and yet your heavenly Father feeds them.
Are you not much more valuable than they?   *Matthew 6:26*

Evidence From PSYCHOLOGY

Psychology, the study of the mind of man, points to the uniqueness of man in creation. **Since man was made in the image of God, he has capabilities far beyond any other creature.** The following is a partial list of attributes that are uniquely human:

Complex emotions
  Individual creativity
    Moral consciousness
      Appreciation of beauty
        Ability to think abstractly
          Capacity to love and worship God
            Ability to articulate symbolic speech

No animal shares these characteristics. Man stands above the rest of creation in his abilities, attributes, and accomplishments. Man's very uniqueness is a stamp of God's handiwork.

THE GENESIS RECORD, P.74

Then God said, "Let us make man in our image, in our likeness..."

GENESIS 1:26

Evidence From PHYSICS

Scientists have been measuring the earth's magnetic field since 1835. **Indirect measurements show that the overall strength of the earth's magnetic field has consistently decreased with time.** It is the rate at which the earth's magnetic field is decreasing which is astounding–it has lost 50% of its strength in the last 1,400 years!

This is not a problem as long as the earth is relatively young; but if the earth is much older than 10,000 years, no life could have existed on earth, because the magnetic field would have been so strong. If the earth is almost five billion years old, why is its magnetic field less than 10,000 years old? **Could the earth be much younger than we have been led to believe?**

Observations of rapid reversals of the earth's magnetic field are also a problem for scientists who believe in an earth of great age. Various observations have shown that in the past the earth's magnetic field has reversed over a very short time period (days to months). Catastrophic upheavals in the earth's molten core during a worldwide Flood can easily explain these rapid reversals. **No other mechanism can adequately explain the short time period reported for these reversals.** These magnetic field reversals would have caused an even more rapid decay of total field strength–indicating a maximum possible age for the earth even less than 10,000 years.

PROC. OF THE 2ND INTERNATIONAL CONFERENCE ON CREATIONISM, "PHYSICAL MECHANISM FOR REVERSALS OF THE EARTH'S MAGNETIC FIELD DURING THE FLOOD," VOL. II, 1991

"The Almighty is beyond our reach and exalted in power..."

JOB 37:23

Evidence From COMMON SENSE

If evolution is true, then the earth must be billions of years old, the solar system must be billions of years old, and the universe must be billions of years old. Furthermore, the more we understand just how complex life is, the more *time* evolution needs to make the impossible seem possible. Since Darwin first proposed his controversial theory more than 160 years ago, the accepted age of the earth and universe has steadily risen. **As each new dating method has come along with an older date, the new date has been rapidly accepted and the previous methods simply discarded.** By hiding the "origins question" behind billions of years, the unsolvable problems of evolution are made to look more feasible.

Our media and textbooks have implied for well over a century that this almost **unimaginable age** is correct. Rarely do they examine the shaky assumptions or examine the mounting evidence for a *young* earth, solar system, and universe. Most people naively accept the idea that the earth and universe are extremely old and base all of their perceptions on this assumption.

The majority of dating techniques indicate that the earth and solar system are quite young–probably less than 10,000 years. **The primary reason a young age is rejected is *not* lack of evidence.**

In the Beginning, 7ᵀᴴ Ed., p.31

...Has not God made foolish the wisdom of the world?

1 Corinthians 1:20

Evidence From ANTHROPOLOGY

Paleontologists have been searching for transitional bones linking modern man to some apelike creature for over a century. **Java Man, discovered by Eugene DuBois in the early 1890s, was one of the first** *proposed* **links.** DuBois reasoned that if he was going to find the ancestor of an apelike creature in the process of turning into a man, he should go to where apes currently lived. DuBois went to the South Pacific island of Java and found a variety of fossilized bones. For decades he promoted these fossils as proof of the existence of "apeman".

These bones consisted of a very *apelike skull cap* found in the same vicinity of a *humanlike thigh bone.* The thigh bone was found one year later and about 46 feet away from the skull cap. It wasn't until many years later, when very little additional evidence had been found to support the apeman concept, that Dubois' find was widely accepted as evidence for the existence of apeman. **Only after this wide acceptance had occurred did DuBois reveal that** *fully human bones* **had been found in the** *same deposit.* If fully human bones were found in the same location, how could Java man be the ancestor of humans?

This is the quality of the evidence which is still being used to promote the idea that man evolved from animals. The Bible clearly states that man was created from the beginning–in God's image. **The physical evidence** clearly supports this biblical truth.

BONES OF CONTENTION, P.86-120
THE ILLUSTRATED ORIGINS
ANSWER BOOK, P. 36

Then God said, "Let us make man in our image, in our likeness..."

GENESIS 1:26

Evidence From BOTANY

Gypsy moth caterpillars can rapidly strip every leaf from a large number of trees. **Since trees are rooted to the ground and cannot escape, it would appear that trees are helpless against such hungry insects.** Yet seldom is an entire grove of trees destroyed. Scientists have wondered why individual trees, rather than whole groves, are usually affected. Perhaps the trees are not as defenseless as we thought.

Botanists have discovered that when facing a threat, even trees can begin to defend themselves. A variety of trees–including beech, poplar, sugar maple, and red oak–communicate with each other by releasing chemicals called pheromones into the air. Before insects attacking one tree move on, the second tree has already begun to defend itself. **When notified by other trees of the attack, many trees begin to manufacture an array of poisons.** Some of the poisons make their leaves impossible to digest, while others kill insects on contact. Some trees can make as many as eight poisons at once, and many can change the types of poison that are made from year to year.

It is difficult to believe that all of these defense mechanisms could have simply evolved. Isn't it far more logical to attribute such design to an intelligent Designer who created specific defense systems so that organisms could survive in our fallen world?

LETTING GOD CREATE YOUR DAY
VOL. 2, P.39

Let the field be joyful, and all that is therein: then shall all the trees of the wood rejoice.

PSALM 96:12 KJV

Evidence From BIOLOGY

The insect commonly known as the locust is a remarkable creation. One type of female locust has an ovipositor (a sort of knife) located in front of her mid-section. When she is ready to deposit eggs she will land on a suitable tree branch and use the ovipositor to make slits in the bark. She then deposits her eggs inside the bark and goes away, never to see her offspring. After the baby locusts hatch, they crawl down the tree, burrow into the ground, and live on the juices from the roots of the tree. **_Seventeen years later_ they come to the surface of the ground as full-grown locusts.**

It has been reported that some locusts come to the surface seventeen years later *to the day*! The theory of evolution can not account for the locust. God's creativity is beyond comprehension.

EVOLUTION IN THE LIGHT OF SCRIPTURE, SCIENCE AND SENSE, P.37

Praise be to the LORD God...who alone does marvelous deeds.

PSALM 72:18

Evidence From
PHYSICS

The little publicized fact of radiocarbon dating is that all organic matter has a "background level" of radiocarbon. To understand the incredible implications of this fact, you must understand how radiocarbon dating works.

As nitrogen in our upper atmosphere is bombarded by cosmic rays, some of it is turned into radioactive ^{14}C molecules, which are uniformly dispersed throughout all living things. **Once an organism dies, it stops taking in ^{14}C. It begins to deteriorate at a rate of 50% every 5,730 years.** A million years later there could not be a single atom of ^{14}C remaining.

Radiocarbon labs have found that essentially *every* previously living organic molecule has approximately 0.3% of the ^{14}C that we find in today's atmosphere. Coal, natural gas, oil, shells, even unfossilized dinosaur bones still have measurable levels of ^{14}C. At the known ^{14}C deterioration rate, for 0.3% ^{14}C to be left in organic molecules, they must be less than 46,000 years old. **They could not possibly be millions of years old.**

Radiocarbon experts have taken extreme measures to eliminate all possible sources of modern contamination, yet they have been totally unsuccessful in eliminating this "inherant" ^{14}C. The implication is staggering. Since radioactive carbon is still present in every buried organic molecule (all of which are assumed to be many *millions of years* old), these molecules must have been alive quite recently. This inescapable conclusion from the data collected from radiocarbon labs around the world is not publicized, because scientists are trained to believe that the earth is billions of years old.

PROC. OF THE 5TH INTERNAT. CONF. ON CREATION, "MEASURABLE ^{14}C IN FOSSILIZED ORGANIC MATERIALS...", P.127-142

[Instruct people] not to occupy themselves with myths and endless genealogies that promote speculation rather than the divine training...

1 TIMOTHY 1:4   RSV

Evidence From ASTRONOMY

Stars are thought to have taken millions of years to form after the initial "big bang" spewed matter through the expanding universe. According to the current theory of stellar evolution, a star goes through several stages. First, under the effects of gravity, gas molecules supposedly come together until they ignite a nuclear reaction in the star's interior. No one really understands how this can happen. Next the star burns brightly for hundreds of millions of years before expanding into a "red giant." Eventually this red giant slowly collapses to form a white dwarf. Sirius B is said to be a white dwarf star. **Sirius B is a huge mystery for those who believe the accepted theory of stellar evolution.**

Both Egyptian astronomers (2000 B.C.) and the Roman senator Cicero (50 B.C.) described Sirius B as a red star. Other ancient writers called Sirius B "more red than Mars." One of the most famous astronomers in history, Ptolemy (150 A.D.), listed Sirius as one of six red stars. There can be no question that Sirius was red. Yet today Sirius B has become a white dwarf star. **According to modern evolutionary assumptions, it should take at least 100,000 years for a red giant to collapse into a white dwarf star.** It is still hotly debated how the red giant Sirius B became a white dwarf in less than 2,000 years.

Sirius B shines forth as a beacon, casting doubt on the most basic theories of stellar evolution and the gradual formation of our universe.

LETTING GOD CREATE YOUR DAY,
VOL. 2, P.133

"My own hand laid the foundations of the earth, and my right hand spread out the heavens; when I summon them, they all stand up together."

ISAIAH 48:13

Evidence From
PHYSICS

Many people believe that the universe is infintely old and has been around forever. They believe that the universe does not have a creator, because the universe is all there is. The fact that the universe is not uniform in temperature disproves this belief.

One of the most fundamental laws of nature is that heat always flows from hot to cold. In other words, left to itself, a hot object eventually cools down. Yet our universe is full of hot objects. If the universe were infinitely old, the temperature throughout the universe should be uniform. Several logical deductions can be drawn from this observation:

- **Since the temperature of the universe is not uniform, the universe is not infinitely old.**

- **If the universe is not infinitely old, it must have had a beginning.**

- **Since the universe had to have a beginning, it must have had a creator; because something cannot come from nothing.**

The Bible is the *only book* which describes the character, methods, and purpose of that Creator. We owe it to ourselves to study both the universe which He made and the book that He has inspired. Both will allow us to know this Creator better.

In the Beginning, 7ᵀᴴ Ed., p.24

O LORD, you are my God; I will exalt you and praise your name, for in perfect faithfulness you have done marvelous things, things planned long ago.

Isaiah 25:1

Evidence From GEOLOGY

There are numerous places in the geologic column where rock material from deep underlying rocks has "oozed" up through cracks into the rock layers above. Solid rock, after being buried for millions of years, would not ooze through cracks.

According to evolutionary geological interpretation, there is a sandstone layer near Colorado's Ute Pass fault which was supposedly laid down under an ancient ocean 500 million years ago. The rock layer directly over this sandstone is allegedly *only* 70 million years old. Some of the sandstone from the "500-million-year-old" rock supposedly oozed up through cracks in the overlying "70-million-year-old" rock layer. To explain this, evolutionary geologists are forced to believe that the underlying sandstone failed to solidify for 430 million years.

A better explanation is that the two rock layers were laid down within a short time span of each other. The lower sandstone layer oozed up through the cracks because the underlying sand had not yet hardened. The structure of the sandstone in the cracks is identical to the structure in the underlying rock. This indicates that both layers had to have hardened close to the same time and millions of years have not passed between the formation of these rock layers. These structures, called clastic dikes, are quite common around the world. Rock layers such as these support the conclusion that almost all sedimentary rock is the result of a flood of global proportions.

Why is this better explanation not considered? Could it be because accepting this explanationwhich is the most straightforward interpretation of the datainvalidates the evidence for evolution and an old earth?

Proc. of the 1st International Conference on Creationism, p. 3-15

"Where were you when I laid the foundation of the earth? Tell Me, if you have understanding, who set its measurements...on what were its bases sunk..."

Job 38:4-6 NASV

Evidence From ASTRONOMY

Evolution requires vast amounts of time to make the impossibility of chemicals forming life by themselves seem reasonable. A young earth, however, would have to be the work of a Creator. **There are many ways in which our universe witnesses to its young age**, thereby bringing glory to God, rather than to random-chance processes.

The space probe Mariner 10 studied the magnetic field of the small planet Mercury in 1974 and 1975. **Based on the assumption that the solar system is almost 5 billion years old, scientists assumed that this small planet should long ago have come to equilibrium and lost all of its magnetic field.** To their amazement, scientists discovered that Mercury's magnetic field was still active. If Mercury is only about 6,000 years old (which is consistent with the Bible's history of things), it is no mystery why Mercury would still have a measurable magnetic field. No other satisfactory explanation exists.

LETTING GOD CREATE YOUR DAY, VOL. 4, P.28

The heavens praise your wonders, O LORD, your faithfulness too, in the assembly of the holy ones. For who in the skies above can compare with the LORD?...

PSALM 89:5-6

Evidence From BIOLOGY

There is an amazing relationship between certain types of elephant ear plants and the scarab beetle. It has only been recently learned that many elephant ear plants depend completely on the scarab beetle for pollination. Elephant ears make a flower stalk, called a spadix, which has three different kinds of flowers: male, female, and sterile. The beetles are drawn to help in the pollination process by the sterile flowers, which they love to eat. In the process of crawling around on the spadix to get to the sterile flowers, the beetles also pick up pollen from the male flowers and pollinate the female flowers.

It is amazing that **none of the male or female flowers are ever eaten, even though they look exactly like the sterile flowers!** The plant has produced a sacrificial look-alike in order to attract a specific pollinating insect which has no interest in its reproductive flowers. How could the plant have known to do this? Why would it ever produce a flower useless except for the actions of another creature? This miraculous interdependency had to have been specifically designed.

LETTING GOD CREATE YOUR DAY, VOL. 4, P.29

O Sovereign LORD, you have begun to show your servant your greatness and your strong hand. For what god is there in heaven or on earth who can do the deeds and mighty works you do?

DEUTERONOMY 3:24

Evidence From
BIOLOGY

Scientists have found that schools of the colorful reef fish called wrasse sometimes have no male fish present. At just the right moment, a fully grown adult male suddenly appears. Ocean biologists wondered where these male fish came from. To their amazement, it was discovered that **when there is a shortage of males, one of the females turns into a fully functional male!**

Leaving aside the incredibly complex physical and biological mechanisms required to make this transformation, it takes **astounding faith to believe that a school of female wrasse could have evolved the mental ability to recognize a shortage of males, decide that a sex change was necessary, and then select which female was to become a male.** The physiological ability to change into the opposite sex on demand is in itself an evolutionary impossibility.

God placed incredible creatures such as the wrasse on the earth for our enjoyment and amazement. It also leaves mankind without excuse for believing in their Creator.

LETTING GOD CREATE YOUR DAY, VOL. 4, P.33

Declare his glory among the nations, his marvelous deeds among all peoples. For great is the LORD and most worthy of praise; he is to be feared above all gods.

PSALM 96: 3-4

Evidence From ARCHAEOLOGY

Those who reject the idea that God was the Creator of man *(Genesis 1:26; 2:7)* **claim that man was really the creator of God (or gods).** Atheists argue that man was polytheistic (believed in many gods) at first and that he personified these multiple gods from various forces of nature that he feared and didn't understand. They believe that the Jews were the first people to develop the idea of monotheism (belief in one God). Archaeological investigations do not support this.

Historical surveys show that even the earliest records of human civilization believed in one God, and that polytheism crept in to replace this original belief. Noted Egyptologist Sir William M.F. Petrie affirmed that monotheism has been found to be the original belief of all cultures that can be traced back to their roots. The evidence clearly supports biblical teaching.

God created man to worship Him alone. As man disobeyed God and began worshiping other "gods," he has harmed himself in innumerable ways.

Biblical Studies in the Light of Archaeology, p. 5,6

If you violate the covenant of the LORD
your God, which he commanded you,
and go and serve other gods and bow down to them, the
LORD's anger will burn against you, and you will quickly
perish from the good land he has given you. *Joshua 23:16*

Evidence From
COMMON SENSE

Spontaneous generation (the emergence of life from nonliving matter) has never been observed. All observations have shown that life comes only from life. This has been observed so consistently that it is called the *law* **of biogenesis.** The theory of evolution conflicts with this law by claiming that life came from nonliving matter through natural processes. Yet all of our knowledge of chemistry, thermodynamics, and probability says that this could not possibly happen.

Even though this law of science states that life does not come from nonlife, evolutionists choose their belief in evolution over observable science. **Evolution is clearly faith masquerading as science.**

The Bible says God created all life and that He created it instantaneously during creation week. **What we observe in nature confirms what we read in God's Holy Word.**

In the Beginning, 7th Ed., p.5

Then God said, "Let the earth sprout vegetation, plants yielding seed, and fruit trees bearing fruit after their kind...and every living creature...and every winged bird...cattle and creeping things and beasts of the earth after their kind"; and it was so.

Genesis 1:11,21,24 NAS

Evidence From
MICROBIOLOGY

Inside of the intestinal track of termites live vast numbers of microscopic protozoa. These microorganisms enable termites to digest wood. **The microscopic parasites eat the cellulose wood structure but share enough nutrients to keep their termite host alive.** In order to confirm the relationship between the termites and their protozoa, scientists exposed termites to conditions that killed the protozoa but not the host termites. Everything seemed normal and the termites continued to eat wood until they dropped dead 10 to 20 days later. Both the termites and these specific protozoa within the termites survive because of a mutually beneficial relationship. Neither can live without the other.

This type of mutually beneficial arrangement is quite common in nature. It is also a strong argument against the evolutionary hypothesis. **How did either of these creatures survive without the other one present?** No one knows. According to evolution, termites and their parasites are so different that they would have evolved independently. The mechanisms of evolution do not explain how either creature could have evolved separately, let alone both at once, each dependent on the other.

EVOLUTION IN THE LIGHT OF SCRIPTURE, SCIENCE AND SENSE, P.39

...you have done marvelous things, things planned long ago.

ISAIAH 25:1

SEPTEMBER 17

Evidence From
THE FOSSIL RECORD

A fascinating set of humanlike footprints was found in mud that had turned to rock at Laetoli in the east African country of Tanzania. A team headed by Mary Leaky found a sequence of apparently modern human footprints, which were dated at 3.7 million years–long before humans should have evolved. **Experts looking at the prints confirmed that these footprints were identical to those made by modern humans who habitually walk barefoot.**

National Geographic Magazine even featured these footprints on its monthly cover in April 1979. The footprints themselves looked like completely modern, barefoot human footprints. Yet they were found in rock strata where humans were not yet supposed to exist. So what did National Geographic feature on its cover? You guessed it–the picture of an apelike creature making the prints.

If human feet made any of these prints, then evolutionary chronology is drastically wrong. Rather than deal honestly with this possibility, the artists placed an apelike creature in the tracks. We need to let the facts direct our conclusions rather than let our bias blind us to the evidence.

In the Beginning, 7ᵀᴴ Ed., p.30
www.Apologetics Press.org

How great is God–beyond our understanding! The number of his years is past finding out.

Job 36:26

Evidence From BIOLOGY

The loon is designed quite differently than almost all other birds. While the bodies of most birds are designed as light and aerodynamic as possible, the loon's body is heavier, allowing it to sink until only its head is above water. **It controls its ability to float by inflating or deflating tiny air sacs under its skin.** When flying at high altitude, where the air is thin, the loon can conserve oxygen by limiting the flow of blood to its massive leg muscles.

The loon also has a perfectly developed reflex which limits the flow of blood to its wings and digestive tract during underwater dives. This allows the loon to hold its breath for long periods of time. Although an average dive lasts about 40 seconds, three-minute dives that cover 300 to 400 yards are quite common. **Astounding dives have been documented where loons have held their breath for as long as 15 minutes while swimming underwater for over 2 miles.**

Both common sense and the laws of probability tell us that these many unique abilities could not have evolved by chance processes such as random mutations. The loon could not have developed its unique diving ability in some step-at-a-time manner. It would have starved to death long before it caught its first fish. The system had to work perfectly from the beginning.

Character Sketches, Vol.III, p.49

For you are great and do marvelous deeds; you alone are God.

Psalm 86:10

Evidence From BIOLOGY

The octopus has no bones, so it can slip through any opening large enough to allow its hard beak to pass. The rest of the organs contained in the dome-shaped head are so soft they can be flattened almost to the thickness of a sheet of paper! **A 60-pound octopus can pass through a two-inch hole!** (This would be like pushing an eight-year-old child through an opening the size of a silver dollar.)

The octopus has eight arms independently controlled by self-contained nervous systems. If an arm is torn off, it can move away from the body and protect the octopus by distracting its enemies. The remote nervous system within the limb quickly seals off the blood flow to limit bleeding. The octopus can also quickly regrow lost limbs.

Each octopus arm has a double row of up to 240 suckers, which range in size from a pinpoint to two and one half inches in diameter. **The combined gripping strength of the arms is over 2,000 pounds.** Because the suckers can lose their gripping strength when the lining becomes worn, the octopus regularly rubs its arms together by coiling and uncoiling them rapidly. This removes the old skin and allows it to be replaced with a new smooth lining.

One truly wonders how all of these unique characteristics simply evolved by chance. The unique characteristics of the octopus point to a creature of design, not random-chance mutational processes.

CHARACTER SKETCHES, VOL. III, P.59-62

Many, O LORD my God, are the wonders you have done....

PSALM 40:5

Evidence From
BIOLOGY

The octopus has three distinct layers in its skin, and each layer contains remarkable tiny elastic sacs of red, yellow, and blue coloring. When threatened, the octopus can make each sac 60 times larger than its original size. An adult octopus can have as many as two million of these tiny spots of color spread over its entire body. **By shrinking some sacs and stretching others, an octopus can change color almost instantly.** When frightened, all of the sacs shrink, making the octopus white. When angry, only the red sacs open, turning its whole body red. When hiding in the green seaweed, it can mix blue and yellow to produce green. When crawling on a gravel ocean floor, it turns to a salt-and-pepper color. **It can even make stripes and polka dots** when resting on patterned backgrounds.

This ability to camouflage helps the octopus hunt for food and hide from its enemies. Is there any reasonable probability that this complicated mechanism could have evolved by chance mutations?

CHARACTER SKETCHES, VOL.III, P.59-62

How many are your works, O LORD! In wisdom you made them all; the earth is full of your creatures. There is the sea, vast and spacious, teeming with creatures beyond number—living things both large and small.
PSALM 104:24-25

Evidence From PSYCHOLOGY

In his best-selling novel *The Closing of the American Mind*, Alan Bloom made the following startling conclusion; "There is one thing a professor can be absolutely certain of: almost every student entering the university believes, or says that he believes, that truth is relative."

Once absolute truth is rejected, truth becomes situational and subjective. In other words, each of us can decide, based on our current situation, what we want to be true at a given moment. This is called "maximum autonomy." Any notion that God has authority over our will, spirit, or actions is considered narrow-minded and limiting. Such ideas can be very inviting. But there is a catch that comes with all this freedom: it comes attached to the idea that we are an accident and that everything that exists (including ourselves) are mere products of time plus chance. Once this idea is accepted, it is impossible to believe that anything really matters, for whatever anyone *does*, *creates*, *changes*, or *enhances* is no less an accident–because it is being done by an accident. So where is the value of anything? Of what value is life?

When people substitute their own arbitrary values for the absolute truths which our God and Creator revealed to us through the Bible, they selfishly do what is most beneficial for themselves, to the detriment of society.

Closing of the American Mind, P.25
Piercing the Darkness, P.566

Trust in the Lord with all your heart, and lean not on your own understanding; In all your ways acknowledge Him, and He shall direct your paths.
Proverbs 3:5,6 NKJV

Evidence From ANATOMY

The brain has over 10 billion nerve cells and 100 billion glia cells (which provide the biological "batteries" for brain activity). These cells float in a jellied mass, sifting through information, storing memories, creating what we call consciousness, etc. Over 120 trillion connections tie these cells together. **The brain sends out electrical impulses at almost 300 mph and receives 2,000 responses per second from each nerve center in the body.** The brain continuously receives signals from 137,000,000 light receptors in the eyes, 100,000 hearing receptors in the ears, 3,000 taste buds, 30,000 heat sensors on the skin, 250,000 cold sensors, and 500,000 touch sensors.

The brain does not move, yet consumes 25% of the blood's oxygen supply. The brain is constantly bathed in blood and receives 20% of all the blood pumped from the heart. If the blood flow is interrupted for 15 to 30 seconds, unconsciousness results. If blood flow is cut off to the brain for more than four minutes, permanent brain damage results.

How can anyone believe this magnificent structure was not designed?

The Revelation of God and Nature, p.11-12
Fearfully and Wondrously Made, p.188-189

He performs wonders that cannot be fathomed, miracles that cannot be counted.

Job 9:10

Evidence From
THE WORLDWIDE FLOOD

Is there enough water to cover all of the earth's preflood mountains in the global Flood that the Bible talks about? For many years experts doubted this.

It was only after the ocean depths were mapped that scientists realized the enormous volume of water on this planet. There is ten times more volume of water in our oceans than the total volume of land rising above the water. Most of the earth's mountains consist of tipped and buckled sedimentary layers. Since these sediments were initially deposited underwater as nearly horizontal layers, the mountains must have been pushed up after the sediments were deposited.

If the mountain ranges around the world were to return to their pre-flood, non-buckled state while the ocean basins were allowed to rise in compensation for this downward flow of mass, **the oceans would again flood the entire earth with water over a mile deep!** There is plenty of water on our planet to account for the Flood described in the sixth, seventh, and eighth chapters of Genesis.

IN THE BEGINNING, 7ᵀᴴ ED., P.40

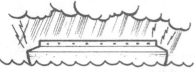

**And the waters prevailed
exceedingly upon the earth; and
all the high hills, that were under the whole heaven, were covered.**

GENESIS 7:19 KJV

Evidence From
CREATION FOUNDATION

Many Christians accept one form or another of a "gap theory" to try to accommodate the supposed evidence for an almost five-billion-year-old earth. According to the gap theory, there are billions of missing years between Genesis 1:1 (when God created the heavens and the earth) and Genesis 1:2 (when the earth was formless and void). This time gap is supposedly when Satan fell and the entire earth was later re-created. Those who accept this idea believe the missing gap of time harmonizes the biblical claim of a recent creation and the evolutionary claim of an old earth. **However, the gap theory ignores biblical contradictions and undermines much of Scripture.** For instance:

1. Noah's Flood (referred to repeatedly throughout the Bible) laid down the current worldwide fossil record. There is no evidence for any previous catastrophe. The idea of any catastrophe before Noah's Flood is pure speculation, because the more recent Flood mentioned throughout Scripture would have destroyed all of the evidence.
2. All of the scientific dating methods indicating a young earth must be ignored.
3. Exodus 20:11 states that the heavens and the earth and all that is in them were created in 6 days. Plants were created on day 3 and the sun on day 4. How does this allow billions of years for an enormous gap of time?
4. Romans 5:12 says death entered the world by the sin of one man, Adam. Yet the gap theory implies that there were billions of years of death prior to mankind. Therefore man's rebellion is not responsible for death. Either the Bible or the gap theory is wrong.

THE REVISED ANSWERS BOOK, P.57-74

• **Wherefore, as by one man [Adam] sin entered into the world, and death by sin; and so death passed upon all men, for that all have sinned.**

ROMANS 5:12 KJV

Evidence From
BOTANY

Imagine a factory capable of converting nothing but dirt, air, water, and sunshine into millions of different useful and/or edible products! The inventor would become a billionaire!

As it turns out, the invention has already happened. These factories not only produce edible goods, but textile fibers, lumber, rubber, oils, and innumerable derivative products from the basic raw materials of dirt, air, water, and sunshine. **It all happens continuously in the most efficient manufacturing system imaginable: plants.** In addition to providing almost every imaginable necessity for life, plants also allow us to breathe. If it weren't for plants, we would suffocate, because plants produce the oxygen we need while using up the carbon dioxide which we exhale.

Take time to ponder and wonder at the incredible balance of this system which has been so skillfully conceived by our Creator.

UNLOCKING THE MYSTERIES OF CREATION, PREM. ED., P.44-45

He makes grass grow for the cattle, and plants for man to cultivate–bringing forth food from the earth.

PSALM 104:14

Evidence From ARCHAEOLOGY

Although there are many references to crucifixion in literature of the early centuries of the Christian era, the first physical evidence was found in June of 1968.

"On Ammunition Hill in northeastern Jerusalem, an ossuary (stone box) was found containing the bones of a young man named Johanan, who had plainly been crucified. This find has been dated between 6 and 66 A.D. A crease in the radial bones revealed that he had been nailed in the forearms (*cheiras*, rendered 'hands' [John 20:27] can also mean 'arms'). The ossuary also contained the heel bones still transfixed by a four and one-half inch iron nail. The leg bones had also been shattered, as in the case of the thieves who were crucified on either side of the Lord (John 19:31-32)."

Every finding of archaeology confirms the documentation of the Bible. The cruel method of execution by crucifixion was indeed common in the ancient Roman empire. Understanding that the all-powerful mastermind Creator of the entire universe suffered this incredibly cruel form of death, specifically as payment for our sins, is tremendously humbling and beyond our ability to comprehend.

BIBLICAL STUDIES IN THE LIGHT OF ARCHAEOLOGY,
P.43

Here they crucified him [Jesus], and with him two others—one on each side and Jesus in the middle.

JOHN 19:18

Evidence From
BIOLOGY

Consider just a few of the abilities of the red squirrel and judge for yourself whether design by a Creator or random-chance mutations seems more likely to have produced it:

1. When falling, the red squirrel's **tail and legs** spread out to catch as much air as possible. This slows down the fall and distributes the impact evenly over the squirrel's body, so it can withstand a 100-foot fall without injuring itself!
2. The squirrel's **eyesight** is so exact that it can determine precisely how far something is by a process called "parallax." This is a process whereby the exact position of an object is located by looking at it from two different angles. The squirrel lifts its head several times to estimate the exact distance before jumping.
3. **Sensory hairs** located on the squirrel's feet, forelegs, underside, and on the base of its tail can sense the difference between a strong and weak branch so it can run along branches and instantly leap to another one if a weak branch is detected, all without missing a step.
4. It uses its **whiskers** to measure the size of a hole so that it may enter without getting stuck.
5. It has specially equipped **sharp claws** and grows a **winter cover of hair** on its feet, which allow it to hold on to branches without falling off, even in a 40-mile-per-hour wind.

CHARACTER SKETCHES, VOL.III, P.71-74

Your love, O LORD, reaches to the heavens,
your faithfulness to the skies....O LORD, you
preserve both man and beast.

PSALM 36:5-6

Evidence From ARCHAEOLOGY

The story of the conquest of Jericho as the children of Israel entered the Promised Land seems to have been vindicated by archaeology. According to the Bible, the Israelites marched around the city of Jericho seven times before offering a great shout. At that very moment the walls of this well-fortified city simply fell down. The Bible also states that the Isrealites burned the whole city.

Excavation of the ancient city reveals that at one occupation level, probably corresponding to Joshua's time, the walls of Jericho were found to have literally fallen "down flat" (Joshua 6:20). It was also found that the city had been *burned* at that time, rather than looted. Once again we find agreement between archaeology and the biblical account of history.

SCIENCE AND THE BIBLE, P. 97

When the trumpets sounded, the people shouted, and at the sound of the trumpet, when the people gave a loud shout, the wall collapsed.... Then they burned the whole city and everything in it....

JOSHUA 6:20,24

Evidence From ASTRONOMY

Theories on the specifics of how God created can change as more information becomes available. Many original measurements of the sun's diameter indicated that it was shrinking far too fast to have allowed its age to be billions of years old. Furthermore, the original measurements of the neutrinos (a subatomic particle produced during nuclear fusion) produced by the sun seemed to confirm that nuclear reactions did not account for all of the energy being emanated by the sun. However, more recent measurements of both shrinkage and neutrinos have confirmed that nuclear power does indeed account for the energy emanated from stars and there is no rapid shrinkage of the sun occurring.

Yet, it is the modern scientific assumption of naturalism which have produced most major blunders of modern science. For instance, the area of the horse-head nebula within the constellation of Orion was for years thought to be an area of "star formation" because new points of light seemed to appear within the nebular gas field. However, it is now acknowledged that the "new stars" are actually stars behind the gas cloud which became visible as the nebula spread out and dissipated. Not a single new star has ever been shown to have appeared, yet thousands have disintegrated in supernovas. This is a strong support of the creation model which states that God made the stars on day 4 of creation. Hydrogen gas simply does not condense to form stars within the vacuum of space.

ANSWERS MAGAZINE, DECEMBER 4, 2007

And this is my prayer: that your love may abound more and more in knowledge and depth of insight, so that you may be able to discern what is best and may be pure and blameless until the day of Christ...

PHILIPPIANS 1: 9-10

Evidence From
GEOLOGY

High oil, gas, and water pressures exist in pockets under the surface of our planet. This is why gushers occurred in Texas and Oklahoma in the early 1900s. Once the rock containing the oil was penetrated, oil would shoot hundreds of feet into the air due to the extremely high pressure in the underground oil reservoir.

The problem for evolution is that this pressure should not be there if the rocks are millions of years old. Observe what happens to helium-filled balloons. Even highly impermeable aluminum-coated balloons lose helium with time and sink to the floor. Based on the known permeability of rock layers, the same thing should have happened long ago to underground oil, gas, and water reservoirs. If these fluids had been trapped more than 10,000 years, leakage would have dropped the pressure far below what it is today. This indicates that underground oil, gas, and water must have been trapped much more recently.

IN THE BEGINNING, 7th ED., P.31

For this is what the LORD says–he who created the heavens, he is God; he who fashioned and made the earth, he founded it...he says: "I am the Lord and there is no other."

Isaiah 45:18

October OCTOBER

The Full Armor of God

I'm a little armadillo;
  My armor is quite strong.
If used as it's intended,
  It helps me get along.

The Bible speaks of *armor*
  That Christians all should wear.
God says it will protect us
  If worn with utmost care.

The pieces of this armor
  Are written in God's Book.
We all can find each item
  If we take time to look.

The TRUTH is what's first needed;
  We put it in our hearts.
God helps us to be RIGHTEOUS;
  Obedience is our part.

We also should be ready.
  This GOSPEL we should give:
  *"Only through FAITH in Jesus
  Can we in heaven live."*

SALVATION is our helmet;
  It guards our thoughts and minds.
We must know we're God's children
  If *peace* we want to find.

The BIBLE is the last piece.
  Our armor's now in place.
For what we practice from it
  Protects us in life's race.

Therefore put on the FULL ARMOR of God, so that when the day of evil
comes, you may be able to stand your ground. . .   Ephesians 6:13

Evidence From CREATION FOUNDATION

There is much about God that cannot be fully appreciated unless we take time to study and understand what He has created. Romans 1:20 tells us that **man can clearly see God's eternal power and divine nature through what He made and no man will have any excuse for not subjecting himself to God's authority, because of this evidence from creation.**

It is our responsibility to not only study God's Word but also His marvelous creation. We should meditate on what we learn from it if we truly desire to appreciate and know God. Too often we waste our God-given time and abilities. We concentrate on entertaining ourselves and satisfying our physical desires instead of getting to know the One who made us and the world around us. Sadly, we are all too often captivated by man-made things, rather than the awesome creation which is right before our eyes. **We miss so much if we do not cultivate a proper interest in the natural world around us.**

RICH AND TINA KLEISS

"...O LORD, open his eyes so he may see."

2 KINGS 6:17

Evidence From
BIOLOGY

Grunion are fish that lay their eggs on land! Right after the peak of the highest spring tide, the grunions throw themselves onto the beach. Once on land, the females bury themselves up to their gills in the sand and lay their eggs about four inches below the surface. At that moment the males appear, twisting and flopping sideways across the beach. As soon as they bump into the egg-laying females, they saturate the sand with milt in order to fertilize the eggs.

The grunion can survive out of water for 20 minutes, which is plenty of time to lay eggs on the sandy beach and return to the water. The total spawning process usually takes less than three minutes! **Within 24 hours the eyes of the baby fish are already visible in their yolk sacs. Soon after that, blood can be seen circulating in their threadlike bodies.** Ten to fourteen days after the eggs are laid, the pounding of waves on the seashore signals the eggs to hatch. The next high tide returns just in time to wash the fully developed baby grunions back into the water.

Why would the first grunions have ventured onto land? Why lay their eggs on land? How could the males have learned to fertilize the eggs in this way? How did the fish learn to time things so perfectly? Evolution has no answers. Give the glory to our intelligent Creator!

Character Sketches, Vol.III, p.185-187

...**"Holy, holy, holy is the LORD Almighty; the whole earth is full of his glory."**

Isaiah 6:3

Evidence From
ANATOMY

Believers in evolution point to *useless* features, such as the wings of a flightless bird or the tailbone of a human, in an effort to prove that an all-wise and all-powerful God could not have made life. This poor logic assumes that because some things now seem to have no purpose, they were not designed, but just happened.

In reality, it is impossible to prove that any feature is useless. The function may not be known, but additional study inevitably reveals its use. This has happened to almost 200 formerly alleged vestigial organs in humans. For instance, our tailbone is the attachment point for important muscles which allow us to walk in a fully upright manner. The "useless" wings of some birds, such as the ostrich, are said to perhaps have been leftover features from a previously flying creature who has lost the ability to fly. This is a loss of information, not an evolutionary advancement. A better explanation is that the ostrich was designed to show the grand creativity of its Designer and the wings function perfectly as designed–for balance while running, warmth, mating rituals, and scaring predators in our fallen world.

"Useless" organs show a *loss* of functioning features, not the development of new features. This means "useless" organs are actually the opposite of what evolutionists need in order to validate their theory–that is, *increasing complexity* and *information* being added to a creature's DNA code.

THE REVISED AND EXPANDED ANSWERS BOOK,
P.122-125

"Hear this, you foolish and senseless people, who have eyes but do not see, who have ears but do not hear: should you not fear me?" declares the LORD....

JEREMIAH 5:21-22

Evidence From BIBLICAL ACCURACY

Beginning in 1947, more than 500 ancient documents were found in a cave in the region just west of the Dead Sea. These are collectively known as the Dead Sea Scrolls. They include many of the writings we find in the Bible as well as other nonbiblical texts. About 100 of these scrolls, which are written in Hebrew, contain portions of every Old Testament book except Esther. One of the scrolls contains the complete book of Isaiah. These manuscripts date from the last few centuries B.C. to the early part of the 1st century A.D. *The Biblical Archaeologist* (May 1948) called this find "the most important discovery ever made in Old Testament manuscripts..."

The primary impact of this discovery is to show how precisely these scrolls duplicate more recent sources of Old Testament Scriptures. For instance, the Isaiah scrolls, which were written about 125 years before the birth of Jesus, are essentially identical to later copies, transcribed hundreds of years after Christ's birth, from which we have translated modern Bibles. This shows the amazing accuracy and care taken by copyists of the Scriptures. Indeed, God's hand has guided the preservation of the Bible throughout history.

BIBLICAL STUDIES IN LIGHT OF ARCHAEOLOGY, P.3

ADDITIONAL INFORMATION IS FROM
EVIDENCE THAT DEMANDS A VERDICT, P.57
THIS BOOK IS AN EXCELLENT RESOURCE ON
BIBLICAL ACCURACY.

Heaven and earth will pass away, but my words will never pass away.

MATTHEW 24:35

OCTOBER 5

Evidence From
BIOLOGY

Certain jellyfish and polyps (coral) have poisonous stinging capsules called nematocysts which explode when it is necessary for defense or acquiring food. These nematocysts are extremely complex biological structures. In fact, Dr. Thomas A. Stephenson, Professor of Zoology at University College in Wales, says, "They are among the most extraordinary structures in the animal kingdom." Jellyfish with these poisonous nematocysts are the favorite food of some sea slugs, which swallow the highly poisonous nematocysts intact. **The sea slug then transfers the unexploded nematocysts from its digestive system to special sacs in its skin; there they are held ready to explode in defense of the slug.**

How did the first sea slug survive swallowing a poisonous jellyfish? How did the sea slug learn to steal its defense mechanism from another creature? How did the complex transfer mechanism, with special storage sacks, develop? Evolution seems to make sense on the surface, but falls apart as soon as the details are examined. **The complete system of poison handling had to be working perfectly in order for the sea slug to have survived.** Evolution ignores these problems and assumes it all "just happened." God must have created all of these abilities simultaneously, either as latent abilities before the Fall or for survival after the Fall.

EVOLUTION IN THE LIGHT OF SCRIPTURE,
SCIENCE, AND SENSE, P.42-43

I will meditate on all your works and consider all your mighty deeds.

PSALM 77:12

Evidence From
BIOLOGY

The turkey vulture has incredibly farsighted vision capable of seeing dead or dying objects several miles beyond what the human eye can detect. Yet it is designed with dull, weak talons and a thin beak, forcing it to eek out an existence eating rotting flesh or decaying vegetables. Since the vulture eats the remains of animals that have died of disease, it has a digestive tract designed to destroy deadly bacteria (including anthrax!). **The turkey vulture also has the ability to sanitize itself and its surroundings using a special disinfectant found in its own excrement.** The same chemicals which kill the deadly bacteria in its stomach continue to kill the germs outside its body!

Because the vulture's head is usually covered in blood, pieces of rotten flesh, and bacteria, it is especially vulnerable to disease. Therefore, this particular bird was created without feathers from the neck up. As the turkey vulture stands in the sun, the ultraviolet radiation kills any remaining bacteria.

By removing the carcasses of decaying animals, the turkey vulture serves an important purpose of limiting the spread of disease and preventing potential epidemics among both man and beast. One wonders how the turkey vulture could have evolved all of these specialized characteristics. The creation solution is that they were created with the original vulture-type bird. The survival characteristics needed for our fallen world were either given after the Fall or developed from originally created abilities.

Character Sketches, Vol. III, p.121-124

The LORD is righteous in all his ways and loving toward all he has made.

Psalm 145:17

Evidence From
BIOLOGY

The aphid and certain ants are uniquely designed to depend on each other. When an aphid taps into the sap of a plant, the pressure in the plant often pumps more liquid sugar into the aphid than it can use or hold. The excess sap simply flows through the aphid's body and results in droplets of "honeydew" at its tail end. **Aphids allow ants to collect and store this honeydew in their "social stomachs."** The honeydew can be regurgitated and shared with other ants.

When plants no longer provide an aphid with sap, ants will guide the aphids to new plants as far as 150 feet away. Ants have even been known to build fences around aphids to protect them from intruders. During the warm months, aphids bear live young. However, when cold air signals the approach of winter, the aphids switch to producing young by laying eggs. **The ants carry the aphid eggs to their own underground nursery, where they hatch and are cared for until spring.** The aphids are then transported back to the surface, where the ants place them on healthy plants.

God made such mutually beneficial relationships not only to show us His creative power, but also for man to observe and learn from.

CHARACTER SKETCHES, VOL.III, P.135-138

Go to the ant, you sluggard; consider its ways and be wise!

PROVERBS 6:6

Evidence From BIOLOGY

Female aphids come in winged, wingless, and clone varieties. Most female aphids are born wingless; but when food becomes scarce or particular plants become overpopulated, winged females are born. Their ability to fly allows them to leave and begin new colonies where conditions are more favorable. Winged females are also produced in the fall when they mate and lay shiny black eggs. The eggs hatch into nymphs, which go through a complete insect metamorphosis to become adult aphids the next spring.

Aphids exhibit a unique type of reproduction called parthenogenesis. This long name simply means that a female can make exact copies of itself without mating. In warm weather a wingless female can produce 25 identical female clones of itself every day. Within seven to ten days these daughters can begin producing their own babies without mating. **Theoretically, if the young are undisturbed, there could be over 3,700,000 offspring from a single parent in less than a month.** If all lived, aphids could cover the face of the earth in a single summer. Fortunately, these clones are more vulnerable to environmental changes. God provided many mechanisms which hold the aphid population in check. Even in the world before the Fall there must have been mechanisms to control the insect population, although we can only speculate what these mechanisms could have been.

How could the aphids' unique reproductive abilities have evolved by mutations? Does evolution offer any reasonable explanation for how all this developed? If not, how reasonable is the evolutionary belief that nature just did it?

CHARACTER SKETCHES, VOL.III, P.135-138

I know every bird in the mountains, and the creatures of the field are mine.

PSALM 50:11

Evidence From ASTRONOMY

The big bang is a totally inadequate theory of origins because of its apparently irreconcilable problems. These difficulties are seldom talked about in popular literature on the subject. Instead, **the big bang is presented as a fact.** The following are just a few of the many major problems with the big bang theory:

1. **Missing Origin** - Where did the energy originate?
2. **Missing Fuse** - What ignites the big bang?
3. **Missing Star Formation** - No mechanism has been suggested to adequately explain how the planets, stars, and galaxies formed.
4. **Missing Time** - Most dating methods show that the earth, stars, galaxies, and solar system are young, and many methods indicate an age less than 10,000 years. If this is true, there was not enough time for the big bang to have taken place.
5. **Missing Life** - In an evolving universe, life should have developed in many different places apart from Earth. Where is everybody else?

How can science speak about "origins" with such authority when there is so much that man does not understand nor can explain?

ASTRONOMY AND THE BIBLE, P. 89-91

Do you know the laws of the heavens? Can you set up God's dominion over the earth?

JOB 38:33

Evidence From
GEOLOGY

Salt concentration in seawater can be used as a chronometer, because the oceans are getting saltier each year as rivers dump dissolved salts from the continents into the sea. Traditionally, evolutionists have assumed that life evolved in a salty sea, some two to four billion years ago. It is even taught that the mineral composition of our blood is similar to ancient seawater, because this is where the first living cell developed. This belief is wrong, because the composition of our blood is not even remotely similar to the concentrations or types of the various salts in the oceans. Furthermore, **by measuring the rate at which salt is flowing from rivers into the ocean, scientists can estimate the maximum possible age of the current oceans.**

Drs. Steven Austin and Russell Humphreys have done just that in a research paper called *"The Sea's Missing Salt: A Dilemma For Evolutionists."* In their research, they systematically identified all known mechanisms and rates for the addition and removal of salt from the oceans. **This work has shown that there is nowhere near enough salt in the oceans if they are really thousands of millions of years old.** This is true even if the oceans started out as pure distilled water! The oceans could not possibly be old enough for evolution to have taken place.

THE YOUNG EARTH, P.85-87
CREATION MAGAZINE, SEPT. 2000

"In the beginning You laid the foundations of the earth..."

PSALM 102:25

Evidence From THE FOSSIL RECORD

Evolutionists have great difficulty explaining why fossilized animal remains are often found together in what appears to be huge graveyards. Entire shoals containing billions of fossilized fish have been found. They are frequently found in distressed postures with no sign of a scavenger's attack. In other locations billions of fossilized clams can be found washed together and tightly closed (normally when clams die they open up and are eaten by scavengers). Duck-billed dinosaurs (which are not water creatures) have been excavated in a swimming position with their heads thrown back as if something catastrophic killed them. In Sicily, fossil hippopotamus bones are so plentiful that they have been mined as a source of charcoal! Such graveyards are found nowhere in the world today containing organisms awaiting fossilization.

Most modern geologists attempt to explain such finds within the framework of uniformitarianism (the belief that geological phenomena happened in the past at the same very slow rate at which they are occurring today). This assumption, however, cannot explain why such large numbers of fossils are found in graveyards worldwide. Nor does this denial of a worldwide flood adequately explain why so many organisms were buried so rapidly. **A flood as described in the Bible would result in exactly the type of worldwide fossil graveyards that we find.**

EVOLUTION: THE BONE OF CONTENTION, P.11

The waters flooded the earth for a hundred and fifty days.

GENESIS 7:24

Evidence From BIBLICAL UNIQUENESS

Biblical Christianity is absolutely unique because of the nature of its founder, Jesus Christ. Jesus is unique in all of history and literature as seen by this partial list of attributes:

1. More than **300 specific prophecies** of His first coming were written hundreds of years prior to His birth. Each was fulfilled with 100% accuracy.
2. **The virgin birth** stands as unique throughout history.
3. His repeated **claim of divine-human nature** was like no others. He was Creator, Sustainer, and Sacrifice for all. Christ alone claimed to be both fully man and fully God. His miracles were never denied by those who witnessed them.
4. His **sinless life** was attested to by His closest friends, worst enemies, the apostles, and Christ Himself.
5. He both **predicted, arranged, and instituted His death** in a way that could not have been anything but voluntary. (John 10:18)
6. **His resurrection** was the final and greatest proof of His absolute uniqueness and can be documented in both biblical and secular history.

MANY INFALLIBLE PROOFS, P.12-14

O LORD, there is none like You, nor is there any God besides You, according to all that we have heard with our ears.

1 CHRONICLES 17:20 NKJV

Evidence From GEOLOGY

When Mount St. Helens erupted on May 18, 1980, the resulting blast cloud snapped off huge trees for 150 square miles around the mountain. At the same time an avalanche of mud sped down from the top of the mountain into Spirit Lake, causing a wave almost 900 feet high which scraped trees from the slopes adjacent to the lake. Many of these trees ended up in Spirit Lake buried at various levels on the bottom as they slowly sank in an upright position after becoming water-logged. Scuba investigation and side-scanning sonar have identified up to 100,000 upright deposited tree stumps buried at various levels of ash and peat deposits at the bottom of Spirit Lake. **Since Mount St. Helens continues to be active (depositing more material in the lake with time) these upright trees will be buried in what looks like separate geological layers, even though they all came from the same forest.**

Years from now if sediment were to fill the lake and bury the trees in such a way that they became petrified in their present positions, these trees would look like multiple forests buried on top of each other over tens of thousands of years. This is exactly what was assumed to be the origin of the petrified forest at Yellowstone National Park's Specimen Ridge. Many geologists now acknowledge that the Yellowstone petrified trees were from the same standing forest, transported into their current positions by a massive flood catastrophe.

THE YOUNG EARTH, p.115-116
SEARCH FOR THE TRUTH, II-9

The waters flooded the earth for a hundred and fifty days.

GENESIS 7:24

Evidence From GEOLOGY

Visitors on cave tours are almost always told that the large **stalactites and stalagmites have taken tens of thousands or even millions of years** to form. Recent discoveries have shown this is not necessarily so. Consider the following:

1. **A bat (not yet decomposed)** was found cemented inside a stalagmite in Carlsbad Caverns, New Mexico This had to have formed recently and VERY rapidly.
2. **A stalactite a foot long was found hanging under a railroad bridge** in Alliance, Ohio. It obviously formed in a few years, but evolutionary methods would date a foot-long stalactite in a cave as being thousands of years old.
3. In a cave in the Tehuacan Valley of Mexico there is a vast chamber called Hall of the Dead. **Skeletons found in that cave are covered with stalagmites which** scientists have dated almost 3,000 years old.
4. **A five-inch stalactite was found in the man-made Hetch Hetchy tunnel** in California. This stalactite had to have formed in less than 20 years, since this is when the tunnel was built. According to evolutionary dating of caves, a five-inch cave stalactite should be thousands of years old.

Stalactite and stalagmite formation provide no evidence that the earth is extremely old.

EVOLUTION IN THE LIGHT OF SCRIPTURE, SCIENCE, AND SENSE, P.102 - 104

...[God] gives wisdom to the wise and knowledge to the discerning.

DANIEL 2:21

Evidence From BIOLOGY

The more we learn about life, the greater the complexity we find. There were no sophisticated microscopes 150 years ago. Consequently, the leap of complexity from single-to multiple-cell organisms was greatly underestimated. The development of the computer has given us an even greater appreciation for the enormous complexity, extreme miniaturization, and vast storage capabilities of the brain. Consider **a few other giant leaps** that evolutionists must accept in order to hold onto their faith in evolution:

1. **Flight** somehow evolved on at least four different occasions (birds, insects, reptiles, mammals).
2. **Photosynthesis** somehow developed.
3. **Cold-blooded animals** somehow turned into warm-blooded animals.
4. **Floating marine plants** somehow changed into complex plants with roots, stems, and leaf systems.
5. **Placental animals** (the off-spring develop inside of their mother) somehow turned into marsupial animals (their off-spring develop within a pouch).
6. **Egg-laying animals** somehow developed the ability to give live births.
7. Insects somehow learned to totally rearrange themselves and change form in a process called **metamorphosis** (such as a caterpillar transforming into a butterfly).
8. Land mammals and reptiles such as whales, seals, dolphins, ichthyosaurs, and plesiosaurs **somehow crawled back** into the sea and developed all of the specialized organs needed for sea survival.

IN THE BEGINNING, 7<small>TH</small> ED., P.17

Blessed is he...whose hope is in the LORD his God, the Maker of heaven and earth, the sea and everything in them...

PSALM 146:5-6

Evidence From BIBLICAL ACCURACY

God says He chooses the weak things of the world to shame the strong, so no one can boast before Him. The truth of this statement can be seen when we consider the incredible abilities of people with what is called savant syndrome. Such people usually must live with caregivers, because they have developmental disorders and are totally incapable of living in society. Yet they possess extraordinary talents far beyond so-called "normal" people.

1. One "savant" can't count, yet can **instantly sum** the total of the registration numbers on all the boxcars of a train speeding by.
2. A four-year-old blind savant heard a Mozart sonata and went to the piano and played the entire sonata without a mistake. He then went on tour and could play any of **5,000 piano pieces by memory.**
3. A pair of savant twins could **instantly total** the number of letters when shown a printed page.
4. Two brothers who couldn't add the simplest numbers could **instantly name which day of the week** any date in the past or 40,000 years in the future would fall.
5. One savant could listen to **long passages in any language** and repeat them flawlessly without understanding a single word.

God continues to give great and unexplainable intellectual gifts. Yet one has to wonder what abilities we have lost since we rebelled against our Creator–how far we have fallen since the Garden of Eden.

HELPING CHILDREN UNDERSTAND GENESIS AND THE DINOSAURS, P.11-13

...God chose the weak things of the world to shame the strong. He chose the lowly things of this world and the despised things...so that no one may boast before him.

1 CORINTHIANS 1:27-29

Evidence From
MICROBIOLOGY

Science News, Nov. 18, 1994, reported that dinosaur DNA had been identified within unfossilized dinosaur bones found 2,000 feet below the surface of the earth in a Utah coal mine. The DNA did not match any known creature currently alive on Earth. **The find was disputed on the grounds that dinosaur DNA should not have survived the supposed 80 million years.** The DNA fragments also had no similarity to bird DNA (from whom the dinosaurs supposedly evolved). Therefore, this evidence has been largely ignored.

Science News, May 20, 1995, reported that scientists have extracted and revived live bacteria from the stomach of a bee which was encased in amber "over 25 million years ago." Although the work was done with the greatest of efforts to prevent any "modern" bacteria from contaminating the results, many biochemists refute the find because **"DNA spontaneously degenerates to short fragments over a period of several thousand years at moderate temperatures."** Thus, this work has also been ignored because it does not fit the old-earth model.

These are just two examples showing how the assumption of evolution hinders the progress of knowledge. Evidence which does not fit into the "evolutionary mold" is ignored on the basis that it shows evolution–*with its requirement of an ancient earth*–to be wrong. The evidence fits perfectly into the biblical model of Earth history with a relatively recent worldwide burial of organisms. **DNA fragments can still be found, because the earth is relatively young.**

World by Design Newsletter,
Vol 2, no 6; Vol 3, no.3

The fear of the Lord is the beginning of wisdom, and the knowledge of the Holy One is understanding.

Proverbs 9:10

Evidence From ANATOMY

The heart is an eleven-ounce muscle about the size of a large fist. It is the strongest muscle in the body. **Every day this relentless organ beats about 100,000 times and pumps about 1,800 gallons of blood.** A small patch of tissue called the sinus node causes the heart to beat. The function of this node is to send an electric current every 0.8 seconds to certain nerve fibers in the heart muscle. These fibers stimulate muscular contractions that send blood flowing up to 10 miles per hour throughout the body. The blood moves through the body, supplying oxygen to every cell, and then returns to the heart. From the heart it is pumped to the lungs, where it is re-oxygenated and then sent back through the body.

If it took time and intelligence for man to design the fuel pump, cooling system, and lubrication system in a car engine, how can we believe that the human circulatory system (which is a far more complex engineering marvel) happened by the blind forces of nature?

THE HUMAN BODY: ACCIDENT OR DESIGN?, P.38-41

...the life of the flesh is in the blood....

LEVITICUS 17:11 KJV

Evidence From
GENETICS

Mendel's laws of genetics (with slight modern-day refinements) explain the physical variations observed in living things. Mendel's law shows that there is no problem explaining how the great variations in skin, hair, eye color, facial structure, and body size within the human family could have developed beginning from just one man and one woman. Mendel discovered that a gene (unit of heredity) is merely reshuffled from one generation to another. **It is a proven fact that reproduction produces different *combinations of genes*, never *different genes*.**

Evolution requires new and useful genes, but such new information is not created by random recombinations of information within existing genes. This has never been observed by scientific experimentation. Different gene combinations produce the many variations within each "kind" of life (such as the wide variation within the dog "kind"), but a new class of animal has never been produced. It is a fact of science, demonstrated by Gregory Mendel's experiments, that there are limits to such variation.

Breeding experiments and common observations confirm these boundaries. In the book of Genesis God said that He created all life to reproduce after its own kind. Once again, science has proven the Bible to be absolutely correct.

IN THE BEGINNING, 7ᵀᴴ ED., P.5

And God made the beast of the earth according to its kind, cattle according to its kind, and everything that creeps on the earth according to its kind. And God saw that it was good.

GENESIS 1:25 NKJV

Evidence From ASTRONOMY

There are more than 10^{22} stars in the universe, but each one is unique. No two stars have exactly the same properties. This may sound like guesswork, since we have analyzed very few stars in detail; but the conclusion is a certainty. **A star has so many variables that the probability of two identical stars is essentially zero.** These variables include the total number of atoms, the exact composition of elements, its size, and its temperature. Some stars show obvious color and brightness differences. Others require spectroscopic study to detect each star's particular identity or fingerprint.

The Bible states in I Corinthians 15:41 that "star differs from star in splendor." How could ancient man have known this? It is only logical to conclude that the Creator of the stars chose to tell man to include this in the Bible. In Psalm 147:4 the Bible also says that God "determines the number of stars and calls each by name." Truly God's abilities have no limit.

ASTRONOMY AND THE BIBLE, p.56-57

The sun has one kind of splendor, the moon another and the stars another; and star differs from star in splendor.

1 CORINTHIANS 15:41

Evidence From CHEMISTRY

One of the toughest environments in which to maintain adhesion is underwater. Water is known as the universal solvent. It tends to prevent adhesion between two surfaces by diluting, dissolving, dispersing, or simply forming an interface between adhesive layers. **So how do creatures which God created adhere to objects underwater?**

Much to a shipbuilder's chagrin, the mussel is God's champion of underwater adhesive systems. When a mussel wants to attach to a surface, it uses its plunger-shaped foot to find the spot that will make the best bond. The foot cleans the point where glue will be attached and then presses down upon the surface, forcing all of the water out. Next the mussel lifts the center section of its plungerlike foot, forming a vacuum to hold itself tightly in place. The final step is for the mussel to pump a chemical adhesive down through its foot, depositing the glue into the vacuum area. This adhesive forms a foamy, shock absorbing foundation, bonded together with individual threads of glue.

The glue itself is made from several different proteins which are mixed in the correct proportions to provide the optimum combination of strength, flexibility, and compressibility for the selected anchor spot. Scientists believe that the specific proteins used *change properties* as conditions change. This has recently been coined a "smart" material.

Modern science can learn much about glue by examining the mussel. The mussel is both a wonder of God's design and a sophisticated chemist.

LETTING GOD CREATE YOUR DAY, VOL. 2, P.56

For with God nothing shall be impossible.

LUKE 1:37 KJV

Evidence From
BIOLOGY

Although coral appears to be a plant, it is actually an animal. A coral reef is made up of millions of tiny animals (called poylps) living inside of interconnected limestone skeletons. **Yet coral cannot maintain its existence without the help of a completely different organism–called algae.** Thousands of single-celled algae, which are plants, live within the stomach of each tiny coral polyp. The polyp uses the waste from the algae to produce the calcium needed to build its protective reef. In return, the polyp's stomach provides an ideal protected living place for the algae. It is the algae in the polyps' stomach which provide the wonderful colors seen in living reefs.

Evolutionists have claimed that it would require a million years to produce such structures as the Great Barrier Reef in Australia. This structure is 1,300 miles long and is considered the largest structure ever produced by a living organism. In contradiction to what evolutionists have taught for years, experimental measurements have shown that coral polyps are capable of doubling their weight every ten days. As a result, the Great Barrier Reef could easily have been produced well within the last 10,000 years. The real question is, why it is not much larger if the earth is really billions of years old?

Almost all dating methods used by evolutionists to justify the belief in an ancient earth need to be revised drastically downward as we learn more.

LETTING GOD CREATE YOUR DAY,
VOL.2, P.90
CREATION 25(1), DEC.2002-FEB.2003, P.29-33

I will praise you, O LORD, with all my heart; I will tell of all your wonders.

PSALM 9:1

Evidence From
COMMON SENSE

The theory of evolution has hindered the advancement of human knowledge since it was first proposed by Charles Darwin in 1859. The idea that one type of creature has changed into a completely different type of creature by the accumulation of small changes over time has been at least partially responsible for many of the following travesties:

1. The **removal of supposedly useless organs** (such as tonsils) based on the assumption that they were evolutionary leftovers.
2. The **idolizing of animals** to the point of animals being considered equal in value to humans, which has resulted in the devaluation of human life.
3. The **devaluation of human life** such that the abortion of babies is considered nothing more than the removal of excess tissue. Biology texts still teach that embryos go through "evolutionary stages" before becoming human.
4. The **promotion of self-love** and survival-of-the-fittest mentality at the expense of others, creating a self-centered society. If we have evolved, why not focus on self?
5. The **distortion, misunderstanding, and redefinition of the word "family"**–leading to broken homes, dysfunctional families, and insecure children.
6. Any **basis for determining good vs. evil** or right vs. wrong has become relative. Truth shifts as easily as moving sand.

Maintaining a creation foundation, as taught by the Bible, prevents all of these problems from occurring.

REASON EMOTION

BRUCE MALONE

...every good tree bears good fruit, but a bad tree bears bad fruit. A good tree cannot bear bad fruit, nor can a bad tree bear good fruit.

MATTHEW 7:17-18 NKJV

Evidence From
GEOLOGY

Topsoil consists of weathered rock and organic material (decomposed from plants and animals). Millions of years should have produced extremely thick layers of soil throughout the geological record. **However, ancient topsoil layers are missing between virtually all rock layers.** The geological record shows layers of sedimentary, metamorphic, or igneous rock deposited directly on top of one another. There are very few places where topsoil is found between these rock layers. So where is all the topsoil from millions of years of Earth history?

Standard geology teaches that land surfaces, supporting lush life, have been here continuously for hundreds of millions of years. Where is all the topsoil between the sedimentary, metamorphic, and igneous layers which make up the geologic column? **The layers of rock in the geologic column, with essentially no layers of topsoil in between them, seem to indicate that little time occurred between the deposition of these layers.** In those few places where soil-type sediments are present between rock layers, there is evidence that they were deposited by flood waters.

The best explanation for the geological column is that these layers were deposited over a short period of time, one layer right after another, which allowed no time for topsoil to form between the layers. The virtual absence of topsoil within the geological column is excellent evidence in support of the biblical claim for a young earth.

THE YOUNG EARTH, P.97-98

By wisdom the LORD laid the earth's foundations, by understanding he set the heavens in place....

PROVERBS 3:19

Evidence From ASTRONOMY

By the 1980s our optical capability had advanced such that telescopes could be built which were sensitive enough to see a speck of dust *two miles* away. **"Such a telescope allowed scientists to discover three gigantic dust rings,** 100 million miles wide, circling the asteroid belt between Mars and Jupiter, 200 million to 300 million miles from the sun." The dust bands were never seen before, because they were made of particles too fine to adequately reflect light back toward Earth. The rings are a mystery, because they seem to defy the laws of physics by circling the asteroid belt in three extremely stable and symmetrical rings. According to Frank Low of the University of Arizona, **"Particles this small can only survive in stable orbits for a few ten-thousands of years before they are pulled apart by the sun.** There must be something that replenishes the ring, because three stable bands that large cannot exist in any other way."

Thus scientists blinded by the presuppositions of evolutionary time scales are forced to rely on blind faith in some **unknown replenishment mechanism** rather than the obvious answer that the rings are there because the solar system is quite young.

IT'S A YOUNG WORLD AFTER ALL, P.46

"...I am He; I am the first and I am the last.
My own hand laid the foundations of the earth,
and my right hand spread out the heavens; when I
summon them, they all stand up together."

ISAIAH 48:12-13

THE FOSSIL RECORD
Evidence From

A microscopic sea creature known as a diatom has a shell which does not decompose when it dies. Instead, the shells gradually accumulate on the ocean bottom; and under just the right conditions they form deposits called diatomaceous earth. Such deposits have been found hundreds of feet thick and can be remarkably free of other contaminants. The existence of these deposits seemed a dilemma for young-earth creationists, because it was not believed that such thick deposits could form rapidly.

A 1976 discovery confirmed that rapid formation of thick diatomaceous earth deposits are possible. At a diatomaceous earth quarry in Lompoc, California, workers of the Dicalite Division of Grefco Corporation uncovered the fossil skeleton of a baleen whale. This fossil is about eighty feet long. **Billions of the tiny diatom shells could not have gradually buried the skeleton over millions of years, because the skeleton would not have lasted that long.** Dead ocean creatures do not become fossils, because they rot and even their bones disintegrate. In order for a fossil the size of this whale to form, it would have to be buried deeply and quickly. **Only quick burial could have sealed the remains from the effects of atmosphere, bacteria, and scavengers.** The formation containing this whale fossil had to have been deposited quickly. The better scientists understand the fossil record, the more reasons they have to believe in a worldwide flood and to abandon the old-earth theory.

It's a Young World After All, p.81-83

"This is what the LORD says, he who made the earth, the LORD who formed it and established it–the LORD is his name: 'Call to me and I will answer you and tell you great and unsearchable things you do not know.' "
Jeremiah 33:2-3

Evidence From BOTANY

The common seed would hardly cause one to take any special notice. But within that tiny case lies the miraculous power to perpetuate life itself. A single kernel of corn can produce hundreds of seeds within a few months. A dot-sized poppy seed can make thousands like itself in one summer. **Every plant is programmed to produce its own special seed.**

Scientists can analyze and take apart the many chemical compounds within a seed, but no scientist has ever been able to produce a synthetic seed. **This is because even the "simplest" seed is entirely too complex for mankind to reproduce.** Every seed is produced only by an amazing process of sexual union determined by the special construction of the parent plants.

Most seeds appear to be pieces of dead organic matter. Yet even wheat seeds sealed inside of Egyptian tombs for 4,000 years bring forth new life when planted and watered.

Seeds are truly marvels of God's design.

UNLOCKING THE MYSTERIES OF CREATION,
PREMIER ED., P.45

"...unless a kernel of wheat falls into the ground and dies, it remains only a single seed. But if it dies, it produces many seeds. The man who loves his life will lose it, but the man who hates his life in this world will keep it for eternal life."
JOHN 12: 24-25

Evidence From ANTHROPOLOGY

The first human institution established by God was marriage. The prolonged period of human infancy requires the careful protection and training of children by their parents. God ordained that the home, built on mutual love and respect of husband and wife, should be the basic human unit of authority and instruction.

Both ethnologists and anthropologists find evidence that the permanent union of a single man to a single woman is the ideal arrangement upon which to base society. Whenever this pattern is broken, problems result. The history of previous civilizations shows that when the family unit deteriorates, so does the society. We need only look around to see that this is a fact.

THE GENESIS RECORD, P.98-102

For this reason a man will leave his father and mother and be united to his wife, and they will become one flesh.

GENESIS 2:24

Evidence From
ARCHAEOLOGY

"Higher critics" are scholars who study the sources of biblical text. Beginning in the mid-eighteenth century, these scholars often approached this study in a biased and negative manner. **For decades, higher critics taught that the Priestly Code and legislation recorded in the first five books of the Bible were far too developed to have been written by Moses.** They alleged that it wasn't until about the first half of the Persian period (538-331 B.C.) that such detailed legislation developed. **Since 1974, however, 17,000 tablets have been unearthed from the era of the Ebla Kingdom (2000 B.C.) which prove the critics wrong.** Ebla shows that at least 500 years before Moses was recording laws for the Israelites, other complex laws and customs were recorded in writing from the same area of the world.

Why did these higher critics of the biblical record assume that people could not have produced such complex written laws? Only because they had been blinded by evolutionary assumptions and believed ancient mankind was too primitive and ignorant (compared to "more evolved" modern man). This is one of many examples where evolutionary assumptions led researchers to the wrong conclusions. Archaeology clearly supports the biblical record.

THIS INFORMATION IS CONDENSED FROM
EVIDENCE THAT DEMANDS A VERDICT, P.68
THIS BOOK IS AN EXCELLENT RESOURCE ON
BIBLICAL ACCURACY.

And he wrote there upon the stones a copy of the law of Moses, which he wrote in the presence of the children of Israel.

JOSHUA 8:32 KJV

Evidence From THE FOSSIL RECORD

Buried beneath the tundras in Siberia and Alaska lie the remains of hundreds of thousands of frozen animals, including the extinct mammoth. **Many of the mammoth carcasses are still preserved to such a degree that they have been used as animal feed.** Although these northern tundras are now cold and barren wastelands, there are many indications that they were much warmer in the past. Fossil evidence has been found of plants that grow today as far south as Mexico, indicating the possibility that these tundras were once covered with lush vegetation.

The freshness of the mammoths and other animal carcasses indicates that they were rapidly buried during a time when the climate was warmer and preserved by a sudden and permanent drop in temperature. One well-preserved carcass was found in 1901 near the Siberian Beresovka River. Identifiable plant fragments were found in the mammoth's mouth and between its teeth. Twenty-four pounds of excellently preserved plants were also discovered in its stomach.

Although mammoths have a "holding stomach" which allows lengthy preservation of undigested food, the preservation of entire animals, testifies to drastic and rapid climatic changes. The Ice Age was one of the results of the worldwide Flood, and apparently these mammoths were frozen during this period of time. The discovery of these caracasses, found thousands of years after their frozen burial, testifies to the global Flood.

Its a Young World After All, p.96-97

Then God said, "Let the earth bring forth grass, the herb that yields seed, and the fruit tree that yields fruit according to its kind, whose seed is in itself, on the earth"; and it was so.

Genesis 1:11 NKJV

OCTOBER 31

Evidence From
ASTRONOMY

The evolutionist theory that the earth is billions of years old can be ruled out by the observations of some star clusters. The most dramatic evidence is the cluster of four stars in the Trapezium of the Orion nebula.

These stars are moving away from a common point at high speed. **If their motion is projected backward at their present speed, their paths lead to a common point of origin in less than 10,000 years.**

With the exception of the biblical timetable for creation, no mechanism is known to explain what could have created or moved these stars away from each other in less than 10,000 years. The evidence suggests that this star cluster is less than 10,000 years from their point of origin because they were created less than 10,000 years ago.

This is only one of the hundreds of observations which support the literal biblical chronology concerning the age of the universe.

IT'S A YOUNG WORLD AFTER ALL, P.60

Lift your eyes and look to the heavens: Who created all these? He who brings out the starry host one by one, and calls them each by name. Because of his great power and mighty strength, not one of them is missing.
ISAIAH 40:26

NOVEMBER

November

Thankfulness From the Heart

Thankfulness grows within our heart
  as we give God control.
It reshapes thoughts, removes complaints,
  and plays an active role.

It knows God's standards for mankind
  were made so we could see
His HOLY nature, pure and just;
  and true to this He'll be.

It, too, can sense the awesome wrath
  our sins on us impose.
Our pride, rebellion, selfishness—
  just what we are God knows.

It's here where thankfulness is born;
  it comes from knowing well
How MUCH in debt we are to Christ,
  who saved our souls from hell.

It also knows our best attempts;
  our debts can't satisfy.
The works we think will gain us life
  are simply Satan's lie.

This mystery we can't explain:
  that knowing mankind's heart,
Our Lord still chose to die for us
  and grace to us impart.

This awesome truth, if we just look,
  will teach us of God's love.
It makes us WANT to do His will
  and PRAISE the Lord above.

It prompts our hearts to give our best
  and read His Word with care
So we can learn about our Lord,
  whose home we'll someday share.

Lord, as we view the world around,
  please make our eyes to see
The wondrous things that you have done
  so we'll *more thankful* be.

Evidence From
CREATION FOUNDATION

Design means that the components within an object are arranged in a such a way as to accomplish some useful or artistic purpose. By this definition, the earth with all of its interrelated systems shows design. The "Law of Teleology" is a principle of logic that has to do with design or purpose in nature. This law of science states that **where there is complex and interdependent design, there must be a designer.** Both the religious and the nonreligious have been forced to acknowledge this principle.

Intelligent functional design *demands* a designer. Therefore, whenever design is discovered in the fabric of Earth's environment, one would have to conclude, if intellectually honest, that there must be a grand Designer ultimately responsible for this design.

THE HUMAN BODY: ACCIDENT OR DESIGN?, P.1

...but they have no regard for the deeds of the LORD, no respect for the work of his hands.

ISAIAH 5:12

Evidence From
GEOLOGY

The Grand Canyon is a showcase of geological change. If there is any place on Earth where the history of our planet can be seen and read, it is within the walls of this great canyon. The Colorado River is commonly reported to have cut the huge canyon as it slowly, one grain of rock at a time, dug deep into the earth over millions of years. Yet this interpretation of the canyon contradicts much of the evidence. For instance:

- **The Colorado River flows through a plateau which geologists acknowledge was uplifted long before the river flowed through the area.** Only a huge and sudden flow of water could have carved through the area, because any river would have flowed around the plateau.

- **There are many folded rock layers in the canyon.** Solid rock does not fold without fracturing, but soft sediment does. In other words, the sediment was recently formed and was not solid when the canyon was carved.

- **According to the evolutionary time scale, there are 500 million years of missing sediment between certain rock layers in the canyon.** Evolutionists assume this sediment was simply washed away. Yet the missing interface is a smooth, flat surface covering hundreds of thousands of square miles. No such flat interface between sediment layers is observed on our planet today, yet this would be the expected consequence of a huge flood of worldwide extent.

There is much evidence pointing to a worldwide Flood. The Grand Canyon was carved out as huge quantities of water broke through an earthen dam and **rapidly gouged out the canyon**.

GRAND CANYON: MONUMENT TO CATASTROPHE, P.1-110

God is our refuge and strength, a very present help in trouble. Therefore we will not fear, even though the earth be removed, and though the mountains be carried into the midst of the sea...

PSALM 46: 1-2 NKJV

Evidence From GREAT SCIENTISTS

It has been said that John Dewey had a greater influence on our public school system than any other man in the twentieth century. John Dewey was also an avid humanist who believed that truth did not exist.

John Dewey was one of the first signers of the Humanist Manifesto in 1933. This document began with the foundational assumption that evolution explains all of reality and that God has no place in the affairs of mankind. John Dewey almost single-handedly transformed the American educational system to conform with these humanistic ideas. Building upon the foundation that John Dewey laid, both the Bible and prayer were banned from public schools shortly after his death. John Dewey was also responsible for promoting evolution in the American educational system, which has resulted in the current situation where no other alternatives are allowed.

After Bible reading and prayer were removed from public schools in the early 1960s, every indicator of social decay began to increase. In the two decades following this removal of absolute moral authority from public schools, the nation's divorce rate increased 100%, drug use increased 500%, violent crime increased 350%, unwed pregnancies climbed 500%, standardized test scores dropped 18 years in a row, premarital sex zoomed 1000%, and suicide increased 250%.

Are any of these trends surprising, once the source of moral standards (the Bible) was eliminated from schools? The absolute truths of the Bible are the only thing that tie moral reality to the physical world.

SEVEN MEN WHO RULE FROM THE GRAVE, P.151-180
AMERICA: TO PRAY? OR NOT TO PRAY?, P.4-106

And you shall remember the Lord your God, for it is He who gives you power to get wealth, that He may establish His covenant....

DEUTERONOMY 8:18 NKJV

Evidence From
BOTANY

Twisted and weather-beaten bristlecone pine trees cling to life in one of the harshest environments on Earth. **High in the arid White Mountains bordering California and Nevada, these rare and rugged trees have been growing for about 4,500 years!** Their annual growth rings have been studied to give a reasonably accurate idea of their history. Because of the hardiness of the bristlecone trees, it is fair to say they will likely go on living for thousands of years longer (barring any catastrophe that would remove them.)

Why don't we find a grove of trees somewhere in the world dating back to 8,000, 10,000 or 15,000 years? If trees like this have lived 4,500 years, they could have certainly lived longer. **It's almost as though all these trees took root on a virgin Earth just 4,500 years ago!** The Bible gives a clear historical record of the global Flood about 4,500 years ago. With all animal and plant life destroyed during this Flood, it stands to reason that the trees of greatest longevity would date back only to that time and no further.

UNLOCKING THE MYSTERIES OF CREATION, PREMIER ED., P.54
CREATION MAGAZINE, 25(1), DEC. 2002 - FEB.
2003, P.10-13

And the waters prevailed exceedingly on the earth, and all the high hills under the whole heaven were covered.

GENESIS 7:19 NKJV

Evidence From
BIOLOGY

The bombardier beetle uses an incredible series of complex chemicals to protect itself. Biologists have discovered that inside the beetle's body are two separate chambers that make two special chemicals, hydrogen peroxide and hydroquinone. **When these chemicals are mixed and ejected through a tube at the rear of the beetle's body, they explode at 100°C (212°F) in the face of would-be attackers.** The beetle also produces a third chemical, called an "inhibitor," which keeps the chemicals from reacting too soon. A final chemical, an enzyme catalyst, sets off the violent reaction that protects the beetle by scalding its attacker.

How could this extremely complex defense system have evolved piece by piece into a functioning apparatus? It had to be fully functional the very first time it was used. If the chemicals were not just the right strength or in the right place, the beetle would have been killed by its predators, because it couldn't have protected itself. If the inner chambers or tubes weren't perfectly designed and placed from the onset or if the inhibitor technology wasn't quite ready in time, the beetle would have blown itself to pieces. A multitude of precise details had to be working perfectly from the start. This insect is truly a testimony to our Creator.

WORLD BOOK ENCYCLOPEDIA'S SCIENCE YEARBOOK, 1981
UNLOCKING THE MYSTERIES OF CREATION,
PREMIER ED., P.114-115

For you make me glad by your deeds, O LORD; I sing for joy at the works of your hands.

PSALM 92:4

Evidence From
BIOLOGY

Consider the probability of all of the following characteristics evolving simultaneously into an effectively functioning system in the woodpecker:

1. **Its beak** is connected to its skull with a resilient shock-absorbing tissue that is not found in any other bird.
2. **The beak** is much harder than the beaks of other birds, enabling it to bang away a hundred times a minute without hurting itself.
3. **The tongue** is barbed in most of the 200+ species and is about four times longer than the beak. In certain species the tongue wraps around the back of the bird's skull, enabling it to reach deep into tree trunks and remove insects.
4. **A sticky coating** on some woodpecker tongues helps them grab insects.
5. **Its tail feathers** are constructed so that they are stiff enough to help brace against trees as it climbs.
6. **Its keen senses of smell** and **hearing** help detect insects crawling around under the bark of the trees.
7. **Its short legs and powerful claws** are uniquely designed to help it climb tree trunks.

The engineering behind **such a technological wonder** as the woodpecker boggles our minds. Try to imagine the obstacles the first bird, which was trying to turn into a woodpecker, would have had to overcome!

UNLOCKING THE MYSTERIES OF CREATION,
*PREMIER ED, P.*117

The eyes of all look to you, and you give them their food at the proper time.

PSALM 145:15

Evidence From GENETICS

Each of us have 46 long portions of DNA (called chromosomes) within our cells which we inherited from our parents. The coded information on this DNA contains unique instructions which determine exactly what each of us looks like, much of our personality, and how every cell within our body will function throughout our life. Copies of this same information are written within the coiled DNA molecules contained within each of the 100 trillion cells within our bodies.

If the DNA in one of our cells could be uncoiled, connected, and stretched out, it would be about seven feet long. It would also be so thin that details could not even be seen under an electron microscope. **If all of the densely packed and coded information from one cell were written in book form, it would fill a library with approximately 4,000 books.** Yet the DNA code from every person who has ever lived, if placed in a single pile, would weigh less than an aspirin tablet! Our knowledge of the marvel of the DNA molecule is just one of many reasons that we can confidently know that we are *"fearfully and wonderfully made."*

Is it reasonable to believe that this complex information transferal system and all of the useful information coded into it could have developed as a result of chance mutations?

IN THE BEGINNING, 7ᵀᴴ ED., P.3

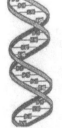

For you created my inmost being; you knit me together in my mother's womb. I praise you because I am fearfully and wonderfully made....

PSALM 139:13-14

Evidence From THE WORLDWIDE FLOOD

Many people claim that Noah's Flood was just a relatively small local event. Yet God clearly stated in Genesis 6:17 that the coming judgment would be a mighty flood of waters (mabbul mayim). The word for flood *(mabbul)*, used in Genesis 6:17 for the first time, is only used for *Noah's Flood*; other floods are denoted by different words in the Bible. The Genesis Flood was the "mabbul," *unique in all history.* **God not only used a unique and exact word for the worldwide Flood, but also made it clear that the waters covered the highest mountains.**

God promised to never send another flood upon the earth. Yet there have been countless local floods throughout history. Either the Genesis Flood was something different, unique, and worldwide–or God is a liar.

Enormous and widespread geologic features around the planet also testify to the global extent of this Flood. From the rapid formation of the Grand Canyon as backed-up waters rushed off the continents...to widespread coal deposits...to oversized river valleys around the world–it is apparent that this planet was once covered with water.

THE GENESIS RECORD, P.183

"I will never again curse the ground on account of man... and I will never again destroy every living thing, as I have done."

GENESIS 8:21 NASV

Evidence From CREATION FOUNDATION

The book of Genesis is the foundation of man's meaning and existence. It sets the boundaries of his spiritual nature and tells him where he fits into the scheme of creation. God, *as Creator*, becomes the basis for all morality–all meaning. He establishes the right of revelation and lawgiving. Man, *the created*, has his purposes set before him–to live according to the plan of his Maker, to obey, and to glorify Him. Remove Genesis, and man is left with nothing but his own foundation. Indeed, it can be argued that the first question all men must deal with is this: What will you do with Genesis?

It takes courage to oppose the theory of evolution. You will be ridiculed by academic elitists and those with fancy titles. You must understand that there is no objectivity here, but a set of conclusions based on faith alone–faith that there is no God, no supernatural. If you oppose evolution, do so on the basis of the myriad of objective evidence that is around you. Oppose evolution with conviction, for the stakes are the highest of all–the eternal resting place of our souls.

THE DARWIN CONSPIRACY, P.243,253

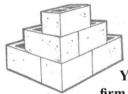

Your word, O LORD, is eternal; it stands firm in the heavens.

Psalm 119:89

Evidence From ARCHAEOLOGY

The Bible says man was created in the image of God. He was made from the start as a creative, intelligent, and rational being. Evolutionists believe that either random-chance mutations turned a primitive apelike creature into man or (if they are theists) that *God* used random-chance mutations to change some sort of apelike creature into a man. **What does archaeology tell us?** Consider just a few examples:

1. Mayans (c. 2000 B.C.) used advanced mathematics to calculate the **exact length of a year** to within 99.98% of the modern value.
2. Relics from ancient Egypt dating back to around 2500 B.C. were found **electroplated**.
3. Chinese weapons dating back over 2,000 years were found treated with a preservative that **prevented corrosion**.
4. Travel between continents took place thousands of years ago. **Ancient maps** and stone monuments inscribed with ancient languages attest to this.
5. On the remote and barren Easter Island 2,300 miles off the coast of Chile, there are massive 180,000-pound **sculptures** of human heads smoothly carved from iron-hard volcanic rock.

These and many other archaeological discoveries indicate that **ancient man had a keen understanding of astronomy, mathematics, and engineering.** Also, evidences of **medicines, surgery, and the use of electricity** indicates man's intelligence from the beginning of his existence.

UNLOCKING THE MYSTERIES OF CREATION, PREMIER EDITION, P.176-225

What has been will be again, what has been done will be done again; there is nothing new under the sun.

ECCLESIASTIES 1:9

Evidence From ANTHROPOLOGY

Contrary to evolutionary thought, evidence indicates that ancient man lived at a high level of civilization from the very start. The Bible and historical writings describe these advanced ancient civilizations. **The pattern we see repeated throughout history** (in ancient civilizations like the Egyptians, Babylonians, Hittites, Phoenecians, Syrians, Persians, Romans, Incas, and many others) **is that of increasing depravity as man rejects God and his accountabilty to Him in favor of satisfying his own selfish desires with accountability to no one.**

Careful examination of the physical remains of these cultures shows evidence of widespread **violence** and **gross immorality**. As these societies continued to fall into deeper levels of degradation, **demonic manifestations** and **human sacrifice** became commonplace. Virtually every civilization of the ancient past reached a point of destruction and ruin. The Bible is 100% accurate in its view of mankind and his ultimate end whenever God is rejected.

UNLOCKING THE MYSTERIES OF CREATION,
PREMIER ED., P.180-181

Furthermore, since they did not think it worthwhile to retain the knowledge of God, he gave them over to a depraved mind, to do what ought not to be done. They have become filled with every kind of wickedness, evil, greed and depravity....

ROMANS 1:28-29

Evidence From ARCHAEOLOGY

Many people look at the ***accomplishments of modern man*** and assume that the ***enormous advances in technology*** over the last few centuries are indicators of increasing human intelligence. This idea is propagated by evolutionists who portray early man as a hairy, bent-over, unintelligent beast. **In contrast to this perception are the factual archaeological finds** of the earliest human civilizations, which reveal that mankind has always been highly intelligent and resourceful. For instance:

1. *Some ancient skulls reveal that successful **brain surgery** was performed by the ancient Inca people of South America.*
2. *Silk cloth has been found with **designs** printed 3,000 years before Gutenburg invented the printing press.*
3. *The Aztecs of Mexico (2000 B.C. to 900 A.D.) monitored the orbit of Venus closely and integrated a **calendar** with the cycles of Venus.*
4. *Unbelievably **precise calculations** went into building the Great Pyramid of Egypt. This single structure contains more quarried stone than what is contained in all of the cathedrals and churches in England. Some 4,000 years ago they were moving cut stones (each weighing up to 100 tons) from 60 miles away.*
5. *Ancient Egyptian **battery cells** (made from clay vessels) show that mankind has known about and made use of electricity for thousands of years.*

There can be no doubt that mankind was created with unique intelligence and abilities from the very start.

UNLOCKING THE MYSTERIES OF CREATION,
PREMIER EDITION, P.176-225

...Jubal: he was the father of all such as handle the harp and organ. And Zillah, she also bare Tubalcain, an instructor of every [craftsman] in brass and iron....

GENESIS 4:21-22 KJV

Evidence From PROPHECY

Israel's detailed history is foretold in many prophetic Old Testament Bible passages. "In Deuteronomy 28, even before the Israelites had entered the Promised Land, Moses predicted their future *season of happiness* in the land, their *repeated suffering* and punishment for disobedience to God's law, and finally their great *worldwide dispersion* among the Gentile (non-Jewish) nations. This dispersion of the Jewish nation was also foretold by many later prophets and finally by Christ Himself (Luke 21:20-24)." There are also specific details numbering their *years in exile* and foretelling of the destruction, rebuilding, and second *destruction of the Temple.*

Jeremiah predicted that the Jews would *never lose their identity or be absorbed by other nations* (as were the Edomites and Philistines) and that their *national identity would be restored.* The eventual restoration of Israel as a nation was also prophesied in many other biblical passages. **After almost 2,000 years as a nation with no homeland, Israel was miraculously reestablished as a recognized nation in 1948 and even regained its ancient capital of Jerusalem in 1967.** The very existence of Israel as a nation and the Jews as a distinct people is perhaps the greatest proof of God's divine intervention and protection.

SCIENCE AND THE BIBLE, P.122

"...I am with you and will save you," declares the LORD. "Though I completely destroy all the nations among which I scatter you, I will not completely destroy you...."

JEREMIAH 30:11

Evidence From COMMON SENSE

Evolution is presented in school textbooks as if it were a *proven fact* with no problems and no controversy surrounding it. As a result, many students are left with the impression that evolution cannot be questioned or debated. **Honest science would reveal the enormous problems surrounding the theory of evolution** and challenge young minds to look for answers to these problems. For instance:

- If one type of **animal slowly and step by step turned** into a completely different type of animal, where are the enormous number of transitional fossils as one animal is changed into another?

- How could **random changes add information** to the DNA molecule? There is no other branch of science where it is assumed that random changes could add useful information to a system.

- Why do nine out of ten **possible ways to date the earth** yield results much younger than the "accepted" date? Why aren't these methods and the problems with radiometric dating shared with students?

- Why did **highly advanced civilizations** suddenly appear all over the planet approximately 4,500 years ago?

If these and many other unsolved mysteries were honestly presented to students, they would be challenged to look at all of the evidence and see that there is still much to discover and contribute in finding solutions.

BRUCE MALONE

Train up a child in the way he should go, and when he is old he will not depart from it.

PROVERBS 22:6 NKJV

NOVEMBER 15

Evidence From CHEMISTRY

Proteins have been called the building blocks of life, because every living cell contains a large percentage of large, complex molecules. Proteins are made by combining a very precise sequence of 20 different kinds of amino acids similar to stringing different colored beads onto a necklace. **Since 1930 it has been known that amino acids cannot react to form proteins in the presence of oxygen.** In other words, proteins could not have evolved by chance chemical reactions if oxygen had been present in the atmosphere.

The chemistry of the earth's rocks, both on land and below ancient seas, show that the earth had oxygen before the earliest fossils of living cells formed. Even earlier, oxygen would have been present by a continuous process whereby solar radiation breaks water vapor into oxygen and hydrogen. The hydrogen could have escaped into outer space, but the oxygen would have remained in our atmosphere. Therefore, from the moment the earth had an atmosphere, it must have had oxygen. It is chemically impossible for even the building blocks of life (proteins) to have developed on Earth. This is an enormous, "elephant in the living room" problem for evolution which is simply ignored.

In the Beginning, 7th Ed., p.12
The Icons of Evolution, p.9-27

Praise him, you highest heavens and you waters above the skies. Let them praise the name of the LORD, for he commanded and they were created.

PSALM 148:4-5

Evidence From
BIOLOGY

Birds of the heron family accumulate a thin layer of oily slime on their feathers. To clean this condition, **they have three patches of feathers that break down into a powder that works** like talcum powder. The birds apply the powder to their feathers to absorb the slime. Afterwards it is combed out of the feathers using a comb-shaped toe designed for this purpose. The birds then waterproof their feathers by applying oil from a specially designed and located oil gland.

In addition to this remarkable feather-cleaning process, many birds have an amazing method for applying a pesticide to get rid of parasites. Hundreds of species of birds will sit motionless near ant hills and allow ants to crawl over them, releasing formic acid. This acid drives mites and most other pests off of the birds.

Is it *reasonable* to believe that these complex and interdependent systems of hygiene could have evolved? Even in our fallen world filled with pests and parasites, God has provided mechanisms for protection.

LETTING GOD CREATE YOUR DAY, VOL. 4, P.208

All you have made will praise you, O LORD....

PSALM 145:10

Evidence From
ARCHAEOLOGY

Dr. Robert Dick Wilson (1856-1930), a graduate of Princeton University at age 20, spent 45 years of his life making a scientific study of the Old Testament. He was one of the most brilliant language and Bible scholars of all times. In order to accurately understand the Bible, Dr. Wilson not only mastered Hebrew and all related languages, but was fluent in every language into which the Bible was translated up to 600 A.D. His primary goal was to be qualified to speak with authority in matters relating to the text of the Bible. Wilson wanted to "reduce Old Testament criticism to an absolutely objective science; something that is based on evidence and not opinions." One of the many areas he researched was the records of the 29 kings of Egypt, Israel, Moab, Damascus, Tyre, Babylon, Assyria, and Persia which are referred to in the Bible and found on monuments.

After studying documents that were up to 4,000 years old, he found that the Bible correctly named every one of these ancient kings, placed them in the correct country, and listed them in correct chronological order. No other document even comes close to the accuracy of the biblical account. Since the original names in the Old Testament frequently carried specific meanings, all that is connected with them has tremendous significance. Robert Wilson's painstaking work formed the foundation for proving the accuracy of these Old Testament passages. Dr. Wilson concluded that the Bible's perfect accuracy reflects the *absolute truth* of Scripture and a Mastermind as its author.

BIBLICAL STUDIES IN THE LIGHT OF ARCHAEOLOGY, P.61-63

"Every word of God is flawless; he is a shield to those who take refuge in him."

PROVERBS 30:5

Evidence From
EARTH'S ECOLOGY

In the book of Genesis, God tells us that mankind was originally put in charge of the animals. **It is interesting to see how animals serve man and are actually under his control, just as God decreed.** For example, look at how creatively the Indians learned to use every part of the bison. They used the meat for food and the tendons for bowstrings, thread, and webbing. Hides were used for clothing, moccasins, tepees, bedding, and boats. The long hair was made into rope; and the stomachs, bladders, and other internal organs were made into containers for holding food. The tallow was used for waterproofing. Bones provided tools, bows, and toys, while ribs were used to make runners for dogsleds. Bile was used to make yellow paint, and the bison's hooves were used to make glue. Dried dung could be stored indefinitely and used as a fuel. Stomach juices were substituted for water in life-or-death situations, and the horns provided spoons and drinking utensils.

The Bible warns that misuse and greed bring ruin. This is exactly what happened in the case of the bison. Man hunted and shot bison in such large numbers between 1865 and 1884 that the former bison population decreased from sixty million to near extinction. It was man's sinful nature that drove this majestic creature to near extinction.

CHARACTER SKETCHES, VOL.II, P.84

"**The fear and dread of you will fall upon all the beasts of the earth... they are given into your hands. Everything that lives and moves will be food for you....**"

GENESIS 9:2,3

Evidence From
BIBLICAL UNIQUENESS

No other book in the history of mankind has been more attacked than the Bible. In both ancient and modern times, kings and priests have tried to *destroy it*, unbelieving people have *mocked it*, and academics have tried to *prove it wrong*. Untold numbers of Bibles have been destroyed, and people who believe what it says have been and still are being persecuted and murdered.

In spite of this suppression, the number of copies and languages into which the Bible has been translated is far greater than *any* other book in existence. It continues to be read and believed by people worldwide, **remaining the world's best seller.** What could account for this incredible fascination, in spite of extreme opposition?

MANY INFALLIBLE PROOFS, P.15
EVIDENCE THAT DEMANDS A VERDICT, P.17-22

"Heaven and earth will pass
away, but my words will never pass away."

MARK 13:31

Evidence From
GEOLOGY

The mapping of the ocean floor–with its awesome mountain ranges and deep caverns–shows a gigantic fissure (crack) spanning the entire globe, called the Mid-Oceanic Ridge. The Bible says when the Flood began, "all the fountains of the deep were *broken up*" (Genesis 7:11). The Hebrew word used for *broken up* also means "to rip open" or "burst forth." This implies that massive quantities of subterranean waters existed below the surface of the earth and that these waters broke forth to fill our present sea basins. Some creationists believe that these Mid-Oceanic Ridge fissures are possibly what remains of the scar from which all of this water burst forth. This theory is known as the hydroplate theory, which is one of the creationist models explaining the rapid changes that happened to the earth's crust during the global Flood.

It is interesting to note that the very word *ocean* is translated from the original Hebrew word that literally means "that which burst forth from the womb." **Scientific discoveries heighten one's appreciation for the Bible**, especially when we find that *every* word and phrase has a specific meaning which fits perfectly with the world around us.

Science and the Bible, p.21 (Grady)
In the Beginning, p.87-119

...the same day were all the fountains
of the great deep broken up, and the
windows of heaven were opened. And the
rain was upon the earth forty days and forty nights.

Genesis 7:11-12 KJV

Evidence From
BIBLICAL ACCURACY

The Bible is full of scientific insights revealed long before man discovered them. One example is a question God asked Job, "Have you walked in the recesses of the deep?" In another passage, David referred to the "channels of the sea" (2 Samuel 22:16). The Hebrew word for *recesses* refers to that which is "hidden, and known only by investigation." **What are these recesses of the deep** (the Hebrew word for *deep* is the same word used for seas or oceans)?

For thousands of years mankind considered the ocean as nothing more than a relatively shallow, sandy extension from one continent to another. It wasn't until the Glomar Challenger expedition (1973-1976) that the first comprehensive scientific exploration of the ocean floor took place. One of the discoveries was a five-mile-deep canyon under the Pacific Ocean. **Numerous other "recesses" have been found since that time, including one near the Philippines which is almost seven miles deep!** One wonders how the writer of Job knew there were "recesses in the deep?" Was it just a lucky guess, or was it revealed to him by our Creator?

A STUDY COURSE IN CHRISTIAN EVIDENCES, P.128-129

"Have you journeyed to the springs of the sea or walked in the recesses of the deep?"

JOB 38:16

Evidence From LANGUAGE

Scientists have discovered that both hearing and deaf children babble in the language used in their homes. How can deaf children who have no hearing communicate? They do this by learning to use sign language with their hands. Hearing infants produce sounds, then syllables, and eventually meaningful words using their vocal cords. The deaf infants can do the same using their hands. Deaf children first learn to make the hand signs for basic letters and numbers and string these signs together without meaning. **However, at the same age when hearing infants begin to make meaningful words (usually by their first birthday), the deaf infants have gained the ability to produce meaningful words using hand signs.**

Researchers were shocked when they realized the implications of this discovery. **It indicates that the human brain comes with a built-in, unified ability to learn language.** This surprised behavioral scientists, because they are trained to assume that mankind has come from some apelike creature, who in turn came from a single-celled organism, which in turn is a result of a random combination of molecules. Why would the end result be a creature with the built-in ability to communicate in *any* complex language?

This is perfectly logical for someone who believes the Bible. The Bible says that our Creator gives understanding to the mind (Job 38:36) and calls mankind to communicate with Him (1 Corinthians 1:9). How else could we do this, unless our minds were pre-wired to understand and develop languages?

LETTING GOD CREATE YOUR DAY,
VOL. 2, P.117

God is faithful, by whom you were called into the fellowship *[partnership or communication]* of His Son, Jesus Christ our Lord.

1 CORINTHIANS 1:9 NKJV

Evidence From BIOLOGY

The *Maculinea arion* is a large blue butterfly that goes through an extraordinary life cycle. The female *Maculinea arion* lays eggs one at a time on the buds of the wild thyme plant. In the fall, the caterpillar hatches and feeds on the thyme for about three weeks. Then it leaves the plant, never to eat vegetation again.

On the ground the caterpillar finds a red ant whose colony is near the thyme plant. The ant strokes the caterpillar with its antennae, and the caterpillar gives off sweet milk from the tenth segment of its body. The ant drinks this for about an hour until the caterpillar suddenly hunches up. The ant then puts one leg on each side of the tiny caterpillar, picks it up in its jaws, and carries it back to its nest. **Once in the nest, the ants enjoy drinking the caterpillar's milk while the caterpillar enjoys eating the baby ants!**

The following June, while still in the ant nest, the caterpillar comes out of its pupa state as an adult butterfly. It **squeezes through small passages** to escape to the surface of the ground, where it flies away to start the same life cycle again.

Tremendous faith is required to believe that evolution caused this complex and incredible butterfly life cycle with its interdependence between different forms of life. A wiser faith trusts the creative hand of God to have produced these complex characteristics needed for survival in our fallen world.

EVOLUTION IN THE LIGHT OF SCRIPTURE, SCIENCE, AND SENSE, P.37-38

You open your hand and satisfy the desires of every living thing.

PSALM 145:16

Evidence From
ANATOMY

The human skin is one of the body's most vital organs. It is the largest organ of the human body, weighing more than the brain, liver, or heart. Its many components, which work together to accomplish a plethora of specific functions, clearly indicate that our skin was designed. Consider the following:

1. The skin keeps out harmful bacteria.
2. It serves as a waterproof wall to hold in our body fluids.
3. Its pigment shields us from the sun's harmful rays.
4. Our skin absorbs the sun's ultraviolet rays and uses them to convert chemicals into vitamin D.
5. Its many nerve endings make us sensitive to touch, heat, cold, pain, and pressure.
6. The body's two to five million sweat glands help to eliminate waste products and to cool the skin.
7. Oil glands lubricate our skin and keep it soft.
8. About 1/3 of the body's blood circulates through the skin The blood vessels expand and contract to regulate body temperature. (A body temperature increase of only 7° F to 8° F can cause death.)

The various features of our skin, and the skin of all other animals, reveal planning and design.

THE HUMAN BODY: ACCIDENT OR DESIGN?, P.17-18

Your hands made me and formed me; give me understanding to learn your commands.

PSALM 119:73

Evidence From
THE FOSSIL RECORD

Evolutionists believe that dinosaurs died out some 65 million years before man came into existence. Yet the fossil record provides much evidence to support the biblical claim that dinosaurs lived at the same time as mankind.

Throughout history there have been records of man's encounters with dinosaurlike creatures. From Africa to Europe to the Orient these encounters have been captured in historical accounts, stories, legends, and drawings.

Dinosaur remains have also been found that are still not completely fossilized. Large dinosaur bones have been found in Colorado with traces of unfossilized blood. If dinosaur bones were 65 million years old, they would be completely fossilized. **These unfossilized bones, with traces of blood and DNA fragments, indicate that dinosaurs died much more recently than the commonly repeated 65 million years ago.**

By looking objectively at the biblical account, the fossil record, and historical data, one cannot help but reach the conclusion that man and dinosaurs have indeed coexisted. It is only by ignoring much of the evidence and uncritically accepting evolutionary beliefs that the opposite conclusion can be reached.

THE GREAT DINOSAUR MYSTERY AND THE BIBLE,
P.36-44

CREATION EX NIHILO, SEPTEMBER 1997, P.42-43

"Look at the behemoth, which I made along with you....His tail sways like a cedar....His bones are tubes of bronze....He ranks first among the works of God....When the river rages, he is not alarmed; he is secure, though the Jordan should surge against his mouth."
JOB 40:15,17,18,19,23

Evidence From
PROPHECY

Many previously great nations have been the subject of Bible prophecies. "For example, Edom was a strong nation located next to the Israelites in Palestine. The Edomites, as descendants of Esau, were related to the Israelites, but were idolatrous and treacherous, frequently warring with the Israelite nation. Their land was rugged and their capital city, Petra, had a seemingly impregnable position in the rocks of the mountains." It was a rich trade center; and even today its ruined palaces, carved out of solid rock, are an imposing and magnificent testimony to human ingenuity.

This nation seemed unconquerable. Yet during the height of its power, the Scriptures (Ezekiel 35:1-15; Jeremiah 49:16-22) predicted its ultimate overthrow. Edom was to be destroyed, and all of her inhabitants would disappear. The fulfillment of these prophecies seemed long in coming, because Edom and Petra remained prosperous, even for centuries after Christ. No one really knows the full story of their decline, but their land has been desolate for such a long time that the Edomites are now a people long forgotten. **The prophecy of Edom has been fulfilled exactly as the Bible foretold.**

SCIENCE AND THE BIBLE, P.120

"The terror you inspire and the pride of your heart have deceived you, you who live in the clefts of the rocks, who occupy the heights of the hill. Though you build your nest as high as the eagle's, from there I will bring you down," declares the Lord. "Edom will become an object of horror...."

JEREMIAH 49:16-17

Evidence From
BIOLOGY

How could a creature slowly learn to disguise itself to look like a completely different object? Long before its appearance changed, it would become lunch for a predator. A perfect example is the Amazon leaf fish. Imagine an ordinary fish trying to fool both predator and prey by trying to look like a leaf lying on top of the water and floating down a river. **Long before it evolved the proper appearance, such a fish would become either a bird's meal or starve to death.** The Amazon leaf fish was carefully designed not only to look like a leaf, but to act like one, as well.

This fish has a flat body, very much like a leaf. A black line runs the length of its body, giving the appearance of the midrib of a leaf; and a fleshy growth on its lower jaw looks like a leaf stem. Beyond just *looking* like a leaf, the leaf fish also *acts* like a leaf floating on water. It lies still in the water, drifting along with the current. To hide its identity further, it draws its fins close to its body, removing any hint that it might be a hungry fish looking for lunch. **The leaf fish combines deceptive coloring, appearance, and behavior into one design so that it can survive.** Our fallen world often requires camouflage for survival. Our loving Creator even provided lowly fish with the ability to become masters of disguise.

LETTING GOD CREATE YOUR DAY
VOL. 2, P.41

Your righteousness reaches to the skies, O God, you have done great things. Who, O God, is like you?

PSALM 71:19

Evidence From ANATOMY

The piano can produce different-pitched sounds from 88 keys, but **the human ear can distinguish over 2,500 different tones!** Even more remarkable than the variation in pitch that the human ear can detect is the intensity of sound which the human ear is capable of hearing. **The human ear can detect sound frequencies that move the eardrum as slightly as a billionth of an inch.** This incredibly small movement is less than the diameter of a hydrogen atom. Our hearing is so sensitive that we can hear the faint sound of blood coursing through our veins when standing in a soundproof room. Over 100,000 hearing receptors in the ears send impulses to our brain to be decoded and interpreted.

Could this marvelously designed instrument of hearing have had no designer?

THE REVELATION OF GOD IN NATURE, P.10
FEARFULLY AND WONDERFUL MADE, P. 24-25

Does he who implanted the ear not hear? Does he who formed the eye not see?

PSALM 94:9

Evidence From
BIOLOGY

If a person were to drink even 1/10 the amount of salt water that a sea gull drinks, he would become extremely dehydrated. The secret of the gull's ability to drink salt water lies in a special pair of glands located just above its eyes. **Many fine blood vessels surround these glands, and the glands act as a desalination membrane to extract salt from the blood.**

It has taken mankind thousands of years and enormous amounts of money and research to develop similar membranes for use in saltwater desalination plants. In the sea gull, the salt is removed as a concentrated saltwater solution which rolls down the beak of the sea gull and drops back into the ocean. Each drop is five times as salty as the gull's own blood and twice as salty as seawater. **This complex purification mechanism could not have arisen by chance mutations, because there are too many irreducibly complex components which would all had to have happened at once.** If the gull had not possessed a perfectly working desalination system from the onset, it would never have been capable of living at the seashore. Long before a slowly evolving salt elimination gland was able to operate, all of the sea gulls would have died off, being unable to drink seawater!

EVOLUTION IN THE LIGHT OF SCIENCE, SCRIPTURE, AND SENSE, P.49

"Where then does wisdom come from? Where does understanding dwell? It is hidden from the eyes of every living thing, concealed even from the birds of the air....God understands the way to it and he alone knows where it dwells."
JOB 28:20,21,23

Evidence From
MICROBIOLOGY

One of the evidences used to support evolution is a method of dating biological changes known as the *molecular clock*. The idea of the molecular clock is that the rate of mutations (changes) has always been relatively constant, so determining the molecular differences between two organisms can be used to determine when the organisms appeared. Much of the timing of the modern theory of evolution rests heavily on this clock.

Recent work by microbiologists [*Nature* Journal, 417 (6887):432-436, 2002] totally disproves the usefulness of the molecular clock. These researchers studied bacteria DNA contained in salt deposits which were "dated" at 10 million, 100 million, and 500 million years old (approximately). They went to meticulous extremes to prevent any modern bacterial contamination. Their results show that DNA fragments from ancient bacteria locked within the salt of different depths were almost identical to each other. **In other words, for over an assumed 500 million years, bacteria failed to change by any significant amount.** Yet bacteria with their large population and short generation times should evolve more rapidly than any other organism on Earth. If the molecular clock does not work for these bacteria, why should it be trusted to tell us how long ago any creature has mutated or changed?

The best explanation for similar bacteria in vastly different salt deposits and the survival of DNA fragments within these levels is that all of **the deposits are thousands, rather than millions, of years old**. The DNA is both present and similar because the salt deposits were laid down during the worldwide Flood.

CREATION MAGAZINE, NOV. 2002, P.36-38

Thus the heavens and the earth, and all the host of them, were finished.

GENESIS 2:1 NKJV

DECEMBER

December

Little Light,
Tell All the World

Little light, so clear and bright,
  Make sure your message is heard.
TELL ALL THE WORLD that
  Christ was born;
  It says so in God's Word.

TELL ALL THE WORLD that
  since man sinned,
  God couldn't look at man.
So then He sent His only Son.
  Christ was God's "Perfect Plan."

TELL ALL THE WORLD that while Christ lived,
  He never did a wrong.
His perfect life He sacrificed
  So we'd to Him belong.

TELL ALL THE WORLD we must accept
  Christ's gift upon the cross.
If we love Him, we'll do God's will;
  If not, we'll suffer loss.

TELL ALL THE WORLD there's just one way,
  Through Christ alone we come.
We may not like to hear this truth,
  But Scripture is where it's from.

TELL ALL THE WORLD to read God's Book
  And put its truth to test.
We'll find not one inaccuracy
  And that God knows what's best.

Little light, so clear and bright,
  Make sure the gospel is spread.
TELL ALL THE WORLD that Christ loves us,
  For that is what He said.

Evidence From
CREATION FOUNDATION

According to Webster, *science* is **"knowledge covering general truths or the operation of general laws, especially as obtained and tested through the scientific method."** Science deals with reality. It is the study of how the universe operates, based on experimentation. In one of the strangest twists of truth in human history, *evolution* (most of which is based on speculation and guesswork) is taught as scientific fact, while biblical *creation* (which is based on statements from a book which can be studied and tested) is ignored as religion. Although the Bible is not a science text, it does give us a clear framework of history so that we can know what has happened in the past and better understand why the present universe looks and operates the way it does. The Bible speaks with authority on all matters which it covers, including science and history. **All investigations have shown the Bible to be both historically and scientifically accurate in every minute detail.**

The Bible specifically *warns us to be cautious* **about false knowledge.** Could this have been a prophetic statement warning us of the future day when evolution would be taught as a fact?

UNLOCKING THE MYSTERIES OF CREATION,
PREMIER ED., P.14-15

...avoiding the profane and idle babblings and contradictions of what is falsely called knowledge...

1 TIMOTHY 6:20 NKJV

Evidence From ARCHAEOLOGY

The original text of the New Testament can be verified by comparison with three other original sources: Greek manuscripts, various ancient versions, and quotations from the New Testament in the writings of early Christians. Amazingly, there are some 5,000 partial or complete Greek manuscripts of the original New Testament in existence today. In addition, there are another 10,000 manuscripts of the New Testament in other ancient languages dating back nearly as far as the 2nd and 3rd century A.D. (some within one lifetime of the original writers).

The quotations in the writings of the Greek and Latin "church fathers" are so extensive that the entire New Testament (with the exception of less than a dozen verses) could be compiled from these quotes! Critics claim that the New Testament was written long after the time of Christ. This has been repeatedly proven incorrect by archaeological discoveries. **The accuracy of the Bible far exceeds any book written by man throughout all of history.**

We can be *absolutely confident* that we have an accurate record of God's Word and that God commends those who make the effort to seek the truth and investigate the Bible's claims (Acts 17:11).

BIBLICAL STUDIES IN THE LIGHT OF ARCHAEOLOGY, P. 65-69

[The Bereans] were more noble than those in Thessalonica, in that they received the word with all readiness of mind, and searched the scriptures daily, [to determine] whether those things were so.

ACTS 17:11 KJV

Evidence From GEOLOGY

Large river canyons are assumed to have taken millions of years to form as stream beds were washed away a particle at a time. **When Mt. St. Helens erupted in 1980, it provided a much better model–demonstrating how new river canyons can form rapidly.**

During the Mount St. Helens' eruption, there were numerous mudflows, because water backed up behind newly deposited sediment. When the water broke through in one area, a large mud flow resulted, cutting a new 140-foot deep canyon. **The power of flowing water to create massive geologic features has astounded geologists.** This "little Grand Canyon" is 40 times smaller than the Grand Canyon in Arizona. However, both now have a comparatively tiny stream meandering through a large river canyon. The walls of this new canyon even display the same horizontal bands of sediment commonly seen in road cuts or within the real Grand Canyon.

Mt. St. Helens' little Grand Canyon was not carved out over millions of years, but in one day by a large volume of water. This provides a model showing that other massive geologic features of our planet–like the Grand Canyon in Arizona– were *not* **necessarily formed gradually** over millions of years. Most of the earth's major geological features are a direct consequence of the worldwide Flood.

Creation, Evolution, and the Age of the Earth, p.48

"He [God] moves mountains without their knowing it and overturns them in his anger."

Job 9:5

Evidence From
BIBLICAL ACCURACY

Moses was a prince of Egypt brought up in the Pharaoh's palace. Acts 7:22 states that "Moses was learned in all the wisdom of the Egyptians..." Egyptian medical practices included smearing the blood of worms mixed with donkey dung into open wounds; applying the fat from horses, crocodiles, and snakes mixed with donkey teeth and honey to the scalp in order to grow hair; and drinking water poured over stone idols in order to cure snake bites.

Yet 4,000 years before mankind discovered the existence of bacteria and viruses, the Holy Spirit inspired Moses to institute modern methods of cleanliness. Even nineteenth century doctors were woefully ignorant of the following procedures. They routinely caused the death of patients by moving from dissecting dead bodies to examining live patients without even washing their hands. Here are just a few of the Bible's insights:

- Leviticus 11:35 warns against touching or bringing any **cooking utensil in contact with dead animals.**
- Leviticus chapter 13 details the first **procedures for medical quarantine** in order to prevent the spread of contagious diseases.
- Leviticus 15:13 calls for the prevention of disease by the **washing of the body** and clothes under "running water."
- In Deuteronomy 23:12-13 Moses even writes of the need for **proper sewage disposal.**

How could a man trained in Egyptian medical nonsense have written about such modern procedures unless he was inspired by God?

THE SIGNATURE OF GOD, P. 156-159

Designate a place outside the camp where you can go to relieve yourself. As part of your equipment have something to dig with, and when you relieve yourself, dig a hole and cover up your excrement.

DEUTERONOMY 23:12-13

Evidence From BIBLICAL ACCURACY

A specific chemical in our blood called hemoglobin carries oxygen throughout our bodies. Without this specific chemical, life could not exist. Each one of our red blood cells is capable of carrying 270 million molecules of hemoglobin. **Hemoglobin itself is such a tremendously complex molecule that it could never have developed by random-chance processes.** If even *two* of the 287 amino acids within the hemoglobin molecule are misplaced, a fatal disease called sickle-cell anemia results. If our blood carried less hemoglobin, there would not be enough residual oxygen available to sustain life after, say, a good sneeze or hard pat on the back.

Moses spoke about the blood being the life of our body, yet this wasn't even believed in George Washington's day. Doctors tried to cure George Washington of his illness by draining his blood. Many believe this medical malpractice is what killed him. It is interesting that Moses knew better almost 4,000 years earlier. How could Moses have been so accurate? Was it just a lucky guess?

A STUDY COURSE IN CHRISTIAN EVIDENCES, P.130

SEARCH FOR THE TRUTH: CHANGING THE WORLD WITH THE EVIDENCE FOR CREATION, I-8

" 'the life of every creature is its blood....' "

LEVITICUS 17:14

Evidence From BIOLOGY

There are numerous examples of the interdependence of animals within nature that defy all natural explanations. A perfect example is the activity of a certain mite that feeds upon the ear membranes of moths.

Some moths can hear ultrasonic sounds emitted by bats that the human ear cannot detect. This enables the moths to avoid being eaten by the bats. Moths of the *Noctvidae* family are often infested with mites which destroy the ability of the moth to hear by eating the moth's ear. It is extraordinary that these mites will only infest one ear on each moth.

Biologists, curious about this natural phenomena, placed nine mites on various parts of a moth. All nine mites migrated to the same ear. Next, mold was put onto the infested ear to make it unsuitable for digestion by the mites. **Amazingly, the mites moved to other parts of the moth's body, but they absolutely refused to eat the uninfested ear!** If both ears were destroyed, the moth would lose its defense mechanism, making both the moth and the mites more likely to be eaten. **How could the mites possibly know this?** How could mites learn that it is dangerous to eat both ears (without dying to gain the knowledge)? How could a dead mite warn its offspring to only eat one of the moth's ears so they won't die, as well?

In the original paradise that God meant our world to be, mechanisms such as this would not have been needed for survival. Yet even in our current fallen world God leaves abundant evidence of His handiwork–for anyone willing to see it!

EVOLUTION IN THE LIGHT OF SCRIPTURE, SCIENCE, AND SENSE, P. 40

The fool says in his heart, "There is no God."...

PSALM 53:1

Evidence From GEOLOGY

Petrified wood does not require millions of years to form. Several laboratory experiments have shown that under certain conditions wood can be petrified quite rapidly. During one field experiment, researchers lowered a block of wood into an alkaline spring in Yellowstone National Park. After one year in the hot silica-rich water, a substantial amount of the wood had been converted into stony material.

Furthermore, artificially petrified wood is even being commercially produced to make true "hardwood" floors. During the petrifaction process, minerals fill the pores and cavities of an organic structure. Next the tissue is dissolved, leaving spaces, where it once was. In the final stage, minerals solidify into the voids left by the missing organic matter. **It takes the right conditions, not necessarily long periods of time, to petrify wood.** Ground water percolating through hot volcanic ash (which typically is rich in silica) is thought to be the ideal natural environment for the rapid petrifaction of wood. These conditions would have been found worldwide during and after the Flood of Noah.

Petrified trees in national parks from Arizona to Montana are not a testimony to millions of years of Earth history, but to the **relatively recent worldwide Flood** which our planet has experienced.

The Young Earth, p. 113-114

It is the glory of God to conceal a matter; to search out a matter is the glory of kings.

Proverbs 25:2

Evidence From ASTRONOMY

One of the most straightforward evidences that our solar system is quite young is the presence of comets. With each trip past the sun, a comet loses part of its icy core. A comet's tail is evidence of material being stripped away by the sun's heat. Evolutionary astronomers acknowledge that comets could not be very old, but speculate that they are still around because they are being replenished from a storehouse of comets called the Oort cloud. The Oort cloud is a hypothetical area outside of our solar system where millions of comets supposedly reside. They speculate that some unknown mechanism kicks comets out of this storehouse into orbit within our solar system. **There is absolutely no evidence for the existence of the Oort cloud.**

A recent study published in *Nature* [409(6820): 589-591] shows additional problems for the belief in this imaginary Oort cloud. For such an area in space to statistically have enough comets such that one occasionally enters our solar system, far more would be destroyed by collisions within the Oort cloud itself–not leaving enough to enter our solar system. The Oort cloud does not qualify as a scientific theory, because there is no evidence of its existence. It is just assumed to exist. Yet it is taught as a fact in science textbooks. **The very existence of comets is still excellent evidence that our solar system is only a few thousand years old.**

TJ JOURNAL, VOL.15(2), 2001, P.11

The heavens declare the glory of God; the skies proclaim the work of His hands.

PSALM 19:1

Evidence From
BIOLOGY

Eels are among the most mysterious animals on earth. The prevailing scientific opinion is that all American and European eels lay their eggs under a mass of seaweed 1,500 feet deep in the Sargasso Sea. The pinhead-size eggs hatch to release transparent, ribbonlike creatures with no eyes or mouths. Billions of these tiny, blind creatures are programmed to travel 1,000 to 3,000 miles across the ocean. They get into the Gulf Stream and are carried toward Europe or America. Traveling farther north, they gradually lose their transparency and their eyes and mouths appear. The eels that are not eaten slowly develop hearts and stomachs. Next they swim up rivers and eat everything in sight, dead or alive. They gradually turn yellow and grow up to 3 feet long.

For the first five to eight years, eels are sexless, after which they develop both male and female organs. Once mature, their noses become pointy, they start back downstream, and their skin turns silvery. Apparently they never eat again, because no silver eel has ever been found with food in its stomach. The eels swim thousands of miles to their birthplace in the Sargasso Sea. At this time the eels either become a male or a female as one of their sex organs shrivels up. Once they reproduce, the eels die.

It is beyond comprehension to think all of this could have somehow evolved by random mutational processes. God designed this complex sequence allowing eels to thrive in our fallen world.

EVOLUTION IN LIGHT OF SCRIPTURE, SCIENCE, AND SENSE, P.43-45

"...stop and consider God's wonders."

JOB 37:14

Evidence From
BIBLICAL UNIQUENESS

The Bible was written on material that deteriorates, so it had to be copied and recopied by hand for hundreds of years before the invention of the printing press. **This copying did not diminish the accuracy of the original Hebrew Bible, because of the unique nature of the copying process.**

The Jews preserved Scripture as no other manuscript has ever been preserved. **They meticulously kept track of every letter, syllable, word, sentence, and paragraph** by counting each separate division on every page and comparing all of the tallies with the original before allowing the page to be put into use. Scribes, lawyers, and massoretes were special classes of men within Jewish culture whose sole duty was to preserve and transmit these documents with perfect fidelity. **If you compare the Bible with *all* other ancient writings, you will find it has more copies of the original manuscript, with less variation between manuscripts, than any other 10 pieces of classical literature combined.**

THIS INFORMATION IS CONDENSED FROM
EVIDENCE THAT DEMANDS A VERDICT, P.19
THIS BOOK IS AN EXCELLENT RESOURCE ON BIBLICAL ACCURACY.

As for God, his way is perfect; the word of the LORD is flawless....

PSALM 18:30

Evidence From
THE FOSSIL RECORD

Charles Darwin knew that the fossil record did not support his theory of evolution. In his book *Origin of the Species* Darwin noted that there was an obvious and serious problem with the lack of transitional fossils. He recognized that fossils of animals and plants are fully developed in fossil - bearing rocks. However, both he and early evolutionists expressed optimism that the fossil links between very different types of animals would be found. Yet over 160 years later, after extensive searching, not one undisputable transition between any major animal form has ever been found!

Darwin also admitted he could not explain the serious problem of how highly evolved animals could be found in the *lowest* rock layers. Evolutionists assume that the lowest layers are many millions of years older than higher layers. Therefore, they should contain very simple forms of life. There are many exceptions to this expectation. For example, very highly developed animals, such as trilobites, are found fully formed in these layers.

In light of what is now known about flood geology, it is reasonable to believe the majority of the fossil record was created by the catastrophic action of the shifting and changing Earth during the great Flood of Noah's time. The lowest rock layers are not millions of years older, they are just the first ones laid down during this Flood.

EVOLUTION IN THE LIGHT OF SCRIPTURE, SCIENCE, AND SENSE, P. 68-69

The wicked, through the pride of his countenance, will not seek after God: God is not in all his thoughts.

PSALM 10:4 KJV

Evidence From PHYSICS

Many great scientists have challenged the billion-year claims of the evolutionary time scale. One is Lord Kelvin, the scientist whose brilliant thermodynamic analysis gave us the absolute temperature scale that bears his name. Kelvin's numerous papers and scientific research pointed out many errors of the long-age concepts held by uniformitarian geologists of his day. **Kelvin rejected the ancient timetable of Earth history, not because of its contradiction to the Bible, but because of its conflict with physics.**

Kelvin's studies dealt with the both high temperature of the earth's core and the slowing of the earth's rate of rotation as evidence for a young earth. **He calculated that if the earth had been around for over five billion years, its initial rate of rotation would have been at least twice its present rate** (the days being only 12 hours long). This increased rotational speed would have increased the centrifugal force four times, causing the ancient earth to bulge much greater than is presently found at the equator. There is no physical evidence that the earth's rotational speed was ever this fast.

Lord Kelvin strongly opposed the evolutionary presuppositions of an extremely old earth using science to justify his belief in a young earth. No one has ever been able to contradict his physics.

EVOLUTION IN THE LIGHT OF SCRIPTURE,
SCIENCE, AND SENSE, P.96-97

The LORD by wisdom hath founded the earth; by understanding hath he established the heavens.

PROVERBS 3:19 KJV

Evidence From
ANATOMY

Our liver, which averages a mere three pounds, is the largest organ inside the human body. **This amazing chemical processing facility performs at least 500 known functions within our bodies.** It is such a complicated chemical factory that biochemists have not even remotely approached developing a machine of any size which accomplishes even a fraction of the same functions.

The liver stores vitamins, detoxifies poisons, stabilizes the body's blood sugar level, builds enzymes, and more. The liver filters enough blood in a single year to fill 23 milk trucks. The liver also plays an important role in our digestive process. Digestion could not take place without the interrelated functions of our liver, mouth, tongue, intestines, stomach, and pancreas. If these organs are not all working *in perfect concert,* we will have major (and potentially fatal) problems.

Observing how all of our body parts work together in such harmony should lead everyone to conclude that mankind was intelligently fashioned by a supreme mind–our Creator God.

The Human Body: Accident or Design?, p.37-38

And if the ear should say, "Because I am not an eye, I am not of the body," is it therefore not of the body? ...But now God has set the members, each one of them, in the body just as He pleased.

1 Corinthians 12:16-18 NKJV

Evidence From ASTRONOMY

If the universe is only thousands of years old, how did light from distant stars reach the earth? At its current speed, light would take billions of years to reach Earth from distant galaxies. One solution to this problem, based on the known laws of relativity, was proposed by a Ph.D. physics researcher from Los Alamos National Laboratories.

A former atheist, Dr. Humphreys discovered that combining biblical assumptions with the laws of relativity solved the mystery. He started with these assumptions:
   1. The earth is near the center of the universe.
   2. The universe is not infinite, but limited in size.
   3. The universe has been "stretched out."
The surprising result was the discovery that time moved in extreme "fast forward" for distant galaxies during the formation of the universe. **It is a scientific fact that we live in a universe in which time moves at different rates, depending on your location.** This "time dilation effect" would have been magnified tremendously as the universe was originally expanding. During this expansion, only days were passing near the center, while billions of years were passing in the distant heavens. This allowed light from distant galaxies time to reach the younger earth. The heavens look quite "old," even though very little time has passed here on Earth.

There is no contradiction between modern science and the straightforward statements of the Bible.

STARLIGHT AND TIME: SOLVING THE PUZZLE OF DISTANT STARLIGHT IN A YOUNG UNIVERSE

This is what God the LORD says–he who created the heavens and stretched them out, who spread out the earth and all that comes out of it, who gives breath to its people, and life to those who walk on it...

ISAIAH 42:5

Evidence From
BIOLOGY

Although birds feed on many butterflies and moths, they avoid eating the monarch butterfly. This is because the monarch butterfly has been given a special ability to protect itself. During its caterpillar stage, the monarch feeds *only* on the milkweed plant. This plant contains a powerful poison that can in most cases stop the heart of any creature that eats enough of it. The monarch caterpillar, however, can eat the milkweed and store the poison in its body, where it remains even after the caterpillar has turned into a butterfly.

How do birds know that eating this particular butterfly will cause sickness or death? **How does the monarch caterpillar know which plant to eat in order to take in only the poison to which it is immune?** How could the monarch's ability to avoid the effects of the poison have slowly evolved? All of this had to have worked perfectly from the beginning and points to a Creator who designed creatures for survival in our fallen world.

LETTING GOD CREATE YOUR DAY, VOL. 3, P.14
FROM DARKNESS TO LIGHT & THE LIFE AND ADVENTURES OF MONICA MONARCH, BY JULES POIRIER

You are God who performs miracles; you display your power among the peoples.

PSALM 77:14

Evidence From
COMMON SENSE

The geological record does *not* testify of an old earth, nor does it show any gradual development of life forms. The whole idea of animals evolving slowly over time cannot be supported by the fossil record. There is simply no evidence for the gradual transition of one form into a completely different form.

Another problem for evolution is the absence of animal remains. They *are not* piling up around us in order to eventually form a fossil layer representing what happened during this "geologic age." Instead, remains are ripped apart by scavengers and dispersed. **Of the estimated 100 million buffalo which roamed the great plains over a century ago, not a single one is now in the process of fossilization.**

The only reason we find such a **rich fossil record of life** in the past (a record that shows distinct forms of life, not life in the process of changing from one form to another) is because there was a *worldwide Flood* which rapidly buried this life!

SCIENCE AND THE BIBLE, P.19

..."Teacher, rebuke your disciples!" "I tell you," he replied, "if they keep quiet, the stones will cry out."

LUKE 19:39-40

Evidence From
ARCHAEOLOGY

Seven hundred years before the birth of Jesus, the prophet Isaiah foretold that Immanuel (this Hebrew name means "God is with us") would be conceived by and born to a virgin. In Isaiah 7:14 the prophet used the Hebrew word *almah* for virgin. **For centuries critics denied the fact that *almah* meant virgin,** but argued that it simply meant "a young woman." Even though the apostle Matthew wrote that Jesus' birth fulfilled the Old Testament prophecy (Matthew 1:22-23), critics claimed the prophet Isaiah didn't really have the birth of Christ in mind. Archaeology is now providing additional support.

One of the most competent Jewish scholars of this generation, Dr. Cyrus H. Gordon, has unearthed clay tablets at Ugarit in Syria which clearly use the word *almah* in the parallel Semitic language to mean "virgin" and not "young woman." ***Almah* was being used to specifically mean "virgin" long before Isaiah**. The clay tablet which documents this was written even before the time of Moses (more than 3,000 years ago).

BIBLICAL STUDIES IN THE LIGHT OF ARCHAEOLOGY, P.53

Therefore the Lord himself shall give you a sign; behold, a virgin shall conceive, and bear a son, and shall call his name Immanuel.

ISAIAH 7:14 KJV

Evidence From BIBLICAL ACCURACY

The Lord asked Job, "Where is the *way* to the dwelling of light?" **In Hebrew the word *way* literally means a "traveled path or road."** In the 17th century Sir Isaac Newton suggested that light was made of tiny particles which traveled in a straight line. Christian Huygens proposed that light traveled as a wave. Scientists now know that light is a form of energy called radiant energy, and that it travels in electromagnetic waves at approximately 186,000 miles per second in a straight line. **It takes about eight minutes for light to travel its "path" from the sun to the earth.** There really is a "way" or "path" of light, just as the Bible says.

It is absolutely amazing that the closer we look at each specific word used in the Bible, the more we can't help but stand in awe of its intricate detail, purposeful design, relevance across time, and perfect harmony. Only God Himself could orchestrate the writing of such a book!

A STUDY COURSE IN CHRISTIAN EVIDENCES, P.132

"Where is the way to the dwelling of light?..."

JOB 38:19 NASV

DECEMBER 19

Evidence From
THE FOSSIL RECORD

Within hours of dying, the two halves of a clam's shell begin to open and separate. Clams found with their shells tightly shut can only indicate they had been buried alive. **There are huge clam fossil graveyards all over the world containing millions of fossilized clams which are packed tightly together with their shells clamped shut.** Yet there is no example anywhere in the world today of millions of clams being buried in this condition.

One of the best examples of a clam fossil graveyard can be found near Halkirk, Alberta, Canada. Many of these clams are encased in a closed condition (indicating rapid burial) in sheets of ironstone. In other locations, millions of marine-dwelling creatures are preserved in hot molten rock which poured out onto the ocean floor.

The biblical account of Noah's Flood explains why this type of formation has occurred in so many locations around the world. When the "fountains of the deep" broke up, volcanic eruptions occurred all over the surface of the earth, both on land masses and in ocean beds. In other places massive movements of sediment simply buried the clams. These fossils strongly support the biblical account of a worldwide Flood.

THE EVIDENCE FOR CREATION, P.167-168

...on that day all the springs of the great deep burst forth, and the floodgates of the heavens were opened. And rain fell on the earth forty days and forty nights.

GENESIS 7:11-12

Evidence From
MATHEMATICS

The *science of statistics* testifies to the impossibility of evolution. The evolution of the "first" life form requires that thousands of specific components come together in exactly the right way. If you have only six components that need to be combined in a specific order, the number of possible combinations is six factorial (1x2x3x4x5x6), or 720 possibilities. **The simplest form of life actually requires thousands of specific chemicals, but let's assume it only needs 200.** The odds of 200 chemicals combining in exactly the right way is 1/(1x2x3x4x5...x200). **By natural random processes this is likely to happen once every 10^{375} attempts** (1 with 375 zeros after it). Yet only one of these combinations can be shown to result in a living cell.

By comparison, the total number of electrons that could be packed into the space available within the entire universe would only be 10^{130}. What are the chances of *all* of the millions of parts in *all* of the millions of organisms on Earth *all* arranging themselves by random-chance processes with no intelligence directing them? The science of statistics would tell us that **this probability is actually an impossibility**. Yet this is exactly what every public school child in America is being led to believe has happened to produce life.

UNLOCKING THE MYSTERIES OF CREATION,
PREMIER EDITION, P.86-87

$2\times(3+4)=$

For although they knew God, they neither glorified him as God nor gave thanks to him, but their thinking became futile and their foolish hearts were darkened. Although they claimed to be wise, they became fools...

ROMANS 1:21-22

Evidence From
BIOLOGY

The thousands of members in an ant colony do not run short of supplies, even though there is no apparent central organization. Why don't some ants get fat, while other ants starve? Modern science is learning how the ant's astonishing system works. By giving radioactively tagged sugar water to worker ants, scientists discovered that within a week every member of the colony had an equal amount of the radioactive water. The sugar water that the worker ants injested was shared with nest mates and delivered to the developing young. The water was also used to soak the ground to keep the chamber's humidity high.

Food is also collected and returned to the colony to be shared with every member of the colony, most often by regurgitation. **Through continuous food sharing, every member of the colony always has an equal amount of food.**

It is difficult to believe this highly organized system of sharing both food and water evolved by chance. A better explanation is the intricate, detailed planning of the Creator.

LETTING GOD CREATE YOUR DAY, VOL. 3, P.78

Go to the ant, you sluggard; consider its ways and be wise! It has no commander, no overseer or ruler, yet it stores its provisions in summer and gathers its food at harvest.
PROVERBS 6:6-8

Evidence From PROPHECY

The book of Daniel contains a remarkable prophecy that accurately predicts the *exact* day on which Jesus declared himself Messiah. **This passage, starting at Daniel 9:24, indicates that 483 years would pass from the day that the order was given to rebuild Jerusalem until the day of the declaration of "Messiah the Prince."** We know from other Old Testament texts that the order to commission the rebuilding of Jerusalem was given on March 14, 445 B.C. If we count forward exactly 483 Jewish years (a Jewish year was 360 days long), this equals 173,880 days; and we come to the date of April 6, 32 A.D. **What happened on that day in history?** It was the *exact* day on which Jesus arranged to have Himself declared the Messiah of the Jewish people by riding into Jerusalem on a donkey.

The *Messiah's* entry into *Jerusalem* on a *donkey* was predicted hundreds of years earlier in Zechariah 9:9. **Exactly on the day predicted by Daniel, 173,880 days after the proclamation that Jerusalem be rebuilt, Jesus rode into Jerusalem revealing Himself as this Messiah.** As the people sang a Messianic song, the Jewish religious authorities (understanding what was implied) told Jesus to stop the worship. Jesus responded, "I tell you, if these should hold their peace, the very stones would immediately cry out" (Luke 19:40).

HIDDEN TREASURES IN BIBLICAL TEXT, P.17

...Shout, Daughter of Jerusalem! See, your King comes to you, righteous and having salvation, gentle and riding on a donkey....

ZECHARIAH 9:9

DECEMBER 23

Evidence From
THE WORLDWIDE FLOOD

On the morning of July 15, 1942, six brand new P-38 Lightnings and two B-17 Flying Fortresses took off from a secret airfield in Greenland, heading for a bombing mission in Germany. The squadron became lost in a blizzard, and the pilots were forced to land on a glacier. The crew was rescued nine days later, but **the planes were abandoned to the relentless snow and left on the ice for the next 50 years.**

In 1980 two Atlanta businessmen, Richard Taylor and Patrick Epps, decided to recover the planes. Twelve years and millions of dollars later, the persistent partners succeeded in retrieving one of the eight airplanes. It had taken so long because the airplanes had to be dismantled piece by piece and recovered from underneath 250 feet of solid ice!

The fact that 250 feet of ice could accumulate in only 50 years clearly demonstrates that **hundreds of thousands of years are not required for the formation of our planet's polar ice caps.** Instead of hundreds of thousands of years and multiple ice ages, a single catastrophic event (such as the aftermath of a worldwide flood) easily explains the great depths of ice at the polar caps.

Both evolutionists and creationists recognize that the Ice Age was the last major geologic event to dramatically affect our entire planet. Evolutionists believe in dozens of ice ages over hundreds of thousands of years, but all evidence for these multiple events is purely circumstantial and highly speculative. Evidence is rapidly accumulating (such as the depth of these buried planes) which indicates that a single Ice Age, rather than multiple events, is the best explanation.

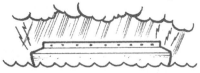

SEARCH FOR THE TRUTH,
p.93

It is the glory of God to conceal a thing: but the honour of kings is to search out a matter.

PROVERBS 25:2 KJV

Evidence From ANATOMY

Even the very smallest bones of our feet testify to specific design by incredible intelligence. One-fourth of all our body's bones are in the feet. Our feet have been ingeniously designed to perform the functions of many modern machines:

1. They **support** a relatively large weight on a very small surface area by the use of arches. This is comparable to the design used in bridges.
2. They operate as **levers** which pivot at the ankle so that we can perform such tasks as pressing the accelerator of a car.
3. They act as a **vertical lift** when we elevate onto our tiptoes.
4. They act as a **catapult** when we jump.
5. They act to **cushion** our legs when we run.

All of these features are extremely helpful–especially in view of the fact that the average person walks about 65,000 miles in his/her lifetime. This is equivalent to walking around the world more than two and one half times.

Anyone doubting the existence of his Creator need look no further than his own feet.

THE HUMAN BODY: ACCIDENT OR DESIGN?, P.21-22

Great are the works of the LORD; they are pondered by all who delight in them.

PSALM 111:2

Evidence From
OUR CHANGED NATURE

The baby whose birth is celebrated around the world on Christmas day...the baby whose birth marks the central focus of all history, as dates count from this event in both directions... the baby whose birth and life were foretold hundreds of years in advance by over 300 prophetic statements...**is the same person that the New Testament declares as the** *Creator* **of the universe.**

The real Christmas is special–not because of the glitz, gifts, and gatherings–but because it is a celebration of the day in which the Creator of the entire universe entered into His creation and became a human being. This historical event loses its ability to give our lives purpose if evolution, rather than Jesus Christ, is responsible for creation. The only physical evidence for God's existence is from His creation and testing the accuracy of His Word. This is why it is absolutely vital for us to study creation and the Bible in order to see for ourselves that God is revealed through both. Christmas will become a "holiday season"–completely devoid of its intended meaning–in direct proportion to the belief in evolution being accepted as a fact. If Jesus is not our literal Creator, then why make Him the center of Christmas by celebrating His birthday?

Truly accepting what God has done for us by becoming human (celebrated at Christmas) and dying for our sins (celebrated at Easter) changes our focus, priorities, and lives. This, in turn, inspires us to reach out to others with the *good news* of who Jesus is and what He has done.

BRUCE MALONE

All things were made through Him.... *JOHN 1:3 NKJV*

For by Him all things were created that are in heaven and that are on earth.... *COLOSSIANS 1:16 NKJV*

[God has] spoken unto us by His Son...through whom also He made the worlds... *HEBREWS 1:2 NKJV*

Evidence From
BIOLOGY

Tropical birds are not only fast and agile fliers but have long, pointed beaks, well-designed to catch butterflies. It would seem that brightly colored butterflies would be easy meals for the much faster birds. Some butterflies are protected by distinctive markings which warn birds they are poisonous. Other nonpoisonous butterflies carry the same markings to fool birds into thinking they are poisonous. But why aren't other bright and tasty butterflies easy meals for birds?

Biologists have discovered that the muscles in nonpoisonous butterfly wings produce more lift-power per unit of weight than bird muscles. Since butterflies also weigh far less than birds, they can fly in tight, darting, erratic patterns that allow them to escape pursuing birds. **What's even more amazing is that edible butterflies have** *50% more* **flight muscle than the poisonous butterflies.**

When one considers how perfectly every living thing has been designed–even after the Fall–to function to its greatest advantage, one must stand in awe of the Master Designer.

LETTING GOD CREATE YOUR DAY, VOL. 3, P.46

"For as the heavens are higher than the earth, so are my ways higher than your ways, and my thoughts than your thoughts."

ISAIAH 55:9 KJV

Evidence From CREATION FOUNDATION

One of many ideas which attempt to combine evolution with the Bible is the *"day-age theory."* **This theory says that the days described in Genesis represent millions of years.** Those who hold to this view believe that the order of geologic history as outlined by the evolutionary theory corresponds with the order of creation in the Bible. **Scripture clearly shows enormous differences:**

1. The Bible states all plant life came into existence on the third day of creation, but fish and marine organisms were created on the fifth day. *Evolution reverses this order.*

2. The Bible states God made the sun, moon, and stars on the fourth day of creation, the day after the creation of plants. *The suggestion that a day of creation could be equivalent to millions of years would not be possible.*

3. The Bible states birds and marine organisms were created on the same day. *Evolution says birds evolved from reptiles millions of years after fish first appeared.*

4. The Bible indicates crawling things (possibly insects) were among the last things created–at the same time as land animals and reptiles. *Evolution puts insects early in the geological record preceding the appearance of animals.*

5. The Bible states that death entered this world through Adam's sin. *The whole concept of evolution is based on the suggestion that death and mutations, working with natural selection, produced mankind.*

6. **In the first chapter of Genesis it is very clear that each creation day is bounded by a morning and an evening.** This could only describe a normal 24-hour day.

THE EVIDENCE FOR CREATION, P.21-23

...but the seventh day is the Sabbath of the LORD thy God. In it you shall do no work.... For in six days the LORD made the heavens and the earth, the sea, and all that is in them, and rested the seventh day....

EXODUS 20:10,11 NKJV

Evidence From PHYSICS

Radiometric dating methods have become an important basis for the claim that the earth is billions of years old. All of radiometric methods are based on three assumptions:

1. The initial amount of the decayed product is known.
2. The rate of decay is known throughout the dating period.
3. None of the decay element has been added to or lost.

These **assumptions are not directly testable**, and therefore no dating method is strictly scientific. It is impossible for anyone to know the initial components of the system or to prove that the decay rate has not changed.

The concept of having a process take place over a long period of time without interference is not reasonable. It is also totally unreasonable to claim that elements have not been added to or taken away from the system over millions of years of time. **The greatest problem with the reliability of radiometric dating methods is the extreme variability of results.** A wide range of dates is often obtained. The date is only "accepted" if it falls within the range which makes evolution seem possible. If the resulting age is not what is expected, it is ignored as a bad or contaminated sample.

The Evidence for Creation, p.34-35

...Has not God made foolish the wisdom of the world?

1 Corinthians 1:20

Evidence From
PHYSICS

Carbon 14 (^{14}C) is a dating method used to measure how long ago a sample of previously living tissue died. As long as any organism is alive, it maintains a fairly constant concentration of ^{14}C with its environment. Once it dies, the radioactive ^{14}C starts to decay; and half of the ^{14}C disappears every 5,730 years. If an artifact is found that has one-half of the modern level of ^{14}C, it is assumed to be 5,730 years old.

Scientists have recently found that the amount of radioactive carbon in the earth's atmosphere is *not constant*. The ^{14}C concentration can be affected by things such as the *total mass of plant life* on earth, the earth's changing *magnetic field, volcanic activity, solar flare activity* on the sun, *nuclear tests* made in the past several decades, *collisions of asteroids or meteorites* with the earth, etc. For example, tree rings from all over the world had an increased variability in ^{14}C level following the 1908 asteroid explosion in Tunguska, Siberia.

Even more important, the concentration of ^{14}C in living things would have changed dramatically right after the worldwide Flood as the total amount of vegetation on the planet readjusted to new conditions. **^{14}C dating is totally unreliable for any date beyond about 4,000 years,** because the assumptions of the technique deny any major change in conditions. It ignores the effect of the worldwide Flood throughout the calculation. **As with all scientific endeavors, if your assumptions are wrong, your conclusions will also be wrong.**

THE EVIDENCE FOR CREATION, P.41-45

Beware lest anyone cheat you through philosophy and empty deceit, according to the tradition of men, according to the basic principles of the world, and not according to Christ.

COLOSSIANS 2:8 NKJV

Evidence From CHEMISTRY

Amino acids are large complex molecules that form the building blocks of our bodies. Amino acids are produced by reactions that result in 50:50 mixtures of right-handed and left-handed amino acids. These amino acids are like identical right and left- handed gloves. The amino acids in all *living things*, however, are made up of almost all *left-handed* molecules. No natural or unguided process can separate these left- and right-handed molecules from each other. So how did life come to select **almost exclusively** left-handed forms when the first cell formed? The mathematical probability that chance processes could produce merely one tiny protein molecule with only left-handed amino acids for even the simplest form of life is virtually zero.

Nucleotides, other molecules necessary for life, also come in the right- and left-handed forms. **Yet nucleotides are only found in the** *right-handed* **form within** *living things*!

Since nucleotides and amino acids are both necessary for life, they must have appeared together in the first living cell. The probability of life forming from a random mixture of chemicals while only using left-handed amino acids and only right-handed nucleotides requires an intelligent Designer.

In the Beginning, 7ᵀᴴ Ed., p.14

"In the beginning you laid the foundations of the earth, and the heavens are the work of your hands. They will perish, but you remain; they will all wear out like a garment...."

Psalm 102:25-26

Evidence From
OUR CHANGED NATURE

One of the foremost evidences of the character of our Creator is His presence in our lives. **Our changed nature should speak volumes.** Our words and our actions should clearly demonstrate that the Creator not only exists, but that His Holy Spirit dwells within us and is continuously working in us to develop our character to be like Christ's. Even the way we choose to spend our time and money should be a testimony of our love for Him.

As God opens our eyes to see the intricate design of everything in His creation and allows us to understand that His Word is *testable*, *accurate*, and *reliable*, we will grow in our knowledge of and love for Him. This will then give us the opportunity to become a strong and powerful witness to the reality of our Creator God. We will be able to share our faith with anyone who asks us why we have the hope within us and will be able to do so *intelligently*, *confidently*, and with *love* and *respect*.

RICH AND TINA KLEISS

And do not be conformed to this world, but be transformed by the renewing of your mind, that you may prove what is that good and acceptable and perfect will of God.

ROMANS 12:2 NKJV

Bibliography

Acts and Facts Newsletter, Instutute for Creation Research, El Cajon, CA, www.ICR.org.

A Study Course in Christian Evidences, Bert Thompson, Ph.D. and Wayne Jackson, Apologetics Press, Inc., Montgomery, AL, 1992.

America: To Pray? or Not to Pray?, David Barton, Wallbuilders Press, Aledo, TX, 1988.

Astronomy and the Bible; Questions and Answers, Donald B. DeYoung, Baker Book House Company, 1991.

The Bible Has The Answer, Henry M. Morris, Ph.D., LL.D., Litt.D. and Martin E. Clark, Ph.D., Creation -Life Publishers, Master Books, El Cajon, CA 1987.

Biblical Studies in the Light of Archaeology, Wayne Jackson, Apologetics Press, Inc., Stockton, CA 1982.

Bone of Contention: Is Evolution True? Silvia Baker, M.Sc., Triune Press Pty. Ltd., 6th Ed., Australia, 1992.

Bones of Contention: A Creationist Assessment of Human Fossils, Martin Lubenow, Baker Books, Grand Rapids, MI, 1992.

Character Sketches, Volume II (1978), Used by permission of the Institute in Basic Life Principles, August 1995.

Character Sketches, Volume III (1985), Used by permission of the Institute in Basic Life Principles, August 1995.

CEA Update Newsletter (Winter 2001), Creation Education Association, Eugene Sattler, editor, Pine River, WI.

The Closing of the American Mind: How Higher Education has Failed Democracy and Impoverished the Souls of Today's Students, Allan Bloom, Simon and Schuster, New York, New York, 1987.

Commonscensescience.org, David Bergman, The electronmagnetic theory of matter, 2002.

The Creation, Don Stewart, Here's Life Publishers, Inc., San Bernardino, CA, 1984.

Creation Magazine, Carl Wieland, Ph.D., editor, Answers in Genesis Ltd., Qld, Australia, answersingenesis.org.

Creation Ex Nihilo Magazine, , editor, Answers in Genesis Ltd., Qld, Australia, answersingenesis.org.

Creation, Evolution, and the Age of the Earth, Wayne Jackson, Courier Publications, Stockton, CA, 1989.

Creation Research Quarterly, Emmett Williams editor, Creation Research Society; P.O. Box 8263; St. Joseph, MO 64508.

Creation's Tiny Mystery, Robert V. Gentry, D.Sc.Hon., Earth Science Associates, Knoxville, TN, 1988.

Darwin's Black Box: The Biochemical Challenge to Evolution, Michael J. Behe, Ph.D., Simon & Schuster Inc. (Touchtone), New York, NY, 1996.

The Darwin Conspiracy, James Scott Bell, Ph.D., Broadman & Holman, Nashville, TN, 2002.

Darwin on Trial, Philip E. Johnson, Ph.D., InterVarsity Press, Downer Grove, IL. (with special arrangement)Regnery Gateway, Washington, D.C., 1991.

The Defender's Bible, Henry M. Morris, Ph.D., LL.D., Litt.D., World Publishing, Inc. Grand Rapids, MI, 1995.

The Evidence For Creation, Examining the Origin of Planet Earth, Dr. G.S. McLean, Roger Oakland, Larry McLean, Full Gospel Bible Institute, Eston, Saskatchewan, 1989.

Evidence That Demands a Verdict, Josh McDowell, Here's Life Pub. Inc., San Bernardino, CA (Nelson Pub., Nashville, TN), 1979.

Evolution in the Light of Scripture, Science, and Sense, Basil Overton, Ph.D., J.C. Choate Publication, Winona, MS, 1988.

Female Piety. A Young Woman's Friend and Guide, John Angell James, Soli Deo Gloria Pub., Morgan, PA, 1994.

From Darkness to Light to Flight, Jules Poirier, ICR, El Cajon, CA, 1995.

The Great Works Catalog, Bryce Gaudian, 21992 810th Ave., Haywward, MN 56043, gaudian@deskmedia.com, 2003.

The Genesis Record, Henry M Morris, Ph.D., LL.D., Litt.D., Baker Book House, Grand Rapids, MI and Master Books, El Cajon, CA, 1976.

God: Coming Face to Face with His Majesty, John F. MacArthur, Jr., Ph.D., Victor Books, SP Publications, Inc., Wheaton, IL, 1993.

Grand Canyon: Monument to Catastrophe, Steven A. Austin, Ph.D., Editor, Institute for Creation Research, Santee, CA, 1994.

The Great Dinosaur Mystery and the Bible, Paul S. Taylor, David. C. Cook Pub. Company, Elgin, IL, 1989.

Helping Children Understand Genesis and the Dinosaur, Erich A. von Fange, Ph. D., Living Word Services, 1992.

Hidden Treasures in the Biblical Text, Chuck Missler, Ph. D., Koinonia House, Coeur d' Alene, ID, 2000.

The Human Body: Accident or Design?, Wayne Jackson, Courier Publications, Stockton, CA, 1993.

Icons of Evolution: Science or Myth?, Jonathan Wells, Regnery Publishing, Inc., Washington, DC, 2000.

ICR Impact Articles, The Institue for Creation Research, El Cajon, CA, ICR.org.

The Illustrated Origins Answer Book, Paul S. Taylor, Eden Productions, Mesa, AZ, 1990.

In The Beginning, Compelling Evidence for Creation and the Flood, 7th Edition, Walt Brown, Jr., Ph.D., Center for Scientific Creation, Phoenix, AZ, 2001.

In The Minds of Men, Ian T. Taylor, TFE Publishing, Toronto, Canada, 1987.

It Couldn't Just Happen, Lawrence Richards, Sweet Publishing Inc., Ft. Worth, TX, 1987.

It's a Young World After All: Exciting Evidences for Recent Creation, Paul D. Ackerman, Ph.D., Baker Book House, Grand Rapids, MI, 1986.

Learn the Bible in 24 Hours, Chuck Missler, Ph.D., Thomas Nelson Inc., Nashville, TN, 2002.

Letting God Create Your Day, Vol. 2, Paul A. Bartz, Bible Science Assoc. Inc., Minneapolis, MN, 1991. (Now Creation Moments, Zimmerman, MN)

Letting God Create Your Day, Vol. 3, Paul A. Bartz, Bible Science Assoc. Inc., Minneapolis, MN, 1992. (Now Creation Moments, Zimmerman, MN)

Letting God Create Your Day, Vol. 4, Paul A. Bartz, Bible Science Assoc. Inc., Minneapolis, MN, 1993. (Now Creation Moments, Zimmerman, MN)

Many Infallible Proofs, Henry M. Morris, Ph.D., LL.D., Litt.D., Creation - Life Pub., Inc. Master Book Division, El Cajon, CA, 1974.

Men of Science Men of God, Henry M. Morris, Ph.D., LL.D., Litt.D., Master Books (Creation-Life Publishers, Inc.), El Cajon, CA, 1988.

Myths and Miracles; A New Approach to Genesis 1-11, David C.C. Watson, Creation Science Foundation Ltd. Sunnybank, Australia, 1988.

The Mythology of Modern Geology, Wayne Jackson, Apologetics Press, Inc., Stockton, CA, Third Printing, 1990.

Noah to Abraham: the Turbulent Years, Erich A. von Fange, Ph.D., Living Word Services, 1994.

Noah's Ark: A Feasibility Study, Woodmorappe, John, The Institute for Creation Research, Santee, CA, 1996.

One Blood: The Biblical Answer to Racism, Ken Ham, Carl Wieland, Don Batten, Master Books, Green Forest, AR, 1999.

Piercing the Darkness, Frank Peretti, First International Press Edition, 1997.

Proceedings of the First, Second, Third, Fourth, & Fifth International Conference on Creationism:1986, 1990, 1994, 1998, 2003, Creation Science Fellowship, Pittsburgh, PA.

The Real Meaning of the Zodiac, D. James Kennedy, Ph.D., Coral Ridge Ministries, Fort Lauderdale, Fl, 1993.

Reason and Revelation, Bert Thompson, Ph.D., Apologetics Press, Inc., Montgomery, AL, 1993.

Refuting Evolution: A Response to the National Academy of Sciences' Teaching About Evolution and the Nature of Science, Jonathan Sarfati, Ph.D., Master Books, Green Forest, AR, 1999.

Refuting Evolution 2: What PBS and the Scientific Community Don't Want You to Know, Jonathan Sarfati, Ph.D., Master Books, Green Forest, AR, 2002.

The Revised & Expanded Answers Book: The 20 Most-Asked Questions about Creation, Evolution, and the Book of Genesis, Answered!, Ken Ham, Jonathan Sarfati, Ph.D., Carl Wieland, Ph.D., Master Books, Green Forest, AR, 2000.

The Revelation of God in Nature, Apologetics Press Inc., Bert Thompson, Ph.D. and Wayne Jackson, M.A., Apologetics Press Inc., Montgomery, AL, 1985.

Science and the Bible, Lee Grady, Maranatha Publications, 1985.

Science and the Bible, Henry M. Morris, Ph.D., LL.D., Litt.D., Moody Press, Chicago, IL, 1986.

Search for the Truth: Changing the World with the Evidence for Creation, Bruce Malone, Search for the Truth Publishers, Midland, MI, 2006.

The Setterfield Hypothesis - A Simplified Explanation, www.setterfield.org, Feb. 2001.

Seven Men Who Rule from the Grave, David Breese, Moody Press, Chicago, IL, 1990.

The Signature of God: Astonishing Biblical Discoveries, Grant R. Jefferey, Frontier Research Publications, Toronto, Ontario, 1996.

Starlight and Time: Solving the Puzzle of Distant Starlight in a Young Universe, D. Russell Humphreys, Ph.D.,Master Books (Creation-Life Publ. Inc.), Colorado Springs, CO, 1994.

TJ: The In-Depth Journal of Creation, Pierre Jerlstrom, Ph.D., Senior Editor, Answers in Genesis Ltd., Qld, Australia, answersingenesis.org.

Tornado in the Junkyard: The Relentless Myth of Darwinism, James Perloff, Refuge Books, Arlington, MA, 1999.

Unlocking the Mysteries of Creation, Third printing revised ed., Dennis R. Peterson, Master Books, El Cajon, CA, 1988.

Unlocking the Mysteries of Creation, Premier Edition, Dennis R. Peterson, Creation Research Pub., El Dorado, CA, 2002.

Why I Believe, D. James Kennedy, Ph.D., Word Publishing, Dallas, TX, 1987.

World by Design Newsletter, Vol. 2, #6, Vol. 3, #3, Creation Research Science Education Foundation, Paul McDorman editor, Columbus, OH.

The Young Earth, John D. Morris, Ph.D., LL.D., Litt.D., Creation - Life Publishers Inc., Master Books Division, Colorado Springs, CO, 1994.

Index of Topics

Subject	Date	Verse	Book/Author
Abortion - evolutionary justification	16-Apr	Proverbs 8:8, 9	Search for the Truth
Absolute Truth - evidence for creation	21-Sept	Proverbs 3:5,6	Piercing the Darkness
Algae - bacteria eating	9-Jul	Psalm 95:3, 5	Letting God Create Your Day
Altruism - evidence against evolution	21-Jun	John 15:13	In the Beginning
Amino acids/Neucleotides	30-Dec	Psalm 102:25-26	In the Beginning
Animal - population stabilization	11-May	Revelation 4:11	The Genesis Record
- interrelationships, snake & gecko	25-Jul	Psalm 147:7,9	Letting God Create Your Day
Anthropic principle - order shows design	22-Jul	Job 25:2	It Couldn't Just Happen
Ants - aphid symbiosis	7-Oct	Proverbs 6:6	Character Sketches
- cooperation shows design	21-Dec	Proverbs 6:6-8	Letting God Create Your Day
Ape-man- history of mistakes	13-Jun	Mark 10:5,6	Letting God Create Your Day
- Java Man	4-Sept	Genesis 1:26	The Bones of Contention
- Neanderthal & others	6-Apr	Titus 1:10,11	In the Beginning
- Nebraska man	3-Jul	1 Timothy 6:20	The Illustrated Origins Answer Book
- Piltdown & other errors	17-Apr	Genesis 1:27	In the Beginning
- vast difference of ape/man	12-Jul	Proverbs 2:3-5	In the Minds of Men
Aphids, unique reproduction abilities	8-Oct	Psalm 50:11	Character Sketches
Archaeopteryx	9-Feb	Proverbs 17:24	Refuting Evolution
Ark - caring for all of animals	28-Feb	Genesis 6:19	The Genesis Record
- project size within man's ability	27-May	Genesis 6:14, 15, 22	The Creation
- size would fit all animals	18-Apr	Genesis 6:19; 7:2,3	Noah's Ark: A Feasibility Study
- stability	15-Jan	Genesis 6:15	The Creation, The Genesis Record
Armillarius - fungus design	31-Mar	Isaiah 66:2	Letting God Create Your Day
Asteroid belt - dust layer shows young age	25-Oct	Isaiah 48:12-13	It's a Young World After All
Bacteria - bdella	17-Mar	Psalm 14:1	Letting God Create Your Day
- E. coli flagella	23-Mar	Psalm 109:27	Darwin's Black Box
- metal corroding	27-Mar	Matthew 6:19	Letting God Create Your Day
- pollution eating	2-Jul	Psalm 8:6-8	Letting God Create Your Day
Bats - ability to identify pups	21-Apr	Job 5:9	Letting God Create Your Day
- sonar system	18-Jul	Psalm 119:68	Character Sketches
- synergism with flying insects	23-Apr	Nehemiah 9:6	Letting God Create Your Day
Bees - ability to make complex nutrients	15-Aug	Psalm 111:2	Letting God Create Your Day
Bible - attempts to destroy	19-Nov	Mark 13:31	Many Infallible Proofs
- evidence for uniqueness	16-Feb	2 Peter 1:20,21	Many Infallible Proofs
- evidence of design	20-Feb	Isaiah 45:21	Hidden Treasures in the Biblical Text
- evidence that written by Holy Spirit	21-Feb	Matthew 5:18	Hidden Treasures in the Biblical Text
- only document that explains origin	1-Jun	Exodus 3:14	Many Infallible Proofs
- reasons for studying evidences	1-Apr	2 Samuel 7:22	Many Infallible Proofs
- resurrection proof of uniqueness	12-Apr	Matthew 28:6,7	Many Infallible Proofs
- unity of thought	12-May	Psalm 119:89-90	Many Infallible Proofs
Biblical accuracy - air has weight	25-May	Job 28:24-25	Myths and Miracles
- archaeology confirming	17-Nov	Proverbs 30:5	Biblical Studies in the Light of Arch.
- copy agreement	21-Jul	Matthew 24:35	Evidence that Demands a Verdict
- Edom, destruction	26-Nov	Jeremiah 49:16-17	Science and the Bible
- exacting copy methods	10-Dec	Psalm 18:30	Evidence that Demands a Verdict
- Genesis reliability	16-Jun	Psalm 33:4	Myths and Miracles
- hare, chews cud	29-Jul	Deuteronomy 14:7	Character Sketches
- Jericho, fall of	28-Sep	Joshua 6:20,24	Science and the Bible
- light follows a path	18-Dec	Job 38:19	A Study Course in Christian Evid.
- long day of Joshua	8-Jul	Joshua 10:13-14	Rivers in the Desert
- mankind literacy	29-Oct	Joshua 8:32	Evidence That Demands a Verdict
- marriage	28-Oct	Genesis 2:24	The Genesis Record
- number of copies	2-Dec	Acts 17:11	Biblical Studies in the Light of Arch.
- number of stars	14-May	Jeremiah 33:22	A Study Course in Christian Evidence
- prophecy	15-Mar	Deuteronomy 18:21-22	Many Infallible Proofs
- Quirinius as governor	7-Jul	Luke 2:2	Letting God Create Your Day
- record of early travel	13-Apr	Acts 17:11	Letting God Create Your Day
- sanitary practices	4-Dec	Deuteronomy 23:12,13	The Signature of God
- sin nature of man	24-Jun	Genesis 6:5	Evidence that Demands a Verdict
- stars uniqueness	20-Oct	1 Corinthians 15:41	Astronomy and the Bible
- Tyre, city destruction	23-Jul	Ezekiel 26:3-14	Why I Believe
- virgin, meaning	17-Dec	Isaiah 7:14	Biblical Studies in the Light of Arch.

Index of Topics (continued)

Subject	Date	Verse	Book/Author
Big Bang Theory - a few problems	9-Oct	Job 38:33	Astronomy and the Bible
Birds - blackbird evidence of design	29-Mar	Psalm 104:31	Letting God Create Your Day
- eagles	28-Jan	Exodus 19:4	Character Sketches
- feather design	28-May	Psalm 47:2	It Couldn't Just Happen
- guillemot eggs	11-Jun	Psalm 50:11	Myths and Miracles
- Hawaiian birds (fossils)	29-Apr	Ecclesiastes 3:1,2	Letting God Create Your Day
- heron, hygiene	16-Nov	Psalm 145:10	Letting God Create Your Day
- hummingbird - obvious design	14-Jul	Psalm 105:4-5	Character Sketches
- loon	18-Sept	Psalm 86:10	Character Sketches
- migration instincts	6-May	Genesis 6:20	It Couldn't Just Happen
- sea gulls	29-Nov	Job 28:20,21,23	Evolution in the Light of Scripture
Bristlecone pine - evidence for recent flood	4-Nov	Genesis 6:19	Unlocking the Mysteries of Creation
Bombardier beetle	5-Nov	Psalm 92:4	Unlocking the Mysteries of Creation
Butterfly - ant symboisis	23-Nov	Psalm 145:16	Evolution in the Light of Scripture
- defense mechanisms	26-Dec	Isaiah 55:9	Letting God Create Your Day
- monarch's awesome design	17-May	Psalm 145:5-6	From Darkness to light to Flight
- monarch's immunity to poison	15-Dec	Psalm 77:14	Letting God Create Your Day
Cain's wife	4-Aug	Genesis 5:4	Search for the Truth
Carbon 14 dating - errors	29-Dec	Colossians 2:8	The Evidence for Creation
- implies young earth	7-Sept	1 Timothy 1:4	5th Intern. Conf. on Creation Proc.
Censorship - of creation in libraries	31-Aug	Romans 1:18	Bruce Malone
Cheetah	27-Jul	Psalm 145:13	Letting God Create Your Day
Chinese language - flood accounts	24-Feb	Genesis 7:13	Search for the Truth
Christ - creates our changed nature	31-Dec	Romans 12:2	Rich & Tina Kleiss
- crucifixion	26-Sep	John 19:18	Biblical Studies in the Light of Arch.
Christianity - elevates the status of women	27-Feb	Galatians 3:26,28	Female Piety
- factual nature	22-Jan	Psalm 119:160	Many Infallible Proofs
Clastic Dikes - evidence of a young earth	10-Sept	Job 38:4-6	1st Intern. Conf. On Creation Proc.
Coal - evidence for flood formation	25-Jan	Genesis 7:4	Unlocking the Mysteries of Creation
- formation	11-Mar	Jeremiah 51:15	Letting God Create Your Day
Comets	8-Dec	Psalm 19:1	TJ Journal
Conservation - Biblical mandate	18-Nov	Genesis 9:2,3	Character Sketches
Continental drift	22-Mar	Genesis 10:25	Bruce Malone
Coral - growth rate	22-Oct	Psalm 9:1	Letting God Create Your Day
Creation - consequence of rejection	11-Nov	Romans 1:28-29	Unlocking the Mysteries of Creation
- implies accountability	1-Jul	Romans 1:20,21	Rich & Tina Kleiss
- importance	9-Nov	Psalm 119:89	The Darwin Conspiracy
- primary evidence for God	1-Jan	1 Peter 3:15	Many Infallible Proofs
- physical evidence for God	1-Oct	2 Kings 6:17	Rich & Tina Kleiss
Christianity - Evolution destroys foundation	4-May	1 Corinthians 15:47	Bruce Malone
Darwin, problems with theory	11-Dec	Psalm 10:4	Evolution in the Light of Scripture
Dating methods - increasing age	3-Sep	1 Corinthians 1:20	In the Beginning
- most show a young earth	1-Aug	1 Timothy 6:20	Rich & Tina Kleiss
- oceans	15-Feb	Ecclesiasties 3:11	The Illistrated Answers Book
- young earth evidence	28-Aug	Genesis genealogy	In the Beginning
Day-Age theory - length of a day	1-May	Exodus 20:11	The Genesis Record
- contradictions to the Bible	27-Dec	Exodus 20:11,12	The Evidence for Creation
Dead Sea Scrolls- biblical accuracy	4-Oct	Matthew 24:35	Evidence that Demands a Verdict
Design - evidence for a designer	1-Nov	Isaiah 5:12	The Human Body: Accident or Design?
- house analogy	14-Jun	Hebrews 3:4	Rich & Tina Kleiss
- fossil record	13-Jan	Romans 1:20-22	In the Beginning
Diatomaceous earth - show young age	26-Oct	Jeremiah 33:2-3	It's a Young World After All
Dinosaur - biblical evidence	15-Apr	Genesis 1:21-31	The Great Dinosaur Mystery
- extinction	21-May	Proverbs 25:2	Refuting Evolution 2
- more young earth evidence	25-Nov	Job 40:15-23	The Great Dinosaur Mystery
- young bones	8-Jan	Job 40,41	Noah to Abraham:The Turbulent Years
DNA - complexity requires designer	20-Apr	Psalm 139: 13,14	In the Beginning
- found in dinosaurs and old bacteria	17-Oct	Proverbs 9:10	World by Design, CRSEF Newsletter
- error correction system	15-Jul	Job 37:14	Letting God Create your Day
- information content	7-Nov	Psalm 139:13-14	In the Beginning
- orgin	30-Jul	1 Corinthians 12:18	It Couldn't Just Happen
- similarity to chimps is not descent	12-Jun	Proverbs 30:5-6	Creation Magazine, Feb. 1997
- deterioration rate	8-Aug	Isaiah 48:12,13	In the Beginning

Index of Topics (continued)

Subject	Date	Verse	Book/Author
Dust - man made from	20-May	Genesis 2:7	The Genesis Record
Earth - carbon dioxide balance	26-Apr	Psalm 115:16	Letting God Create Your Day
- center of universe	28-Mar	Psalm 8:3-4	TJ - The in-depth Journal of Creation
- ideal design	5-Jun	Colossians 1:16,17	Myths and Miracles
- internal temperature	30-Jan	Job 12:8	In the Beginning
- magnetic field decay rate	2-Sep	Job 37:23	Proc. of 2nd Conf. On Creation
- oxygen balance	29-May	Psalm 66:5	It Couldn't Just Happen
- rotation speed shows young age	12-Dec	Proverbs 3:19	Evolution in the Light of Scripture
- vapor canopy	28-Jun	Genesis 1:7	Letting God Create Your Day
Eels - unique creature	9-Dec	Job 37:14	Evolution in Light of Scripture
Electromagnetic Theory of Matter	5-Feb	Colossians 1:17	Common Sense Science
Embryology - E. Haeckel & F. Crick	23-Feb	Psalm 139:13-14	Search for the Truth
Enviromental problems - due to sin	29-Jun	Genesis 2:15	Rich & Tina Kleiss
Evolution - consequences of acceptance	12-Aug	1 Timothy 4:7	Why I Believe
- gaint leaps	20-Aug	1 Chronicles 29:11	In the Beginning
- entirely speculation	1-Dec	1 Timothy 6:20	Unlocking the Mysteries of Creation
- harmful consequences	23-Oct	Matthew 7:17-18	Bruce Malone
- incompatible with Christianity	16-Jul	Proverbs 14:12	Search for the Truth
- meaning shifts	7-Jun	Proverbs 14:7-8	Myths and Miracles
- missing links	15-Oct	Psalm 146:5-6	In the Beginning
- missing "mistakes"	3-May	Jeremiah 10:12	Bruce Malone
- new information is lost	22-Feb	Proverbs 18:17	Creation Magazine
- problems hidden from students	14-Nov	Proverbs 22:6	Bruce Malone
- unanswered questions	5-Apr	1 Corinthians 2:6	Bruce Malone
Fish - Anglerfish	31-Jan	Psalm 92:5	Letting God Create Your Day
- Grunion eggs show design	2-Oct	Isaiah 6:3	Character Sketches
- Wrasse, sex changing	13-Sep	Psalm 96: 3-4	Letting God Create Your Day
Flies - population balance	6-Aug	Exodus 8:24	Character Sketches
Fallen nature	27-Jan	Isaiah 55:8	The Revised Answers Book
Flood all cultures started at end of	3 Jun	Acts 17:26	Unlocking the Mysteries of Creation
- biblical description	8-Nov	Genesis 8:21	The Genesis Record
- traditions and stories worldwide	5-May	Genesis 9:19	The Creation
Fossil - clam graveyards	19-Dec	Genesis 7:11-12	The Evidence for Creation
- flood evidence	13-Feb	Genesis 7:20-22	The Creation
- gaps	20-Jan	1 Corinthians 15:39	Letting God Create Your Day
- graveyards are worldwide	11-Oct	Genesis 7:24	Evolution: The Bone of Contention
- index fossils (geological column)	30-Aug	Ezekiel 13:3	In the Beginning
- missing body types	26-Jan	1 Corinthians 1:25	Search for the Truth
- not forming today	16-Dec	Luke 19:39-40	Science and the Bible
- out of place (presuppositions)	21-Aug	Luke 19:39-40	Creation Ex Nihilo
- same animals alive today	8-May	Genesis 1:20,21	Myths and Miracles
- shows no change	5-Jul	2 Corinthians 10:5	Letting God Create Your Day
- sudden appearance	18-Aug	Psalm 53:1	In the Beginning
Frog - coqui	18-Mar	Psalm 84:3	Letting God Create Your Day
- stomach incubation of young	7-Mar	1 Chronicles 16:9	Letting God Create Your Day
- ability to freeze	25-Apr	Job 12:7,9	Letting God Create Your Day
Fruit fly	2-Aug	Ecclesiastes 3:14	In the Beginning
Gap theory	24-Sep	Romans 5:12	The Revised Answers Book
Gazelle - blood cooling	10-Jan	Exodus 15:11	It Couldn't Just Happen
Gender - origin	8-Jun	Genesis 2:22	Myths and Miracles
Genes - can trigger death of cells	18-May	Hebrews 9:27	Letting God Create Your Day
Genetics - Mendel's law	19-Oct	Genesis 1:25	In the Beginning
Geologic column - index fossils	30-Aug	Ezekiel 13:3	In the Beginning
Grand Canyon - inconsistencies	2-Nov	Psalm 46:1-2	Grand Canyon
Gregor Mendel - one bloodline	19-Jan	Acts 17:26	One Blood
Heat flow indicates young universe	9-Sep	Isaiah 25:1	In the Beginning
Helium - by radiometric decay	3-Apr	1 Thessalonians 5:21	Impact Article #352 - 10/02
Hermit crabs	2-May	Matthew 6:8	Letting God Create Your Day
Honeybee communication	23-Jun	Psalm 145:10	Letting God Create Your Day
Hormone system	7-Feb	Job 10:8	The Human Body: Accident or Design?
Horse evolution - problems	9-Apr	Genesis 1:24	Tornado in the Junkyard
- deception	9-Jun	Genesis 1:20 - 2:3	Icons of Evolution

Index of Topics (continued)

Subject	Date	Verse	Book/Author
Human - baby helplessness	19-Jul	Proverbs 22:6	The Human Body: Accident orDesign?
- blood clotting	17-Aug	1 Corinthians 8:6	Darwin's Black Box
- blood vessels	24-Jan	Psalm 136:4	The Human Body: Accident orDesign?
- brain	13-Aug	Job 11:7	Letting God Create Your Day
- circumcision	4-Feb	Genesis 17:12	A Study Course in Christian Evidence
- ear	10-Aug	Proverbs 20:12	The Human Body: Accident or Design?
- egg and sperm	9-Mar	Genesis 3:15	A Study Course in Christian Evidences
- eye (design)	5-Mar	Psalm 40:5	Letting God Create Your Day
- eye (incredible complexity)	13-Jul	Proverbs 20:12	The Human Body: Accident or Design?
- eye (chemical reaction speed)	8-Mar	Psalm 107:15	Letting God Create Your Day
- eye (lens design)	2-Mar	Psalm 94:8,9	Letting God Create Your Day
- feet	24-Dec	Psalm 111:2	The Human Body: Accident orDesign?
- footprints in old rock layers	17-Sep	Job 36:26	In the Beginning
- healing process	19-Aug	Psalm 119:156	Letting God Create Your Day
- hearing	28-Nov	Psalm 94:9	The Revelation of God in Nature
- heart	18-Oct	Leviticus 17:11	The Human Body: Accident or Design?
- hemoglobin	5-Dec	Leviticus 17:14	A Study in Christian Evidences
- immune system	11-Aug	Isaiah 63:7	In the Beginning
- kidneys	27-Apr	Ecclesiastes 7:13	The Human Body: Accident or Design?
- hair	7-Jan	Matthew 10:29-31	The Human Body: Accident or Design?
- liver	13-Dec	1 Cor. 12:16-19	The Human Body: Accident or Design?
- muscles	7-May	Psalm 119:73	The Human Body: Accident or Design?
- nerve cells (brain)	22-Sep	Job 9:10	Fearfully and Wonderously Made
- nervous system	10-Jun	Isaiah 44:24	The Human Body: Accident or Design?
- nursing (designed system)	30-Mar	Psalm 107:8-9	The Human Body: Accident or Design?
- pheromone organ	19-Mar	Job 11:7,8	Letting God Create Your Day
- skin	24-Nov	Psalm 119:73	The Human Body: Accident or Design?
- sperm	6-Jul	Psalm 139:15,16	Letting God Create Your Day
- spine	29 Aug	Psalm 29:2	Creation Magazine
- stomach	13-May	Psalm 100:3	The Human Body: Accident or Design?
- skeleton	25-Feb	1 Chronicles 16:24	The Human Body: Accident or Design?
- uniqueness compared to animals	1-Sep	Genesis 1:26	The Genesis Record
Human ability - early eye surgery	15-May	Ecclesiastes 1:10	Letting God Create Your Day
- Mayan astronomy	19-May	Ecclesiastes 1:9,11	Unlocking the Mysteries of Creation
Human nature - development of conscience	1-Mar	Romans 2:15	Rich & Tina Kleiss
Hyaluronic acid	10-Mar	Psalm 92:4	Letting God Create Your Day
Ice age	27-Aug	Job 38:22, 29-30	Proc. of 2nd Conf. On Creation
Ice - rapid accumulation at the poles	23-Dec	Proverbs 25:2	Search for the Truth
Iceplant insect	20-Mar	Psalm 83:18	Letting God Create Your Day
Inland salt seas	24-May	Genesis 7:17-18	Myths and Miracles
Io - warmth evidence of young age	18-Feb	Psalm 19:1-2	It's a Young World After All
Irreducible complexity	12-Feb	Psalm 100:3	Darwin's Black Box
Israel - in prophecy	13-Nov	Jeremaih 30:11	Science and the Bible
Jellyfish - design	5-Oct	Psalm 77:12	Evolution in the Light of Scripture
- siphonophores	2-Apr	Psalm 98:1	Letting God Create Your Day
Jerusalem - biblical accuracy	8-Apr	2 Samuel 5:8	Letting God Create Your Day
Jesus - claim to be creator	25-Dec	John 1:3	Bruce Malone
- like no other	12-Oct.	1 Chronicles 17:20	Many Infallible Proofs
- uniqueness	28-Jul	1 Chronicles 16:25-26	The Person of Christ
- evidence for existence	14-Jan	Matthew 2:1	A Study Course in Christian Evidence
John Dewey - founder of modern education	3-Nov	Deuteronomy 8:18	Seven Men Who rule from the Grave
Language - baby's early learning ability	19-Apr	Job 38:36	Letting God Create Your Day
- deaf ability to learn	22-Nov	1 Corinthians 1:9	Letting God Create Your Day
- development	12-Mar	Genesis 2:20	Letting God Create Your Day
- oldest are most complicated	2-Jun	Psalm 139:3-4	Myths and Miracles
Law - biblical influence	29-Jan	2 Timothy 3:16-17	Rich & Tina Kleiss
- of teleogy	1-Nov	Isaiah 5:12	Human Body: Accident or Design?
Leaf fish	27-Nov	Psalm 71:19	Letting God Create Your Day
Light - speed and possible decay	4-Apr	Psalm 74:16	www.setterfield.org
Locusts	6-Sep	Psalm 72:18	Evolution in the Light of Scripture
Louis Pasteur	22-Apr	Psalm 14:1	Letting God Create Your Day
Lungfish	14-Apr	Psalm 9:1	Letting God Create Your Day
Mammoths - recent burial	30-Oct	Genesis 1:11	Its a Young World After All

Index of Topics (continued)

Subject	Date	Verse	Book/Author
Mankind - ancient abilties	25-Mar	Exodus 36:1	Letting God Create Your Day
- early intelligence	10-Nov	Ecclesiastes 1:9	Unlocking the Mysteries of Creation
- more ex. of early intelligence	12-Nov	Genesis 4:21-22	Unlocking the Mysteries of Creation
Matthew Maury - oceanography	26-Feb	Psalm 8:8	A Study Course in Christian Evidence
Mendel, Gregory	19-Oct	Genesis 1:25	In the Beginning
Mental capacity	8-Feb	Proverbs 2:6	In the Beginning
Mercury - magnetic field	11-Sep	Psalm 89:5-6	Letting God Create Your Day
Michelangelo analogy of creation	16-Mar	Proverbs 3:19	The Great Works Catalog
Mid-Oceanic Ridge	20-Nov	Genesis 7:11-12	Science and the Bible
Mistletoe	14-Mar	Colossians 1:16	Letting God Create Your Day
Molecular clocks	30-Nov	Genesis 2:1	Creation Magazine, Nov. 2002
Mongoose	23-Aug	Psalm 77:12	Letting God Create Your Day
Monogamy	23-May	Matthew 19:4-6	The Genesis Record
Monotheism - root of all cultures	14-Sep	Joshua 23:16	Biblical Studies in the Light of Arch.
Mosquito - design	20-Jun	John 21:25	Character Sketches
Moths - design	6-Dec	Psalm 53:1	Evolution in the Light of Scripture
- peppered moths	26-May	Proverbs 14:12	Unlocking the Mysteries of Creation
- pheromones	26-Mar	Hebrews 2:8	Letting God Create Your Day
- ultrasonic hearing	24-Apr	Genesis 2:1,2	Letting God Create Your Day
Mt. St. Helen's - buried forests	13-Oct	Genesis 7:24	The Young Earth
- rapid river formation	3-Dec	Job 9:5	Creation, Evolution and the Age of the Earth
Mussles - natural adhesive	21-Oct	Luke 1:37	Letting God Create Your Day
Mutations - don't cause improvments	18-Jan	Genesis 1:25	Search for the Truth
- fruit fly experiments	2 Aug	Ecclesiastes 3:14	In the Beginning
- no greater complexity	10-May	Job 37:5	In the Beginning
Nuclear forces	22-Jul	Hebrews 1:3	God: Coming Face to Face with His Majesty
Ocean - salt concentration shows young earth	10-Oct	Psalm 102:25	The Young Earth
- trenches	21-Nov	Job 38:16	A Study Course in Christian Evidences
- volume	23-Sep	Genesis 7:19	In the Beginning
Octopus - unique arm abilities	19-Sep	Psalm 40:5	Character Sketches
- unique coloration ability	20-Sep	Psalm 104:24-25	Character Sketches
Oil pressure - evidence of young earth	30-Sep	Isaiah 45:18	In the Beginning
Orion nebula - evidence of young universe	31-Oct	Isaiah 40:26	It's a Young World After All
Pack rats	6-Mar	Psalm 36:6,7	Character Sketches
Penguins	9-May	Genesis 1:21	Myths and Miracles
Pest control	4-Mar	Romans 11:33	Letting God Create Your Day
Petrified wood - Yellowstone	7-Dec	Proverbs 25:2	The Young Earth
Plant - control of photosynthsis	4-Jul	Psalm 145:9	Letting God Create Your Day
- Elephant ear interdependency	12-Sep	Deuteronomy 3:24	Letting God Create Your Day
- manufacturing systems	25-Sep	Psalm 104:14	Unlocking the Mysteries of Creation
- sensitivity	17-Jun	Genesis 1:11,12	Letting God Create Your Day
- tree defense	5-Sep	Psalm 96:12	Letting God Create Your Day
- tree water movement to top	4-Jan	Isaiah 40:28	Letting God Create Your Day
Platypus - mixture of features	3-Aug	Psalm 145:3-6	In the Beginning
Polystrata fossils - flood evidence	14-Feb	Psalm 104:6-8	The Creation
Population growth - young earth	10-Feb	Psalm 119:160	Science and the Bible
Preying mantis	11-Jul	Revelation 15:3	Letting God Create Your Day
Primates - survival instincts	13-Mar	Job 12:7	Letting God Create Your Day
Probability - life could never form	20-Dec	Roman 1:21-22	Unlocking the Mystries of Creation
- cells could never form	17-Jul	Deuteronomy 32:3-4	Energy Flow in Biology
Prophecy- about Jesus (over 300)	9-Jan	Isaiah 14:24	Evidence that Demands a Verdict
- crucifixion	20-Jul	Psalm 22	Defender's Study Bible
- Jesus' entry into Jeruselem	22-Dec	Zechariah 9:9	Hidden Treasures in Biblical Text
Protein formation - probability is zero	7-Aug	Isaiah 55:9	In the Beginning
- impossility with oxygen	15-Nov	Psalm 148:4-5	The Icons of Evolution
Radiohalos - evidence for a young earth	9-Aug	Job 38:4	Creation's Tiny Mystery
Radiometric dating - varying results	28-Dec	1 Corinthians 1:20	The Evidence for Creation
Rattlesnake - infared vision	14-Aug	Psalm 50:11	Letting God Create Your Day
Red Algae	29-Feb	Hebrews 4:13	Letting God Create Your Day
Red squirrel - design	27-Sep	Psalm 36:5,6	Character Sketches
Rock - missing soil layers between	24-Oct	Proverbs 3:19	The Young Earth
Saturn - rings evidence of young age	11-Apr	Deuteronomy 10:14	It's a Young World After All
Savant	16-Oct	1 Cor. 1:27-29	Helping Children Understand Genesis

Index of Topics (continued)

Subject	Date	Verse	Book/Author
Science - antropic principle	3-Feb	Job 34:14-15	God: Coming Face to Face w/
- defined to exclude creation	1-Feb	John 8:31-32	Darwin's Black Box
Scientists - great creationists	21-Jan	Psalm 119:130	Men of Science, Men of God
Sea mammals - the bends	19-Feb	Jeremiah 32:17	Letting God Create Your Day
- whales	6-Jun	Isaiah 14:24	Myths and Miracles
Seasons & Signs - designed for our benefit	30-May	Genesis 1:14	Myths and Miracles
Sedimentary rock	21-Mar	Genesis 7:20	The Bone of Contention
Seeds - evidence of design	27-Oct	John 12: 24-25	Unlocking the Mysteries of Cr.
Selective Breeding	2-Feb	Genesis 1:24	Many Infallible Proofs
Seven day week - origin	4-Jun	Exodus 31:16-17	Myths and Miracles
Sidon	3-Jan	Ezekiel 28: 22,23	Science and the Bible
Skunk cabbage	16-Aug	Psalm 77:12-13	Character Sketches
Snow - shows design	22-June	Isaiah 55:10	CEA Update
Snowshoe rabbit	2-Jan	Psalm 116:5	Character Sketches
Soil - evidence of young earth	26-Jul	Jeremiah 33:2	Unlocking the Mysteries of Cr.
Solar system - formation problems	24-Aug	Psalm 33:6	In the Beginning
- planetary rotation	22-Aug	Job 25:2-3	In the Beginning
- not enough helium present	24-Jul	Psalm 148:4-5	In the Beginning
- composition diversity	31-Jul	Psalm 97:6	Astronomy books
Spadefoot Toad - survival in dry desert	6-Jan	Isaiah 43:20	Letting God Create Your Day
- symbiosis with horsefly	16-Jan	Psalm 104:27	Letting God Create Your Day
Specimen Ridge - tree stump pattern	17-Jan	Proverbs 25:2	The Young Earth
Spider - Bola has complex chemistry	30-Apr	Psalm 104:27	Letting God Create Your Day
- web complexity	24-Mar	Job 5:9	Letting God Create Your Day
Spiny Lizard - recycles waste	27-Jun	Isaiah 43:20	Letting God Create Your Day
Spontaneous generation	15-Sep	Genesis 1:11,21,24	In the Beginning
Stalagmites & stalactites - growth rate	14-Oct	Daniel 2:21	Evolution in Light of Scripture
Stars - evidence for young universe	31-May	Job 38:33	In the Beginning
- Sirius B formation	8-Sep	Isaiah 48:13	Letting God Create Your Day
- problems births vs. deaths	26-Aug	Genesis 1:16-19	In the Beginning
- purpose of constellations/zodiac	11-Jan	Genesis 1:14	Real Meaning of the Zodiac
Stick Insects	17-Feb	Psalm 29:2	Letting God Create Your Day
Sun - diameter evidence of young earth	29-Sep	1 Cor. 3:19-20	Creation Ex Nihilo Magazine
Tea	26-Jun	Genesis 2:15	Letting God Create Your Day
Termites - design	16-May	Psalm 145:17	Letting God Create Your Day
- fossils	10-Jul	Genesis 1:31, 2:1	Letting God Create Your Day
- symbiosis with protozoa	16-Sep	Isaiah 25:1	Evolution in the Light of Scrip.
Thermodynamics - First Law	25-Aug	Ecclesiastes 3:14	In the Beginning
- Second Law	3-Mar	Romans 8:20,22	Letting God Create Your Day
Time dilation - one way to explain a six day creation	14-Dec	Isaiah 42:5	Starlight and Time
Turkey vulture - design	6-Oct	Psalm 145:17	Character Sketches
Turtles - ability to survive freezing	11-Feb	Psalm 86:8	Letting God Create Your Day
Uniformitarianism	12-Jan	2 Peter 3:3-4	Bruce Malone
UV protection of animal s	18-Jun	James 1:17	Letting God Create Your Day
Vapor canopy	15-Jun	Genesis 5:5	Myths and Miracles
Venus Flytrap	23-Jan	Psalm 40:5	Letting God Create Your Day
Vestigial organs - Appendix and various glands	7-Apr	Isaiah 44:24,25	In the Minds of Men
- Tailbone and wingless birds	3-Oct	Jeremiah 5:21-22	The Revised Answers Book
Voodoo Lilly	10-Apr	Psalm 86:10	Letting God Create Your Day
Wasps	25-Jun	Daniel 4:2-3	Letting God Create Your Day
Water - cycle	19-June	Isaiah 55:10	A Study Course in Christian Evid.
- unique properties	5-Jan	Psalm 66:5	Letting God Create Your Day
Whales - sperm	30-Jun	Psalm 65:8	Letting God Create Your Day
William Ramsay	28-Apr	2 Samuel 22:31	A Study Course in Christian Evid.
Woodpecker - diet	5-Aug	Matthew 6:26	Letting God Create Your Day
- evidence for design	6-Nov	Psalm 145:15	Unlocking the Mysteries of Cr.
Writing - evidence for man's intellegence	6-Feb	John 5:46	The Bible has the Answer

Index by Subject

Topic	Date
Anatomy	7-Jan
	24-Jan
	7-Feb
	25-Feb
	2-Mar
	8-Mar
	10-Mar
	19-Mar
	30-Mar
	7-Apr
	27-Apr
	7-May
	13-May
	10-Jun
	6-Jul
	13-Jul
	19-Jul
	10-Aug
	13-Aug
	19-Aug
	29-Aug
	22-Sep
	3-Oct
	18-Oct
	24-Nov
	28-Nov
	13-Dec
	24-Dec
Anthopology	6-Apr
	23-May
	4-Jun
	3-Jul
	4-Sep
	28-Oct
	11-Nov
Archaeology	6-Feb
	25-Mar
	8-Apr
	28-Apr
	27-May
	30-May
	8-Jul
	14-Sep
	26-Sep
	28-Sep
	29-Oct
	10-Nov
	12-Nov
	17-Nov
	2-Dec
	17-Dec
Astronomy	11-Jan
	18-Feb
	28-Mar
	4-Apr
	11-Apr
	14-May
	19-May
	31-May
	5-Jun
	24-Jul
	31-Jul
	22-Aug
	24-Aug
	26-Aug
	8-Sep

Topic	Date
Astronomy (cont.)	11-Sep
	29-Sep
	9-Oct
	20-Oct
	25-Oct
	31-Oct
	8-Dec
	14-Dec
Biblical Accuracy	12-Jan
	4-Feb
	26-Feb
	9-Mar
	13-Apr
	14-May
	22-May
	16-Jun
	19-Jun
	29-Jul
	4-Oct
	16-Oct
	21-Nov
	4-Dec
	5-Dec
	18-Dec
Biblical Uniqueness	29-Jan
	27-Feb
	12-May
	24-Jun
	21-Jul
	12-Oct
	19-Nov
	10-Dec
Biology	2-Jan
	6-Jan
	10-Jan
	16-Jan
	28-Jan
	31-Jan
	11-Feb
	17-Feb
	19-Feb
	22-Feb
	23-Feb
	6-Mar
	7-Mar
	13-Mar
	18-Mar
	24-Mar
	26-Mar
	29-Mar
	2-Apr
	14-Apr
	21-Apr
	23-Apr
	2-May
	6-May
	9-May
	16-May
	17-May
	26-May
	28-May
	6-Jun
	8-Jun
	9-Jun
	11-Jun
	18-Jun
	20-Jun
	21-Jun

Topic	Date
Biology (cont.)	23-Jun
	27-Jun
	30-Jun
	11-Jul
	14-Jul
	18-Jul
	25-Jul
	27-Jul
	3-Aug
	5-Aug
	6-Aug
	14-Aug
	15-Aug
	18-Aug
	20-Aug
	23-Aug
	6-Sep
	9-Sep
	12-Sep
	13-Sep
	18-Sep
	19-Sep
	20-Sep
	27-Sep
	2-Oct
	5-Oct
	6-Oct
	7-Oct
	8-Oct
	15-Oct
	22-Oct
	5-Nov
	6-Nov
	16-Nov
	23-Nov
	27-Nov
	29-Nov
	6-Dec
	9-Dec
	15-Dec
	21-Dec
	26-Dec
Botany	4-Jan
	23-Jan
	29-Feb
	14-Mar
	17-Jun
	26-Jun
	4-Jul
	16-Aug
	5-Sep
	25-Sep
	27-Oct
	4-Nov
Changed Nature	25-Dec
	31-Dec
Chemistry	5-Jan
	12-Feb
	10-Apr
	25-Apr
	30-Apr
	20-May
	29-May
	17-Aug
	21-Oct
	30-Dec
	15-Nov

Index by Subject

Topic	Date	Topic	Date	Topic	Date
Common Sense	13-Jan	**Genetics**	18-Jan	**Physics (cont.)**	25-Aug
	8-Feb		19-Jan		2-Sep
	15-Feb		2-Feb		7-Sep
	16-Mar		5-Mar		9-Sep
	16-Apr		10-May		28-Sep
	29-Apr		18-May		12-Dec
	3-May		12-Jun		29-Dec
	7-Jun		15-Jul	**Prophecy**	3-Jan
	14-Jun		2-Aug		9-Jan
	22-Jun		19-Oct		20-Feb
	12-Jul		7-Nov		21-Feb
	28-Aug	**Geology**	17-Jan		15-Mar
	31-Aug		25-Jan		20-Jul
	3-Sep		30-Jan		23-Jul
	15-Sep		14-Feb		13-Nov
	23-Oct		11-Mar		26-Nov
	14-Nov		22-Mar		22-Dec
	16-Dec		28-Jun	**Psychology**	1-Mar
Comparing Religions	22-Jan		26-Jul		1-Sep
	16-Feb		30-Aug		21-Sep
	12-Apr		10-Sep	**Worldwide Flood**	15-Jan
	1-Jun		30-Sep		28-Feb
	28-Jul		10-Oct		21-Mar
Creation Foundation	1-Jan		13-Oct		18-Apr
	27-Jan		14-Oct		5-May
	1-Apr		24-Oct		8-May
	5-Apr		2-Nov		24-May
	1-May		20-Nov		15-Jun
	4-May		3-Dec		23-Sep
	1-Jul		7-Dec		8-Nov
	16-Jul	**Great Scientists**	21-Jan		23-Dec
	1-Aug		1-Feb		
	1-Oct		22-Apr		
	24-Sep		3-Nov		
	1-Nov	**History**	14-Jan		
	9-Nov		24-Feb		
	1-Dec		15-Apr		
	27-Dec		15-May		
Earth's Ecology	4-Mar		3-Jun		
	31-Mar		7-Jul		
	26-Apr		4-Aug		
	11-May		12-Aug		
	25-Jun		27-Aug		
	29-Jun	**Language**	12-Mar		
	2-Jul		19-Apr		
	18-Nov		2-Jun		
Fossil Record	8-Jan		22-Nov		
	20-Jan	**Mathematics**	10-Feb		
	26-Jan		20-Apr		
	9-Feb		17-Jul		
	13-Feb		7-Aug		
	9-Apr		20-Dec		
	17-Apr	**Microbiology**	17-Mar		
	24-Apr		20-Mar		
	8-May		23-Mar		
	21-May		27-Mar		
	13-Jun		9-Jul		
	5-Jul		30-Jul		
	10-Jul		11-Aug		
	8-Aug		16-Sep		
	18-Aug		17-Oct		
	21-Aug		30-Nov		
	17-Sep	**Physics**	3-Feb		
	11-Oct		5-Feb		
	26-Oct		3-Mar		
	30-Oct		3-Apr		
	25-Nov		25-May		
	11-Dec		22-Jul		
	19-Dec		9-Aug		

OTHER CREATION BOOKS
by Search for the Truth Ministries

Brilliant

Brilliant is a full-color coffee-table style book that brings the Bibles account of history alive by showng how artifacts and cultures throughout history confirm biblical truth. Each two-page spread is a different topic and every page features a biblical timeline. *(hardcover 8 1/2 x 11, 128 pages)*

Censored Science

A stunning, full-color book containing fifty of the best evidences for biblical creation. Examine the information all too often censored, suppressed, or ignored in our schools. Every page is a visual masterpiece. Perfect for students. *(hardcover 8 1/2 x11, 128 pages)*

Search for the Truth

This book is the result of a 15-year effort to bring the scientific evidence for creation into public view. *Search for the Truth* is a compilation of 100 individual articles originally published as newspaper columns, summarizing every aspect of the creation model for our origin. *(softcover 8 1/2 x 11, 144 pages)*

See all of our resources at www.searchforthetruth.net

Search for the Truth
MAIL-IN ORDER FORM
SEE MORE at WWW.SEARCHFORTHETRUTH.NET

Call us, or send this completed order form
(other side of page) with check or money order to:

Search for the Truth Ministries
3275 Monroe Rd.
Midland, MI 48642
989.837.5546 or truth@searchforthetruth.net

PRICES - MIX & MATCH

	Item Price	2-9 Copies	10+ Copies	Case Price
BOTH DEVOTIONAL SPECIAL (2 books)	$12.00	-	-	-
Inspired Evidence (book)	$11.95	$9/ea.	$6/ea.	call
A Closer Look at the Evidence (book)	$11.95	$9/ea.	$6/ea.	call
Censored Science (Sewn Hardback)	$16.95	$9/ea.	$6/ea.	call
Brilliant (Sewn Hardback)	$16.95	$9/ea.	$6/ea.	call
Search for the Truth (softcover)	$11.95	$9/ea.	$6/ea.	call
Protecting His Workmanship (book)	$11.95	$9/ea.	$6/ea.	call
Borrowing God's Glasses (softcover)	$11.95	$9/ea.	$6/ea.	call
All DVDs	$11.95	$9/ea.	$6/ea.	call

MAIL-IN ORDER FORM

Resource	Quantity	Cost each (see reverse)	Total
BOTH DEVOTIONAL SPECIAL (2 books)			
Inspired Evidence (book)			
A Closer Look at the Evidence (Book)			
Censored Science (Hardback)			
Brilliant (Hardback)			
Search for the Truth (book)			
Borrowing God's Glasses (book)			
Protecting His Workmanship (book)			
Creation 101 (DVD)			
A Matter of Time (DVD)			
Explosive Geological Evidence... (DVD)			
Monkey Business (DVD)			
Tax deductible donation to ministry			

Normal delivery time is 1-2 weeks

For express delivery increase shipping to 20%

Subtotal	
MI residents add 6% sales tax	
Shipping add 15% of subtotal	
TOTAL ENCLOSED	

SHIP TO:

Name: _____

Address: _____

City: _____

State: _____ Zip: _____

Phone: _____

E-mail: _____